ASHE-ERIC Higher Education Report: Volume 30, Number 4
Adrianna J. Kezar, Series Editor

Accreditation Matters

Achieving Academic Recognition and Renewal

Jeffrey W. Alstete

Accreditation Matters: Achieving Academic Recognition and Renewal
Jeffrey W. Alstete
ASHE-ERIC Higher Education Report: Volume 30, Number 4
Adrianna J. Kezar, Series Editor

This publication was prepared partially with funding from the Office of Educational Research and Improvement, U.S. Department of Education, under contract no. ED-99-00-0036. The opinions expressed in this report do not necessarily reflect the positions or policies of OERI or the Department.

ISSN 0884-0040   electronic ISSN 1536-0709   ISBN 0-7879-7478-1

The ASHE-ERIC Higher Education Report is part of the Jossey-Bass Higher and Adult Education Series and is published six times a year by Wiley Subscription Services, Inc., A Wiley Company, at Jossey-Bass, 989 Market Street, San Francisco, California 94103-1741.

For subscription information, see the Back Issue/Subscription Order Form in the back of this journal.

CALL FOR PROPOSALS: Prospective authors are strongly encouraged to contact Adrianna Kezar at the University of Southern California, Waite Phillips Hall 703C, Los Angeles, CA 90089, or kezar@usc.edu. See "About the ASHE-ERIC Higher Education Report Series" in the back of this volume.

Visit the Jossey-Bass Web site at **www.josseybass.com.**

Printed in the United States of America on acid-free recycled paper.

Advisory Board

This Issue's Consulting Editors and Review Panelists

Executive Summary

Accreditation matters today because it is the primary means of ensuring the quality of higher education available to its many constituencies. It is a self-regulating system of institutional peer review that is surely better than alternatives involving direct government oversight of academe. To fully understand accreditation today, it is important to know how it began, why it was started, the ways academic accreditation has evolved over the years in response to changing conditions, and the stages of this evolution. In the late nineteenth century, a movement was begun to "accredit" institutions regionally in the United States; the new system met minimal standards and then became a major force after 1901. This period can be viewed as the start of the first generation of academic accreditation in the United States. As the regional accrediting agencies were developing, there was also a movement to establish standards that could be applied across the nation (Bloland, 2001). Some of the difficulties that needed attention include the transfer of educational credit between institutions, admission to graduate schools, and determination of equivalent degrees between the United States and Germany. These issues all gave momentum to the national standardization of higher education in the United States. This period, the early to mid-twentieth century, can be called the second generation of academic accreditation; it was characterized by the attempts at national coordination among the regional agencies and periodic changes in the supraregional oversight coordinating bodies. Today, the purposes are clearly well evolved beyond the goals of early first- and second-generation accrediting agencies; they now seek to ensure that the regional and specialized agencies do more than merely recognize what a college is and the resources available. The Council for Higher Education Accreditation (CHEA), a private, nonprofit, national organization that coordinates accreditation activity, is directing accrediting agencies to employ appropriate and fair procedures in decision making and to continually reassess their accrediting practices. In other words, CHEA wants accrediting organizations to practice what they preach to their educational clients. However, critics of the current system of accreditation oversight by CHEA view it as a compromise with college presidents instead of a rigorous set of common standards to be used by the regional accrediting agencies (Amaral, 1998). It remains to be learned whether the creation of CHEA and this third generation of accreditation will be enough to protect the institutional autonomy valued by postsecondary institutions. The third generation of academic accreditation can also be characterized by efforts to apply quality initiatives such as the Academic Quality Improvement Project (AQIP) and the Malcolm Baldrige awards in addition to focused self-studies, coordinated evaluations with other agencies, and new models of periodic review.

Why Does Accreditation Matter?

The perception of higher education by the public, legislatures, and employers has been an issue in recent years, and a great deal of research has been conducted on public attitudes toward higher education (Eaton, 1999b). The research has focused largely on questions related to the price, value, purpose, and quality of education but little on the public's knowledge of and opinion about accreditation. CHEA commissioned a survey in 1999 to learn what the general public knows or believes about ensuring the quality of education through accreditation. The results found that a large majority of the public believes that colleges and universities must meet moderate or high standards to receive accreditation. Interestingly, a large portion do not know who performs accreditation, but a clear majority said they would not consider taking a course from an institution that is not accredited. The disparity between the public perception of moderate to high standards of accrediting bodies and the internal perceptions by the educational community (and the high percentage of accredited institutions) regarding the perceived low requirements to achieve and renew accreditation need to be addressed and examined by all parties involved. This book explores some of the issues as guidance to both the public and those involved in higher education about the potential true possibilities for renewal and recognition by effective accreditation processes now in place and those under development.

What Matters Are Involved in Accreditation Today?

A recent survey of eighty-one regional and specialized accreditors found that many accrediting agencies are departing from traditional accreditation approaches that are individual to more cooperative initiatives (Safman, 1998). These new efforts are beginning to address how self-studies are developed, how visiting teams are created, how visitation team reports are prepared, and how data are collected and shared among accrediting organizations. Regional and specialized accrediting organizations have been forming collaborative evaluations by jointly designating a single review team that collects information, interviews institution personnel, examines facilities, and writes a single report to both accrediting agencies. However, accrediting organizations retain the authority for the respective decisions on the actual accreditation outcome decision. Although these collaborative self-study reviews offer some advantages, they may be viewed as somewhat of a temporary solution to the overlapping, redundancy, and financial cost problems previously mentioned. Other pressing concerns about accreditation also need to be addressed, such as accountability, thoroughness, and the potential discord between the formative and summative goals. Regardless, educational institutions today must deal with the regional and specialized accreditation systems. Effective facilitation of organizational resources is strongly needed for successful recognition and renewal.

Other recent changes in approach to accreditation matters include three-year collaborative accreditation reviews, international collaboration, alliance of subspecialties, reduced number of site visits, reduced size of visiting teams, and use of annual questionnaires to collect data. Another important improvement that also has gained popularity is the availability of topic choice in the self-study, especially for larger institutions that wish to emphasize and improve particular problems such as fundraising, governance, or strategic planning. Policies for facilitating accreditation should strongly consider leveraging accreditation self-study processes for these purposes as part of their strategy.

How Can Interpretive Strategies Help Achieve Academic Recognition and Institutional Renewal?

The interpretive model of strategic management is developed on the concept that an organization is a network of self-interested participants, both within and outside the organization, and that successful strategic management requires the carefully planned use of all forms of communication and of the symbols used to portray the collective reality of participants. For accreditation goals, it can be a method for helping the accrediting agency, the public, and all the institutional stakeholders to support the institutional mission and believe in the achievements earned and the goals set forth. For colleges and universities seeking recognition from external stakeholders and internal institutional renewal in a challenging, decentralized, change-resistant organizational culture, interpretive strategies are a natural process that many accreditation plans, processes, and results seem to strive for. These efforts seek to shape participants' and potential participants' attitudes.

Accreditation systems in the United States and elsewhere have begun to apply quality initiatives as an alternative and improvement of the traditional process, which has somewhat similar properties to academic audits in that rigorous self-assessment is conducted but also includes a demonstration of higher productivity and quality. Currently, higher education continues to face "universalization" (Trow, 1973) where more people are attending postsecondary institutions. The next generation of accreditation will have to take into account these factors of change while simultaneously increasing the public's trust. Changes in the future of accreditation may actually impact traditional higher education institutions in surprising and perhaps positive ways by forcing institutions to concentrate on their market niche and mission and not attempt to evolve into areas that are beyond their ability and true market to serve. A new, fourth generation of academic accreditation will be needed to ensure that institutions stick to their mission and evolve in an appropriate direction. In the meantime, colleges and universities realize that accreditation does still matter. There are many new options available to assist institutions achieve the renewal and recognition they deserve.

Contents

Foreword

The current political and social environment makes the topics of accountability and accreditation extremely important. Over the past two decades, state and federal governments have been emphasizing the need for some quality assurance and improvement mechanism for higher education. Leaders are concerned whether there are sufficient external and impartial checks on institutions involved in a voluntary process. The recent Enron and other corporate scandals have put accountability back in the forefront. Citizens are concerned whether institutions are being run in an honest and quality fashion. The international community has become more concerned about issues of accountability as well and has turned to the United States for examples, because it has a longer history of addressing issues of institutional standards using a voluntary and collegial approach.

Historically, accreditation has been the main mechanism for ensuring accountability and improvement in higher education. For many years, leaders and policymakers were satisfied with accreditation because it is an approach that respects the various institutional types and different disciplines in higher education. The complex accreditation process has various levels; for example, separate groups can accredit institutions, while various professional schools (such as business) can be sensitive to the specific goals of those differing parts of the institution. Accreditation relies on a set of minimum standards for all institutions and then allows institutions to develop their own set of criteria against which they will be judged. Accreditation teams visit campuses so that they can better understand the specific institutional context as they develop their assessment of institutional performance. Accreditation avoided the problematic approach of applying one standard to all campuses with vastly different missions, histories, and constituents. However, many people are concerned that the minimum standards of accreditation are not sufficient to ensure quality, which has led to new initiatives. And some worry that because members of the higher education community carry out accreditation, external reviews are not impartial enough.

More recently, standardized and external approaches to accountability such as report cards, performance funding, and benchmarking have become popular. Some policymakers would like to abandon accreditation for report cards or benchmarking because of their simplicity and because the quality assurance process could be moved to external groups. Although these newer approaches acknowledge the distinctive mission of campuses, they provide no complex way to account for these differences in measuring performance. It is for this reason that leaders and policymakers should work to alter accreditation rather than abandon this thoughtful, intensive process for simplistic approaches.

This monograph demonstrates ways to make the accreditation press as beneficial as possible. Accreditation will be successful only if a careful implementation process is carried out. Many people ignore the way accreditation is enacted; it is easy to understand why because campuses can get caught up worrying about results, institutional image, and other issues that can sidetrack the institution from accountability, performance, and improvement. In this volume, readers will become familiar with the process of carrying out a quality accreditation program that involves planning, making the campus ready, becoming informed of changes in accreditation procedures (such as the emphasis on outcomes assessment or the Baldrige quality process), and providing adequate information and communication. Far too few texts and resources are available on such an important topic. The author brings this synthesis of the history of accreditation, current approaches, and ways to guide accreditation to ensure a quality process.

Adrianna J. Kezar
Series Editor

Acknowledgments

I want to offer my thanks to everyone who helped make this book possible. I thank my dean, mentor, and friend, Nicholas J. Beutell, for his encouragement, knowledge of accreditation, and extensive experience in the matters discussed here. My editor, Adrianna Kezar, and external reviewers provided me with superb recommendations as the manuscript evolved. The Ryan Library at Iona College was a great resource, and the staff provided strong support in an ongoing quest for books, articles, and documents. The research assistants in the Hagan School enabled me to delegate some of the routine research support and frequent trips to the library for picking up and returning borrowed items. Finally, I dedicate this book to my wife, Marta. She and my daughter, Jessica, kept me going through the demanding process of seeing this book to print.

Why Does Accreditation Matter?

OUR INSTITUTION is doing well, we are successful, and everyone knows it. So why do we need to go through accreditation? How can I successfully perform all my other duties—teaching and administration—and also do this accreditation thing? Administrators and faculty sometimes ask these and other questions. The answers to those questions should acknowledge that accreditation is required for recognition by governmental agencies, demanded by students, parents, and the community, and changing and evolving into an increasingly comprehensive system of self-renewal for institutions. Elementary, secondary, and postsecondary school employees spend most of their adult lives involved with these complex systems of education, and facilitating improvements is not easy. It should be a priority, however, to ensure success, growth, organizational development, and learning for an institution.

Today and in the near future, some of the changes in accreditation are related to the changes in condition that educational systems face (Ewell, 2001). One change is in the methods or modes of knowledge delivery. Technology comes to mind as the primary cause, but in reality technology is more of an *enabler* of change. The method of delivery is changing from an all-knowing teacher-sage model to more active learning wherein students participate in the learning process with resources facilitated by faculty. Changes are also occurring in curriculum design, with traditional semester-based systems now competing with alternative formats and new learning outcomes–based models on the rise. Another change is evident in the student profile; many students today attend multiple institutions over four or more years for their education. These and other changes are forcing organizational structures and faculty roles to evolve in new ways. The greater decentralization of authority (Alstete, 1997) and devolution of budget authority can affect the mission of the institution, because various departments seek different objectives that may or may not be in line with the traditional goals of the institution. In the area of teaching and learning, one of the most common changes in education today is the increase in active student learning and less traditional lecturing by faculty. More emphasis is placed on group work, student involvement, changing roles of faculty, and diverse instructional forms. Other changes include increased assessment of student outcomes, a more diverse student body, and the integration of technology in the learning process (Kezar, 2000). Administrators, faculty, students, and employers are seeing the results of these changes, and accrediting organizations are beginning to learn how to recognize and acknowledge the new learning.

Accrediting organizations and the institutions of higher education that seek accreditation are being forced to acknowledge these changes and to seek new roles and models for themselves in this environment. Even as far back as the early 1980s, changes were accurately predicted (Young, Chambers, and Kells, 1983), including changes in accreditation requirements from a quantitative to a more qualitative approach, relying less on numbers such as graduation rates and number of books in library and more on the processes and systems for institutional improvement. Accrediting bodies are also moving away from seeking institutional conformity to encouraging individuality. Many accrediting agencies now recognize that their mission is to provide guidance for the accreditation review, not to rely on some third-party set of standards. This approach is part of accrediting associations' general movement away from the philosophy of external review of resource inputs to more emphasis on self-evaluation, outcomes assessment, and formative development. Schools, colleges, and universities are now being required to perform more of the evaluation themselves and not rely so heavily on the external accrediting agency. The accrediting agency is now being viewed as less of a judge to more of a facilitator, guide, and mentor for assisting the educational institution in self-improvement.

This kind of image change may be an important improvement, because the system and standards for regional accreditation are normally not challenging for well-established colleges and universities (Dill, 2000). Therefore, institutions must ask themselves what accreditation will involve in the near future. Educators need to consider the accreditation process as a more active learning exercise at the institutional level. Active learning in education today can be broadly defined as students doing more than just listening. They must be engaged in solving problems and actively involved in such higher-order thinking tasks as analysis, synthesis, and evaluation (Bonwell and Eison, 1991). For accreditation, it means more active engagement by institutions in the self-study process, just as active learning assignments mean more involvement by students in their education, learning, and development. Education leaders can help faculty, administrators, and students view the accreditation process as problem-based learning, wherein stakeholders in the institution identify and examine certain challenges, peers from other institutions review them, and together they generate recommendations for improvement. It is up to the leadership of the institution to make the accreditation process become a positive, active learning exercise that is welcomed at the institution. But to achieve this goal, senior faculty and administrators need to provide strong direction and management of the accreditation process and its preparation.

Planning, organizing, supervising, directing, reporting, budgeting, and other activities to facilitate accreditation are not what many academics originally had in mind when they chose their career and entered the field of higher education. But faculty and educational leaders should be strongly motivated to effectively facilitate thorough accreditation processes for several reasons. First, self-regulation through the system of regional accreditation offers institutions the methods and support to continue and reinforce academic integrity, institutional diversity, and academic freedom (Benjamin, 1994). The alternative to this autonomy is government-directed licensing and accreditation of educational institutions that could interfere with their independence as the current system is still evolving. The history, culture, appeal, and strength of higher education in the United States and many other countries is based in large part on the principles of academic freedom, self-direction, institutional diversity, and self-governance. It is therefore important for educational leaders to educate, reinforce, and restate the benefits of self-improvement to faculty.

Martin Trow (1994) wrote that external reviewers often opt for easily quantifiable measures because they appear more objective. But colleges, universities, and individuals should be continually engaged in critical reviews of their own activities and departments. A danger exists that the criteria for success or quality in external reviews tend to be chosen with more quantitative and supposedly objective measures, which unfortunately can result in the decline of quality resulting from the increased amount of bureaucratic reports and the increased efforts of educational institutions to adapt to the simplifying tendencies of the quantification outputs. Trow reasons that departments and individuals shape their activities toward what counts in the external accreditation assessments, which negatively affects the life of the university, because academe is always more varied than any quantitative assessment of outputs can measure.

Others in higher education support the argument that voluntary self-regulation is needed to prevent government regulation, adding that the system can be improved with an "academic audit" (Dill, Massy, and Williams, 1996), that is, an "externally driven peer review of internal quality-assurance, assessment, and improvement systems" (p. 22). Unlike assessment, an academic audit is done not to measure quality but to focus on the processes that are understood to produce quality and the methods by which academics are assured that quality has been achieved. These audits of educational quality normally take place at the institutional level and concentrate on the formalities of quality assurance such as policy statements, rules and procedures, guidance notes, and meeting minutes. However, academic audits do not explore areas such as academic standards, the quality of teaching, or learning outcomes (which many U.S. accreditors now focus strongly on). But audits do evaluate how an educational institution satisfies its own standards and how they are being achieved. In addition, academic audits have the benefit of shorter cycle times than typical accreditation processes, they leave clear audit trails of records that were examined, and they are founded on the principle that good people working with sufficient resources and good processes will produce good results. The system of self-evaluation and self-regulation that most U.S. institutions are involved with must attempt to balance the nearly opposite goals of accountability and improvement, and the system of academic audits offers some new thinking and concepts for these systems to consider. Either system, accreditation or through academic audit, is surely more preferred by the higher education community than pure government regulation.

Therefore, leaders must examine the aspects of accreditation today and look for new ways to make the process an appealing renewal for the internal community, effective in improving the institution and recognized publicly as an important system and well-earned achievement.

The public perception of higher education has been an important issue in recent years, and a great deal of research has been conducted on public attitudes toward higher education (Eaton, 1999b). The research has focused largely on questions related to the price, value, purpose, and quality of education but little on the public's knowledge of and opinion about accreditation. The Council for Higher Education Accreditation (CHEA) commissioned a survey in 1999 to learn what the general public knows or believes about assuring the quality of education through accreditation. The results found that a large majority of the public believes that colleges and universities must meet moderate or high standards to receive accreditation. Interestingly, a large percentage (37 percent) did not know who performs accreditation, but a clear majority said they would not consider taking a course from an institution that is not accredited. The findings of this survey are encouraging for accrediting agencies and educational institutions that are accredited, but there is also a significant need to further educate the public about who the accrediting agencies are and the important value of self-regulatory structures currently in place. In addition, the disparity between the public perception of moderate to high standards of accrediting bodies and the internal perceptions of the educational community (and the high percentage of accredited institutions) regarding the supposedly low hurdle to achieve and renew accreditation needs to be addressed and examined by all parties involved. Accreditation does matter, and this book seeks to explore some of the issues as guidance to both the public and those involved in higher education about the potential possibilities for renewal and recognition by the effective accreditation system now in place and those under development.

The many potential benefits of accreditation and self-study at colleges, universities, and other types of institutions are often unrealized (Kells, 1994), partly because most efforts are burdensome, descriptive, mechanical efforts that are not related to the important problems and do not explore the significant achievements and opportunities that renewal through accreditation can offer. Many participants report that some improvements result from accreditation efforts and that they are useful exercises, but the infusion of continuous self-study as part of a continuous improvement strategy is rarely attempted. (Examples of effective accreditation processes and a discussion of how accreditation can be a useful and change-oriented process rather than a waste of valuable time, energy, and money are provided later in this book.) Educational leaders can motivate members of their institutional communities to be interested participants in the accreditation process if they convey the belief that it is truly regenerative to the individual members and the institution. To succeed, leaders need to prepare the institutional community before the process, expect more than minimal compliance with standards, plan more than the traditional processes usually included by exploring best practices, and keep continuous improvement institutionalized and rewarded.

Background of Accreditation

To fully understand why accreditation matters today, it is important to know how it began, why it was started, the ways academic accreditation has evolved over the years in response to changing conditions, and its fundamental characteristics (Young, Chambers, and Kells, 1983). After exploring the background of accreditation and its history, the effective management and improvement of accreditation practices can be more completely discussed in the context of its continuing evolution as a distinctive social and quasi-governmental enterprise. The historical context of the development of higher education is also important to fully appreciate the need for facilitating accreditation in universities today. Before the late nineteenth century, postsecondary education in the United States and the Colonies was largely a proscribed doctrine based on an ancient course of study at institutions that were primarily religious in nature (Rudolph, 1977). The curriculum normally included such topics as Latin, Greek, Hebrew, logic, and natural philosophy. Oversight of curricula and other matters by intercollegiate agencies or the government did not occur, which began to lead to a large diversity of institutional types, students, and educational quality.

A system of accreditation or government oversight was probably not viewed as needed because there were relatively few colleges and universities, only a small portion of the population attended, and the curriculum was not of concern to many. As the nineteenth century came to an end, however, American universities were changing from a state of near homogeneity to one with distinct differences and wide variability (Veysey, 1965). In addition, the increasing size and complexity of institutions made it inefficient for college faculty to perform much of the administration that they previously were not accustomed to doing, such as student discipline and, especially, admissions. Although institutions such as Harvard established committee systems to handle much of the work, the diversity and complexity of the higher education institutions created a need for coherence and congruity. Around 1890, a movement was begun to "accredit" the institutions that met minimal standards; the movement became a major force after 1901. This period can be viewed as the start of the first generation of academic accreditation in the United States.

The years from about 1873 to 1909 have been described as a period in the history of education that was characterized by educators' growing dissatisfaction with college admission policies and practices and by the need for sensible communication between secondary schools and the colleges of the time (Shaw, 1993). The major areas of confusion largely regarded college admission standards, the appropriate precollege preparatory subjects needed, the appropriate role of the secondary schools, and confusion concerning the competition for college students (Tompkins and Gaumnitz, 1954). Because the federal government lacked the authority to deal with the unresolved educational issues that were beyond the scope of state officials, a movement by members of the collegiate community began to address these issues. Rather than seek governmental oversight and direction, college leaders sought to regulate themselves, which may be partly because of the historically limited role of the federal government in the U.S. system and Americans' strong belief in self-reliance.

The evolution began when accreditation emerged as a national phenomenon on August 3–4, 1906, at a meeting of a joint committee of the National Association of State Universities in Williamstown, Massachusetts (Young, Chambers, and Kells, 1983). The goal of the meeting was to present a plan for creating, preserving, and agreeing to a common understanding of the admission standards and the administration of the standards.

Representatives of the four existing regional associations attended the meeting, along with the recently created College Entrance Examination Board. Attendees at the meeting agreed to recommend that the regional associations have their member colleges accept certificates from accredited schools in other regions. They also recommended encouraging the organization of a college entrance certificate board or a commission for accrediting schools, developing common definitions and standards, and establishing a permanent commission on entrance requirements. These practical matters were related to admissions and intercollegiate cooperation for standardization and mutual recognition. As the number and diversity of postsecondary institutions were growing, these early accreditation concerns in the first generation were a natural part of the development of the complex system of higher education that we see today.

During this early first period of the evolution of accreditation, two main branches of accreditation that we see today had their early roots: institutional (regional) accreditation and specialized accreditation (Young, Chambers, and Kells, 1983). The North Central Association was an early regional leader; it started accrediting secondary schools in 1905. The organization then decided to accredit member colleges and created a set of standards for doing that in 1909. The first list of accredited institutions appeared in 1913 (Pfnister, 1959; Young, Chambers, and Kells, 1983). With regard to specialized accreditation, the health care field has many examples of important early accreditation initiatives, and the medical field was an early leader in specialized accreditation. The importance of setting educational standards quickly became apparent to the leaders of medicine in the United States around the beginning of the twentieth century (Hamm, 1997). The American Medical Association (AMA) Council on Medical Education was formed in 1904 to look into those quality issues in medical education in the United States. At the request of this council, a representative from the Carnegie Corporation prepared a report on the need for common standards in U.S. medical schools. Shortly thereafter, a final report, published in 1910, led to the development of a national accrediting system for medical schools. Many medical schools were subsequently closed as the result of those standards, and the accreditation body (now called the Liaison Committee on Medical Education of the

AMA) has had a major impact on the entire health care delivery system in the United States.

In addition to medical education, the Carnegie Foundation was instrumental in standardizing college-level education in the early twentieth century. In 1905, the wealthy industrialist Andrew Carnegie established the Carnegie Foundation for the Advancement of Teaching and granted it $10 million (Tompkins and Gaumnitz, 1954; Shaw, 1993). The money was to be invested, and the income from it was to provide for retirement of professors in the United States and Canada. As they began their mission, however, the board of trustees of the organization soon learned of the nonconformity and wide array of postsecondary education faculty and institutions in North America. The Carnegie Foundation then declared that to properly carry out its goal, it must decide what truly defines a college education and the standards of meaning and definition for colleges and universities at the time. The private Carnegie Foundation did not have the authority to force colleges to comply with the rules and regulations established by its trustees. If any college wished to be eligible to receive any money from it, however, it had to comply with the stated standards. The result was a set of minimal standards that included a definition of what institutions of postsecondary education must have in regard to faculty, courses, and admission requirements. Although the influence of the Carnegie Foundation on academic standardization was not considered accreditation, it certainly affected higher education in North America significantly and subsequent accreditation efforts by academic associations.

In reality, the push to organize regional accrediting came first from secondary officials in the New England and North Central regions; for the collegiate level, it came first in the middle and southern regions of the United States (Bloland, 2001). The Middle States Association of Colleges and Schools (MSACS) was founded in 1887; the North Central Association of Colleges and Schools (NCACS) and the Southern Association of Colleges and Schools were both founded in 1895. The Northwest Association of Schools and Colleges was formed in 1917, followed by the Western Association of Schools and Colleges in 1962. These regional accrediting agencies differ greatly in size and influence. Today, the six regional accrediting organizations in the United States accredit a total of 3,000 educational institutions, with individual regional agencies having between 149 (Northwest) and 960 (North Central) institutions (Council for Higher Education Accreditation, 1999). A visit to the various Web sites of the six regional accrediting bodies shows some similarity in goals and objectives but large differences in methods, strategies, support, and organizational style. Many educational institutions seek the seal of approval from regional and specialized accreditors for public recognition, government approval, and the improvement of quality. In addition, the specialized and regional accrediting agencies are now accrediting institutions outside the United States (Bloland, 2001).

The characteristics of accreditation and purposes have been evolving over the years, and they continue to change. However, some features have remained constant, such as the aforementioned voluntary nature of the process and the self-regulatory component. Even though colleges and universities are not required to seek accreditation (Young, Chambers, and Kells, 1983), there is a large price to pay for those who do not in areas such as recognition by other organizations, public perception, and funding support. Most important, students enrolled in unaccredited institutions are not eligible for federal student aid, and the public perception of unaccredited institutions is usually low. It is interesting that this complex, thorough, and important system of accreditation is an example of service industry self-regulation and not directly supervised by the government. Members of the higher education community would be wise to keep this trust in mind as they perform self-evaluations, because the alternatives could be much more difficult and not as effective in achieving quality improvement. The current system focuses primarily on judging educational quality through institutional self-evaluation and offering guidance for improvement provided by outside consultation, which is tied to the institution's own mission and vision. As discussed later, many individuals criticize the accreditation system. But this system also has many beneficial features; it is surprisingly robust and somewhat unique in organizational quality oversight and improvement of educational processes.

One hundred years ago, the primary issues were understanding the difference between a secondary school and a college and the standardization of admission criteria. As the regional accrediting agencies were developing, there was also a movement to establish standards that could be applied across the nation (Bloland, 2001). Some of the difficulties that needed attention include the transfer of educational credits between institutions, admission to graduate schools, and the determination of equivalent degrees between the United States and Germany. These issues all gave momentum to the national standardization of higher education in the United States. This period, characterized by the attempts at national coordination among the regional agencies and periodic changes in the supraregional oversight coordinating bodies, can be called the second generation of academic accreditation. By 1949, a national association on institutional accreditation was established: the National Commission on Accreditation (NCA). The regional accrediting agencies were already well established and covered most of the established institutions, however. The regionals were largely not in favor of becoming part of a national coordinating system (Bloland, 2001). The regional associations then formed the National Committee of Regional Accrediting Agencies (NCRAA), with the purpose of aiding their members and addressing the proliferation of national accrediting bodies. The evolution then continued as the NCRAA became the Federation of Regional Accrediting Commissions of Higher Education, representing the nine postsecondary commissions of the six regional associations. FRACHE was perceived as not living up to its potential; it did little to halt the proliferation of professional and vocational accreditation across the nation.

During this period, college and university accreditation needed to address the similar yet somewhat competing interests of the federal government, state governments, and the growing number of accrediting bodies. By 1975, the presidents of many colleges became so disaffected with the complicated system that a new national organization was formed by merging NCA and FRACHE: the Council on Postsecondary Accreditation (COPA). This association encompassed a large array of types of postsecondary education, including community colleges, liberal arts colleges, proprietary schools, graduate research programs, religious schools, and trade and technical schools (Chambers, 1983). COPA had structural and organizational difficulties from its founding because there was no formal role for the staff personnel and the accreditation issues they dealt with conflicted with the source of their funding (the members they also approve for accreditation). The purpose, scope, power, and composition of COPA were regularly contested, and many questions arose whether it was needed at all (Bloland, 2001). A plan of dissolution was created by a special committee in April 1993, which then created the Commission on Recognition of Postsecondary Accreditation (CORPA) to continue its work of recognizing accrediting agencies for the U.S. government and other agencies. After several more years of debate, government leadership changes, and input from different stakeholders, the Council for Higher Education (CHEA) was formally created in 1996 and designated the successor to COPA and CORPA. (For a complete list of accrediting organizations that meet CHEA eligibility standards or were recognized by COPA or eligible for recognition by CORPA, see Appendix A.)

The purposes are clearly well evolved beyond the goals of early first-generation accrediting agencies, and they now seek to ensure that the regional and specialized agencies do more than merely recognize what a college is. CHEA now also wants to move beyond the second generation by directing accrediting agencies to employ appropriate and fair procedures in decision making and continually reassessing their accrediting practices. In other words, CHEA wants accrediting organizations to practice what they preach to their educational clients. But critics of the current system of accreditation oversight by CHEA view it as a compromise to the college presidents instead of a rigorous set of common standards to be used by the regional accrediting bodies (Amaral, 1998). It remains to be seen whether the creation of CHEA and this attempt at third-generation accreditation will be enough to protect the institutional autonomy valued by postsecondary institutions from additional federal and state governance. The third generation of academic accreditation can be characterized by efforts to apply quality initiatives, such as the Academic Quality Improvement Project (AQIP), the Baldrige awards, focused self-studies, coordinated evaluations with other agencies, and new models of periodic review. Exhibit 1 summarizes the generations of accreditation defined in this report.

EXHIBIT 1
Generations of Academic Accreditation in the United States

First generation: 1880s to early 1900s
Focus on admission standards, definition of postsecondary institutions.

Second generation: early 1900s to early 1970s
Attempts at national coordination among the regional agencies and periodic changes in the supraregional oversight coordinating bodies. Increasing number of specialized accreditation agencies. Largely input-driven numerical analysis for meeting standards.

Third generation: late 1970s to present
Diversity of quality standards among regional and specialized agencies, focused self-studies, coordinated evaluations, and other new models for periodic review. Increasing criticism of the accreditation system.

Quality Improvement and Accreditation

As we have seen, the early purposes of accreditation changed during the twentieth century to meet the evolving needs of the public as the number, size, and diversity of postsecondary institutions grew significantly. In the late 1960s and early 1970s, pressures for greater accountability in higher education mounted as the government regulation and reporting of many college functions caused increased costs. This factor, combined with inflationary pressures on institutions to pass along costs to students, resulted in increased examination of accountability and the role of accreditation of colleges and universities. In 1979, a report by COPA called for "accreditation teams to begin to look for evidence of student achievement [outcomes] used for the award of credit and degrees, and make judgements about the quality of the institution in light of the adjudged student achievement compared with degrees awarded" (Casey and Harris, 1979, p. 25). This early call for outcomes assessment, which is so pervasive today in most accreditation standards, continued the evolution of what the role of accreditation was to become. In general, the self-regulation of accreditation efforts was being changed to become more than defensive statements against increasingly meaningless standards.

Also in recent years, employers of college graduates in the business world and the general public have called for accountability and increased quality. These calls, combined with tuition costs and crowded classrooms at many large institutions, led to an increasing awareness of quality issues in higher education that needed to be addressed. For the business world, global competition helped create a large movement to increase quality of American goods and services; an example is the Malcolm Baldrige National Quality award that was created by public law in 1987 (National Institute of Standards and Technology, 1987). The award program, which led to the creation of a new public/private partnership, also includes a special category for educational organization award winners. Principal support for the program comes from the Foundation for the Malcolm Baldrige National Quality Award, established in 1988. The award is named for Malcolm Baldrige, who served as Secretary of Commerce from 1981 until 1987. His managerial excellence contributed to long-term improvement in government efficiency and effectiveness. It is clear that the overall tone and intent of this kind of thinking with regard to quality improvement has affected political leaders', business managers', and the public's push for increased accountability and quality in higher education. Among the five winners of the 2001 Malcolm Baldrige awards, three were educational organizations (National Institute of Standards and Technology, 2001a).

In addition to the Baldrige award, other business-style quality improvement efforts have also impacted accreditation through programs such as the Academic Quality Improvement Project offered by the Higher Learning Commission of the North Central Association, a regional accrediting agency in the United States (Academic Quality Improvement Project, 2002). AQIP uses a quality framework for self-evaluation that demonstrates an educational institution's commitment to systematic improvement. The self-study allows the institution to examine strengths and opportunities for improvement (weaknesses) using set criteria or questions designed around quality principles. Participants can use the AQIP criteria, other criteria such as Baldrige, a feedback report from a state quality program, a report from an independent consultant engaged by the institution, or a process such as the Continuous Quality Improvement Network's (CQIN's) Pacesetter award program (CQIN, 2003).

The self-assessment is usually broad-based and institution-wide and uses the external criteria from these or other sources. (Examples of institutions that use this approach are discussed later.)

Other examples exist of how accountability by corporate managers is becoming more important in light of the ethical issues surrounding corporate scandals of the early 21st century. As early as 1993, Peter Drucker wrote in *Post Capitalist Society* that there will be calls for a "business audit" as a common means for performance checks at companies to compare their performance with their strategic plans and objectives (Drucker, 1993). As mentioned earlier, audits of education organizations, in comparison with traditional accreditation, have also been proposed for higher education (Amaral, 1998). Where the accreditation process determines whether an institution or program has met threshold quality criteria and minimal standards, the European University Association (a merger of CRE–Association of European Universities, formerly known as the Conference of European Rectors, and the Confederation of EU Rectors' Conferences) has developed a system of quality audits (Dill, Massy, and Williams, 1996; Amaral, 1998; Dill, 2000). *Accreditation* compares the observed performance of institutions against preset standards that are usually determined by the accrediting body, whereas an *academic audit* is an externally driven peer review of internal quality assurance, assessment, and quality improvement systems. Unlike assessment, an audit often does not evaluate the quality itself or outcomes; it concentrates instead on the processes that are believed to produce the quality and the methods with which the educational members can assure themselves that quality has been achieved. In the CRE system, the review team is small, usually consisting of three auditors. They normally visit the institution or program twice for a preliminary visit and a main visit, with the goal of reaching a formative judgment about the quality management and strategic management capabilities of the university. The European system has been criticized, however, for the lack of coaching support after the review has taken place and of regular follow-ups of evaluated institutions (Amaral, 1998). In addition, because of the diverse nature of the member countries in the CRE, there is no answer to the problem of improving the transparency and comparability across member states. This situation is somewhat analogous to the concern of American institutions regarding the different evaluative systems in place by the many regional and specialized accrediting organizations. Again, the fear exists that these systems may follow rather than lead the trends in quality improvement as a result of the collegial nature of these reviews (Trow, 1994; Moore and Diamond, 2000). In the United States, some view it as a reason that, after World War II, most colleges and universities began to follow a research model rather than the teaching one many institutions were founded upon. But today, accreditation is evolving into a better quality assurance system that now encourages adherence to institutional roots and mission and even encourages diverse processes and outcomes—provided they are of high quality.

In addition to higher education's adapting some improvement strategies from business, the corporate sector has attempted to use academic accreditation-type systems for quality improvement. Among travel agencies, for example, the Airlines Reporting Corporation (ARC) launched a corporate travel department accrediting program in 1998 (Michels, 1998). ARC is a service company owned by the principal U.S. scheduled airlines. Two of its primary functions are to process and evaluate applications by persons and organizations seeking ARC approval as travel agencies and to approve locations in the United States where ARC agents may conduct business. This corporate accreditation system was set up to approve corporate travel departments in large companies. Despite supposed interest, however, only a handful of corporate travel departments actually were accredited.

Another example from the business world is the call for business accreditation to enhance global labor standards and address international concerns about labor abuses (Raynor, 1999). Private sector accreditation modeled on the accreditation system in academia has been proposed as a possible method to address labor issues. Voluntary accreditation of businesses would be an ongoing process to ensure that labor standards are being met. This solution holds potential, because the accreditation would be international, it could respond faster than other public policy strategies, and it could be used as a marketing tool for companies. Overall, however, the concept of accreditation means less to corporations than quality and success in making the business more profitable. Educational organizations have a less clear definition of what their successful outcomes are for themselves and especially for the general public. In this regard, accreditation is necessary for public confidence and assurance in addition to the more recent goals of improvement and renewal of the institution. Many concerns about perception and fact in the academic accreditation system still need to be addressed, however.

Concerns About Accreditation

Accreditation has been criticized both from within by accredited educational institutions, individuals, and organizations in the educational community and from without by those who do not see the value or worth of the system. As with many issues that are subject to public debate and speculation, some of these concerns are justified and some are not. As far back as 1939, Samuel P. Capen, chancellor of the University of Buffalo, said that educational leaders in various parts of the country are weary of having their institutions' educational and financial policies dictated by irresponsible outsiders who have selfish interests in mind (Capen, 1939; Young, Chambers, and Kells, 1983). Over the years, others involved in accreditation have described the system as elusive, nebulous, superficial, and meaning different things to different people. As mentioned earlier, part of the reason is that accreditation has never been well understood by the general public or even by the institutions that it primarily serves (Young, Chambers, and Kells, 1983). Although some of the criticism has come from misunderstandings about the proper role and authority of accreditation, other negative perceptions are rooted in the belief that the system could achieve far greater things if only certain improvements in accreditation goals and processes were made. This belief is combined with the continual pressure that educational leaders are under to restrain costs and to increase faculty and staff productivity while achieving more and more accreditations for their organization. According to Doerr (1983), "If accreditation isn't slowed as a phenomenon, institutions of higher education may well declare that process is our most important product" (p. 8). Some may argue that process, debate, and discussion are what academics truly enjoy most in their profession. When confronted with a choice for more accreditation process in their organization or more discipline-related discussion and debate, however, most people in academe would probably choose the latter.

The criticisms of accreditation today also include its cost, cumbersome nature, lack of in-depth evaluation for many institutions involved, unfairness of standards, and the perception that it is primarily self-serving (Ewell, 1994, 2001; Dill, 1998). Senior educational leaders in particular such as college and university presidents have been vocal in their negative perceptions about the academic accreditation systems and processes. Lately, these criticisms may have been aimed more at specialized accreditors in business, education, and law rather than the regional accrediting bodies—perhaps because of the positive changes that have occurred in many accreditation standards from measuring inputs to assessing outcomes and providing constructive help to organizations of varying size and development. For many years, the specialized accrediting organizations in higher education, such as the Association to Advance Collegiate Schools of Business (AACSB–International) and the National Council for Accreditation of Teacher Education (NCATE), were driven by quantitative measures of resources instead of more flexible measures of educational quality. It created a competition for resources among the various academic disciplines in medium and large institutions and virtually excluded the smaller institutions from even applying. Specialized and regional accreditation has evolved significantly in recent years, but it is still perceived by some as being too formulaic a process and too broad in scope to delve deeply into real organizational and educational deficiencies in the institutions. Many specialized accrediting organizations and even regional accreditors in the United States are often seen as bypassing the most fundamental of the higher education product: the undergraduate core courses that are usually taught by arts and science faculty. Other negative perceptions include the cost in personnel time and opportunity cost in work hours used by the many administrators and faculty who participate in a typical accreditation self-evaluation study and outside team site visit. The concerns about the value of an accreditation review are particularly strong at many larger and well-established universities whose academic standards are thought to be clearly above the threshold of most accrediting bodies (Ewell, 1994; Dill, 2000).

The accreditation process is also sometimes seen as discouraging innovation and ignoring an institution's distinctive goals and markets served (Dill, 1998). Many accreditation standards have been significantly revised to address this concern (examples of colleges and universities that not only evaluated their educational innovation but also were innovative in the internal accreditation process itself are included later). These positive changes in accreditation organizations and institutional processes, however, do not diminish the perception by many in higher education that accreditation reviews and the reviewers themselves are often ill-informed, biased, and unrealistic in their judgments or requests to the organizations. This perception is particularly troublesome to the highly educated professionals working in postsecondary educational institutions who often have very high standards for objectivity, intelligence, and strong personalities that do not receive outside evaluation well, especially if the evaluation was not conducted in a manner that was perceived as thorough, informed, and useful and the evaluators are not respected by those in the organization under review. In addition, some agencies are perceived as narrowly focused and selfishly driven by accreditation standards that are not applicable to the organization under review (Dill, 1998). This situation adds to already strong beliefs that the whole system is flawed and in need of improvement.

In theory, the literature of higher education envisions accreditation self-evaluation as a continuous process, but in reality this theory is rarely true (Barker and Smith, 1998). Colleges and universities usually consider, plan for, and perform their regional and specialized accreditation processes only when the time is nearing for a required review. There have been calls for integrating accreditation into strategic and operational planning, and several examples are available of facilitating accreditation processes effectively through proper planning, funding, and evaluation (described later). For the majority of institutions today, however, accreditation is viewed as a necessary chore that is promulgated by quasi-governmental agencies that are not viewed as helpful to the institution by many faculty and administrators. Part of these negative perceptions are probably based on the accreditation process and partly on the way that the accreditation system is structured in American higher education. For example, accreditation agencies are widely called "voluntary" (Casey and Harris, 1979), when in fact accreditation is required by the federal government for institutions to offer federal student financial aid and be awarded institutional grants. It seems therefore disingenuous to some that accreditation claims to be unrequired when there is such enormous financial pressure to achieve and maintain regional, if not specialized, program accreditation. The challenge for accrediting agencies is to enlighten members of the educational community and the public regarding the true benefits of institutional self-evaluation, feedback from peers, government recognition, and the opportunities for renewal that properly managed accreditation practices can provide. Similarly, educational leaders are challenged to inform their internal constituents of the benefits of accreditation processes, effective management and integration into the institutional structures, and support of an organizational culture that is continually aware of accreditation expectations, best practices, and implementation of a system that is more than just a periodic review.

Important institutions and individuals have condemned accreditation, including a report in the mid-1990s that was financed by the Mellon Foundation and published by Columbia University (Graham, Lyman, and Trow, 1995). This report called accreditation an overconfident intervention combined with unimportant enthusiasm that encourages self-justification rather than critical self-review of institutions. It recommended changing the accreditation system to involve intense internal reviews focused on teaching and learning and investigating genuine internal improvement processes at colleges and universities. In addition, one of the most thorough, and perhaps important, formal indictments of accreditation in recent years is a report from the American Council of Trustees and Alumni (ACTA) that was presented to U.S. lawmakers who were debating the future of accreditation (Leef and Burris, 2002; Morgan, 2002). A U.S. House of Representatives subcommittee, meeting to assess the role of accreditation in higher education, strongly criticized the U.S. accreditation system, claiming that it fails to ensure academic quality, lacks accountability, and drives up the cost of colleges for institutions and students. The ACTA report went so far as to criticize the link between accreditation and U.S. federal aid and called for severing the tie. Although some lawmakers favored this criticism, others were opposed to moving too swiftly in making such a fundamental change in the importance of accreditation to the U.S. system of postsecondary education. Specifically, the report states that although accreditation began as a voluntary system to set good standards and identify quality schools, it has evolved into a false stamp of government-approved quality that is required for all institutions that wish to offer federal financial aid. The report points out that virtually all postsecondary institutions in the United States have received regional accreditation and that rather than ensuring educational quality, accreditation now merely verifies that a college has what accreditors regard as the proper inputs and internal procedures. In addition, it says that there are significant costs associated with the accreditation system, including direct costs of the accreditation process and opportunity costs for the lost time and effort that institutions experience while pursuing the accreditation approval.

In light of these concerns and issues raised by other organizations and individuals, many reforms are under way by many regional and specialized accrediting agencies, including changes in accreditation standards, more connection to the educational mission of the institution, review processes, expectations, membership qualifications, time lines for reviews, and other aspects. One issue that is currently under increasing scrutiny is examining the evidence of student learning outcomes. The regional associations and various specialized accrediting organizations have been examining ways for colleges and universities to more thoroughly measure student learning in their programs or to create plans to implement these measures and prove that processes are in place to continually enhance learning outcomes. The extent to which it is happening has been called unprecedented (Ewell, 1998).

It has also been proposed that the U.S. Department of Education focus more on reviewing accrediting agencies that are of most concern to federal program interests, such as the proprietary schools, and those that evaluate institutions with high default rates on student loans (Martin, 1994). Despite these efforts at improvement and even as some of the reforms address important concerns raised by the membership and the public, however, some important issues are still not being fully addressed. These issues include expanding the availability of public information about quality and focusing on the non-degree and for-profit providers (Eaton, 2001a). Historically, accrediting organizations have usually provided limited information to the public about the quality of educational institutions in their detailed reviews. The reasons may have been based on the need for trust and candor among peers undergoing evaluations, but increasing calls for accountability, government scrutiny, and explanations of rising tuition costs have created increased pressure for more openness. In addition, the increasing competition to traditional educational providers by for-profit companies has further enhanced scrutiny on the accreditation process, its meaning, and its value to society.

What Is Needed?

Despite the many concerns about accreditation, there is a strong perceived, and real, need for recognition and renewal of educational institutions by governments and the public. A survey of accreditation issues involving 520 institutions of higher education by the American Council on Education in 1986 found that 90 percent of survey respondents agreed that institutional accreditation provides a useful index of institutional quality (Andersen, 1987). It was also found that a majority believed accreditation is seen as a useful tool for self-evaluation and a stimulus for improvement. However, only one-fifth of respondents identified it as extremely useful as a criterion for eligibility for federal funds. This finding raises a question as to whether there may be a conflict between the summative and formative goals of the accreditation process. This potential conflict may be supported by established management theories related to the separation of such goals in performance appraisals (Meyer, Kay, and French, 1965). The primary concept is that evaluation of performance should not be linked closely with development processes so as to maximize the potential benefits of each goal. Can outside peer evaluators in an accreditation process offer legitimate and thorough recommendations for improvement when they are also required to render a formal judgment on institutional or program quality? Some would probably argue that there is no problem in being both judge and consultant, but others might believe that there should be more of a separation to ensure the highest possible quality of the accreditation decisions and the recommendations for improvement. Regardless of the reason for the perceptions by the educational members about the usefulness of accreditation for permission to award federal student financial aid and receive federal funds, the current system is likely to remain for the time being. Proper planning and management of accreditation by educational organizations should consider both the summative and formative goals in design and implementation to achieve the best from both objectives.

Accreditation has been defined as a "voluntary process conducted by peers via nongovernmental agencies . . . to attempt on a periodic basis to hold one-another accountable to achieve stated appropriate institutional or program goals [and] . . . to assess the extent to which the institution or program meets established standards" (Kells, 1994). Therefore, based on the aforementioned reasoning, it can be proposed here that facilitating accreditation, from the perspective of the institution's education leaders, is needed to ensure continuous quality improvement and government recognition through effective planning, budgeting, organizing, and controlling the various regional and specialized educational processes in mutually beneficial consort with organizational development. Facilitating accreditation effectively means moving beyond the viewpoint that accreditation is a periodic annoyance that must be dealt with in minimal effort and compliance. Effective management of the specialized and regional accreditation processes means leveraging the significant knowledge, external power, and driving forces available for making significant improvements in organizational effectiveness and student learning. Recently, student learning has been at the forefront of regional and specialized accreditation requirements, and most institutions should make every effort to focus their resources and strategic planning on making this it of the highest goal on their strategic and operational agendas. Except for a few highly research-based institutions, student learning is and should be the goal of most postsecondary educational institutions today.

These changes are a follow-up to many recent and much needed changes in regional and specialized accreditation that were implemented, nearly all which have been for the better. Approximately twenty years ago, third-generation regional accreditation in the United States was moving away from a more quantitative approach in which input numbers such as budgets and number of library books were counted, toward a qualitative approach that considered broader educational issues (Young, Chambers, and Kells, 1983). Criticisms arose from many institutions under the previous approach because conformity, it seemed, was encouraged over individuality. Conformity of institutions by accrediting organizations in such a diverse educational system as in the United States was seen as a weakness that needed to be addressed and reversed. In light of the history of accreditation and its initial goals of ensuring minimal quality, it is understandable how easily quantifiable organizational numbers were used as a supposed measure for quality. As the educational system has evolved into the complex and diverse range of institutional types, goals, programs, locations, students served, and technologies available today, the traditional second-generation accreditation system was naturally becoming obsolete. The accreditation system itself depended on external review and then moved toward more reliance on self-evaluation and self-improvement by the educational organizations. The accrediting bodies moved from merely judging to encouraging and assisting educational institutions to improve their quality.

Recent third-generation accreditation reforms in regional accreditation have resulted in remarkable changes in the stated and actual relationships to education constituents and their approach to quality review (Eaton, 2001a). Standards have been revised not only to focus on quality improvement but also to use the regional accreditation processes to address national quality review needs. Some of these needs include the increasing presence of distance learning courses at traditional colleges, fully online distance learning programs and institutions, the expanding need for international quality reviews, the expanding attention to teaching and learning, and even the achievement of greater efficiency through coordination among accrediting organizations. Specialized accreditation, such as that used for professional programs in business, education, medicine, and law, necessitate increased institutional attention, funding, and senior-level support. Specialized program accreditation was once seen by many as an expensive, troublesome, but necessary struggle for most institutions that often resulted in great disappointment or a perceived great achievement. The president of a college recently wrote that specialized accreditation was indeed troublesome but also offers hope for beneficial reforms (Dill, 1998). This type of specialized accreditation can now be seen as necessary to spur collective self-assessment, planning, and program improvement. Specialized accreditation is valuable because it not only shows how programs can be improved but also helps the institution to understand and become more committed to the proper resources and delivery requirements for quality education in special fields with unique needs. Today, many institutions are facilitating both regional and specialized accreditations in ways that are fair to both nonspecialized programs and professional degree programs for overall institutional quality, learning results, and organizational success.

The planning and facilitation of specialized accreditation in relation to other accreditation systems and the role of educational leaders in implementing change within organizational and accreditation-sponsored reforms are important to consider. A published study on the managerial role of school deans at colleges and universities on implementing revised accreditation standards by a specialized accrediting body found that faculty involvement can be influenced to support change and accreditation process–related improvements but only to a limited extent (Henninger, 1998). Faculty members are greatly influenced by their academic disciplinary and local institutional restrictions and expectations. Although faculty may be personally in favor of certain changes brought to light by accreditation processes and reforms, their colleagues and pressure from other sources may influence their willingness to fully support and participate in important organizational development activities. The need exists for facilitating accreditation strategies to negate this effect through planning, publicity, budgeting, and personnel selection to minimize the consequence of these factors. In addition, the very structure of higher education organizations today tends to spread the loci of control among institutional standards, specialized accreditation standards, and disciplinary perceptions to influence faculty expectations in a way that may limit the role of educational leaders who are responsible for accreditation. This factor also must be considered when planning for accreditation, interaccreditation strategic cooperation, and innovative reforms in seeking accreditation approval and renewal.

Significant internal and external pressures for facilitating the accreditation processes exist in educational institutions today, among them the very real need for federal funding support, the choices among the many specialized accreditation agencies (and, in some cases, choices among regional and national associations), the increasing costs of accreditation, the internal and external pressure to improve and verify student learning, the value of receiving useful feedback from peer institutions, and the interdepartmental competition for institutional resources. Often, academic (and even nonacademic) departments have the option to pursue specialized accreditation, but institutions must decide, through strategic and operational management policies, whether to fund and support these accreditations for all that seek them. If educational institutions would implement a facilitative and interpretive managerial approach to accreditation, then decisions could be made based on a variety of factors such as the college's mission, long-range strategic plans, short-range objectives, available funding and resources, and staff qualifications. The likelihood is strong that if colleges and universities do not directly address these concerns, outside forces will. Recent hearings by the U.S. Congress on the accreditation system called for more accountability by the government, whether directly or through accreditation agencies (Morgan, 2002). In addition, many states have already begun to call for statewide testing of college graduates as a supposed measure of student learning that may then be tied to state funding support for institutions. If higher education does not manage accreditation internally, then it seems that the world outside academe will. It seems to some individuals that the problem for higher education is not how to build in more testing but how colleges and universities can measure internal standards for performance that are aligned across institutions yet are also credible to the outside world (Ewell, 2001). Facilitative and interpretive managerial strategies for accreditation processes by institutions themselves will address some of these pressures and result in continued recognition by the public and increased internal renewal at educational organizations.

The Matters of Accreditation

MOST COLLEGES and universities have developed their own forms of internal peer reviews as well as participate in regulation-based regional accreditation along with voluntary professional school accreditation (Moore and Diamond, 2000). These various internal and external review processes are often somewhat similar in their details, but for the most part they have led rather than followed the trends in higher education. Accreditation standards today are largely driven by mission and seek to guide institutional development and improvement; many are now becoming more focused on student learning outcomes. Processes that institutions develop as part of an effective strategy for facilitating accreditation should address the mission and student learning goals but also coordinate the timing, planning, staffing, and budgeting of various accreditations sought in conjunction with the internal reviews and the important interpretive strategic and operational goals of the organization. At this point in the exploration of facilitating accreditation strategies, it is important to first examine the details of the accreditation process. The actual processes of the regional and specialized accreditation are often somewhat similar and usually contain common steps.

Accreditation has been defined as "a process by which an institution of postsecondary education evaluates its educational activities, in whole or in part, and seeks an independent judgment to confirm that it substantially achieves its objectives and is generally equal in quality to comparable institutions or specialized units" (Young, Chambers, and Kells, 1983, p. 21). As stated earlier, accreditation arose in the United States as a method of conducting nongovernmental, peer evaluation of educational institutions and programs. The United States, through private educational associations of regional or national (specialized) scope, has adopted criteria that are intended to reflect the qualities of sound educational programs and has developed procedures for evaluating institutions or programs to determine whether or not they are operating at basic levels of perceived quality. According to the U.S. Government, the basic procedure in a typical accreditation system includes setting standards by the agency, a self-study by the institution applying or renewing accreditation, an on-site evaluation, publication of the decision, and monitoring by the agency (U.S. Office of Postsecondary Education, 2002). Accreditation agencies offer detailed guidance and publications for educational institutions seeking accreditation that the chief academic officer should obtain, including handbooks on the self-study, manuals, and guidelines for accreditation standards.

Naturally, from the perspective of the educational institutions, Steps Two and Three are the most critical and require close attention. Institutions normally focus on their upcoming self-evaluation (also called self-study) and the on-site visit by a team of individuals from other institutions who are designated by the accrediting association. However, these steps are only a part of an overall accreditation strategy, later described in this book, for educational institutions that wish to integrate, coordinate, and maximize the effectiveness of the various accrediting processes that most institutions typically experience periodically. Nevertheless, some institutions have used the self-study process itself as an important tool for change. For example, at the University of Vermont, the institution's leadership collaborated with faculty, staff, and students to use the accreditation process as a catalyst, or "chariot," for institutional transformation (Martin, Manning, and Ramaley, 2001). The self-study was reported to be the impetus for change and the foundation for goals that united the disciplines in finding an organizational mission. In this case, the accreditation self-study process was more than an example of continuous improvement. The process was more reactive to accreditation requirements and the stated need for strategic planning than a proactive management approach. In some institutions, this approach may be necessary and useful to make changes happen where there is strong faculty and administration opposition, inertia, or other factors that hinder strategic planning. Because there are so many different patterns of study, approaches to problems, and individual management styles among administrators and faculty in higher education, there are many potential barriers to an effective self-study (Kells, 1994). These characteristics are not unique to colleges and universities; they are quite common in many nonprofit, service-oriented bureaucracies—particularly those that are publicly supported government agencies and research organizations with a high percentage of educated professional staff members (Goodstein, 1978). The potential barriers to self-study that can arise in these environments include:

- Weak organization and governance, which often results in unclear goals, lack of readily available and useful data, staffing issues; and
- Interaction among groups, partly because of the academic nature of in-depth analysis for all problems, tendencies to avoid conflict, histories of poor planning procedures, and a general dislike of direction or guidance from highly educated independent thinkers who are often too proud to accept other opinions.

Regardless of these potential obstacles, self-evaluation studies in accreditation processes can be, and usually are, beneficial to the institution. A great deal of evidence of this is found in journal articles, conference presentations and proceedings, and the feedback stated on many self-evaluation reports. Many accrediting bodies have been implementing changes in accreditation to attempt improvements in their systems that face significant internal institutional obstacles and increasing external criticism.

A recent survey by the Council for Higher Education Accreditation of 81 regional and specialized accreditors found that many accrediting agencies are departing from traditional accreditation approaches that are individual to more cooperative initiatives (Safman, 1998). These new efforts may address how self-studies are developed, how visiting teams are created, how visitation team reports are prepared, and how data are collected and shared among accrediting organizations. In a later chapter, this book describes several examples of cooperative accreditation approaches that can be part of an effective strategy for facilitating accreditation. Regional and specialized accrediting organizations have been forming collaborative evaluations by jointly designating a single review team that collects information, interviews institution personnel, examines facilities, and writes a single report to both accrediting agencies. This collaborative evaluation requires that the institution and accreditors agree on a process calendar, the size of the visitation team, and the focus of the self-evaluation. However, accrediting organizations retain the authority for the respective decisions on the actual accreditation outcome decision. Although these collaborative self-study reviews do offer some advantages, they may be viewed as a somewhat temporary solution to the overlapping, redundancy, and financial cost previously mentioned. Other pressing concerns about accreditation also need to be addressed, such as accountability, thoroughness, and the potential discord between the formative and summative goals. Regardless of these difficulties, educational institutions today must work with the regional and specialized accreditation systems. Furthermore, effective facilitation of organizational resources is strongly needed for successful recognition and renewal.

Other recent changes in approaches to accreditation practice include three-year collaborative accreditation reviews, international collaboration, alliance of subspecialties, choice of self-study topics, reduced number of site visits, reduced size of visiting teams, and the use of annual questionnaires to collect data. The multiyear approach concentrates the accreditation reviews of the participating regional and specialized accreditors for the institution within a three-year time frame so that accreditors can share data and develop common reporting formats. International collaboration entails American visiting teams joining with accreditors from another country to conduct collaborative reviews. This approach may have increasing importance in future years to facilitate understanding of the differences about accrediting and quality assurance in a global economy with increasing internationalization of education organizations. Subspecialties such as allied health and related fields are now seeking to develop common standards of good practice, which can also reduce organizational costs and reduce redundancy. An important improvement that also has gained popularity is the availability of topic choice in the self-study, especially for larger institutions that wish to emphasize and improve particular problems such as fundraising, governance, strategic planning, or other important issues. Leaders implementing facilitating accreditation policies should strongly consider leveraging accreditation self-study processes for these purposes as part of their strategy. Other new strategies such as reducing the number of site visits and visiting team member can also be managed to reduce costs and improve efficiency. However, one area that may increase costs and potential definition problems is the use of annual questionnaires by various accrediting agencies. At least one specialized accreditor, AACSB-International, has recently begun requiring all members to complete lengthy questionnaires each year, which takes considerable time and resources from member schools for dubious returns on their efforts. In addition, some may view questionnaires with large amounts of numerical data as a regression toward quantifiable input measures by accrediting agencies instead of a move ment toward quality improvement through proper external recognition coupled with effective internal renewal.

Traditionally, the academic associations, governing bodies, and other agencies that create and administer accreditation programs have been advised and directed to set certain parameters and goals. It is important for educational institutions and managers of accreditation at colleges and universities to understand what the accreditors are seeking, the value and costs of the particular accreditation under consideration, and what needs to be done to achieve maximum return on the investment in pursuing the accreditation. When the accrediting agencies first create their policies, they normally seek to define the need for the accreditation from the educational market (Hamm, 1997). The mission statements of the organizations are also exam ined, along with the structuring options for accreditation administration. The standards are then set, governance and leadership selected, operational issues defined, marketing and promotion to potential members conducted, and applications for accreditation accepted. Educational institutions must then decide which accreditation, or accreditations, fit with their goals. The educational institutions then may begin the actual process of seeking accred-itation or reaffirmation for continuing to be accredited by applying to the accrediting body. Criteria for eligibility to seek accreditation are listed in Appendix B.

The Self-Study

After applying for accreditation, the next step is an in-depth institutional or program self-evaluation that is conducted by the educational institution under the guidance of the accreditation program being sought. The self-study is the main mechanism that academic accrediting agencies currently use to measure quality and to assist educational institutions for self-improvement. The self-study can provide a foundation for planning at the institution, lead to ongoing institutional research and self-analysis, enhance institutional openness, and provide staff development (Young, Chambers, and Kells, 1983). To be most effective, the self-study should be internally motivated and supported rather than seen by the educational community as a response to an external agency (Jones and Schendel, 2000). It is important for senior leaders of the educational institution or program to be fully committed to the process, a commitment that should be expressed publicly to the community (Rieves, 1999). The faculty, students, and midlevel administrators will then be more motivated to participate fully in the accreditation process and thereby increase the opportunity for institutional improvement. A later chapter describes examples of innovative approaches to self-study as part of an accreditation approach that uses an interpretive strategy (Chaffee, 1985b). However, at this point it is important to understand that the self-study can be designed by the senior administration with not only the accreditation goal in mind but also particular goals of the educational institution. In a traditional linear approach, many institutions use the criteria and norms stated by the various accreditation agencies as the basis for their self-studies. Actually, the accreditation self-study process can use a more interpretive strategy as part of an informed procedure to clarify institutional goals to stakeholders, assess goal achievement, and present the organization's true capabilities. For example, Michigan Tech chose to organize its regional accreditation self-study around eight strategic goals, taking five specific actions in the late summer and early fall of the first year of the self-study (Walck, 1998):

- Selecting the steering committee and subcommittees;
- Creating written committee charges to guide the committee work;

- Developing a strengths, weaknesses, opportunities, threats (SWOT) analysis to focus the committees and departments on evaluation;
- Conducting an orientation to distribute information and create buy-in; and
- Publicizing the self-study process widely.

A SWOT analysis can be an effective accreditation planning tool that asks planners to evaluate the organization in an informed manner; it can also be used to summarize the results of various subcommittee reports in a self-study process. The SWOT analysis that was mandated for Michigan Tech's use is shown in Figure 1.

Examining benchmark institutions is part of the SWOT analysis, and a list of appropriate comparable institutions can be designated by self-evaluation team leaders. The benchmark institutions can be selected based on peer or aspirant institution type, mission, size, and student market. The actual distinctive competencies and competitive disadvantages can be discovered through informal research from primary and secondary sources or through formal benchmarking programs. Government offices, private organizations, and accrediting agencies such as AACSB-International offer comparative statistical services; Educational Benchmarking Incorporated, for example, offers the Stakeholder Assessment Studies, and AACSB offers annual data collected from its Business School Questionnaire. Benchmarking in higher education gained popularity as a management tool to collect comparative data, discover best practices, and adapt improvements to home institutions that perform these studies (Alstete, 1995). This technique can be used as a valuable part of self-study and often demonstrates the areas of significant institutional strengths as well as any areas that may need improvement.

Normally, the self-evaluation process for regional accreditation is the responsibility of the chief academic officer, often called the vice president for academic affairs or the provost. In specialized accreditation reviews, this responsibility normally falls under the school or department leader, such as a dean. Other elements of self-study to consider include the selection of institutional members on the formal self-evaluation team, group dynamics, report writing, and virtual team technology (Young, Chambers, and Kells, 1983). Like the selection of team members for accreditation visits, it is also very

FIGURE 1
Self-Study SWOT Analysis

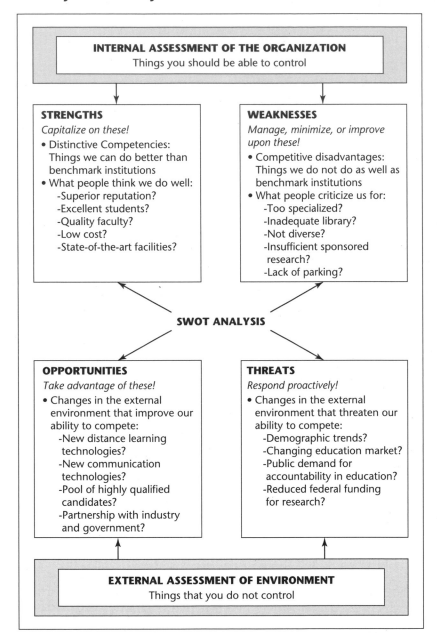

INTERNAL ASSESSMENT OF THE ORGANIZATION
Things you should be able to control

STRENGTHS

Capitalize on these!

- Distinctive Competencies:
  Things we can do better than
  benchmark institutions
- What people think we do well:
  - -Superior reputation?
  - -Excellent students?
  - -Quality faculty?
  - -Low cost?
  - -State-of-the-art facilities?

WEAKNESSES

Manage, minimize, or improve upon these!

- Competitive disadvantages:
  Things we do not do as well as
  benchmark institutions
- What people criticize us for:
  - -Too specialized?
  - -Inadequate library?
  - -Not diverse?
  - -Insufficient sponsored
    research?
  - -Lack of parking?

SWOT ANALYSIS

OPPORTUNITIES

Take advantage of these!

- Changes in the external
  environment that improve our
  ability to compete:
  - -New distance learning
    technologies?
  - -New communication
    technologies?
  - -Pool of highly qualified
    candidates?
  - -Partnership with industry
    and government?

THREATS

Respond proactively!

- Changes in the external
  environment that threaten our
  ability to compete:
  - -Demographic trends?
  - -Changing education market?
  - -Public demand for
    accountability in education?
  - -Reduced federal funding
    for research?

EXTERNAL ASSESSMENT OF ENVIRONMENT
Things that you do not control

SOURCE: Walck, 1988; p. 235. Used with permission.

important to properly select a representative, appropriate, performance-minded internal self-study team from a variety of departments in the educational community. Institutions should seek to involve as many individuals from the community as possible, and it is not uncommon to have more than one hundred faculty and staff involved on the committees and subcommittees (Bartelt and Mishler, 1996). Team members should be experienced in their department, with good oral and written communication skills, and be experienced in working effectively on institution-wide teams that will be formed, such as the self-evaluation committee or subcommittees. The important group dynamics to consider include the stages of group development and formation of group leadership in the self-study team. The final product that the team will produce is a self-evaluation report; therefore, excellent writing skills are needed and should be demonstrated in previous written work before assignment to the self-evaluation team. One interesting and relatively new aspect to consider in the self-study process is the availability of virtual team tools that use today's information technology for communication, research, work flow management, and the written output. It has been shown that team performance can be enhanced using e-learning systems, which have many useful features that a self-study team can use (Alstete, 2001). These features include discussion boards to facilitate intrateam communication, digital drop boxes to exchange documents, an announcement page for the team leader to manage the team, external Internet links to help the team research certain issues, and the ability to hold virtual live chats for real-time communication and instant feedback for informative discussions.

The steps in the self-study process often include preparing for and designing the self-study, organizing the study, monitoring the process, using peers, and integrating the cycles of study and planning (Young, Chambers, and Kells, 1983). In preparation, it is important to establish leadership and internal motivation for the self-study, identify a specific list of institutional needs and issues, and recognize local conditions to reflect in design of the self-study. Two elements of a successful self-study that were recognized at Pikes Peak Community College during its reaccreditation were the full support of the college's president and community and the detection of common threads of concern and direction (Kemling, 1994). This experience showed that the self-study report should not merely be a collection of various committee reports bound together under a common title. A good self-study can bind the institution together in the pursuit of a common direction with strong leadership and active community participation. The self-study must also be organized effectively by defining tasks and roles, establishing the guidance structure (normally a steering committee of task force chairs), and selecting the best people to orient and train, obtain resources, set time lines, and establish coordination and communication mechanisms. Goncalves (1992) points out that it is very important to pay attention to the characteristics of those individuals who are creating the strategy (Goncalves, 1992). Therefore, it is important to wisely choose accreditation managers, team leaders, and participants in the self-study teams. Members should be detail-oriented, thorough in their work, have good writing skills, be critical and evaluative in their outlook, but not hold a political, departmental, or other agenda that may interfere. Honesty and integrity are also very important, and participants should be willing to look at institution-wide problems and seek feasible solutions that can be achieved.

The mechanics of the self-study process itself need attention so that participants stay with the stated intentions and study goals, with clarification, consensus building, completeness, and priority where needed (Young, Chambers, and Kells, 1983). Inputs into the self-study, along with the institutional environment, program, and processes, need to be continually examined and refined. It is important to review accreditation standards once the self-study is under way for use of valid criterion levels applicable to the educational institution that is being studied. The self-study process should examine potential survey or other instruments to assist with gathering facts and opinions, as well as outcomes assessment processes and results that are now required by most accreditation standards. The mechanics of the study should also include a plan to formally discuss the self-study results and preparation of a useful report for implementing institutional changes. During the self-study process, the use of peers as consultants prior to the study is encouraged by some accreditors and often by the visitation team from outside the organization.

The accreditation process, whether regional, specialized, or other, should be promoted within the educational organization to create strong motivation by faculty, administrators, staff, trustees, alumni, and students. One mid-sized comprehensive college in the eastern United States recently achieved accreditation by AACSB International. The institution had sought this prestigious recognition for more than twenty years, without success, until a new leadership team was in place. The new president, chief academic officer, and dean of the business school all made accreditation a top priority, both in words and action. The institution's president went so far as to state publicly during a college-wide presentation that the "train had left the station" (toward achieving accreditation) and that if educational community members were not on board, they would be left behind. The chief academic officer stated publicly that the institution would do "whatever it takes" to achieve accreditation. The school's dean was therefore well supported in seeking the accreditation. Continual persuasion, formal and informal, by the educational leaders of the planning group and the institution itself are necessary to create and sustain internal motivation, especially in the early stages.

As mentioned earlier, accreditation agencies offer detailed guidance and handbooks on the self-study process, which are often the best source of guidance for particular accreditation goals. Figure 2 illustrates the overall schema of planning from the institutional perspective and shows how the prestudy planning fits into a model for effective self-evaluation as part of a framework for effectively facilitating accreditation. This model is based on self-study time lines by Kells (1994) and Bartelt and Mishler (1996), with modifications added by this author incorporating facilitating accreditation objectives.

The planning stage in an individual accreditation process involves creating a prestudy accreditation planning group approximately eighteen months before the visitation team arrives at the educational institution. The institution needs to select and appoint the leadership team for the self-study and to promote internal motivation regarding the accreditation objectives. Local needs for the self-study plan should be established, the study designed, formal governance approval sought, and a budget planned. All of these items are necessary for properly facilitating accreditation and achieving maximum return on the investment in self-evaluation. The typical regional or specialized

FIGURE 2
Self-Study Planning Time Line within Facilitating Accreditation Framework

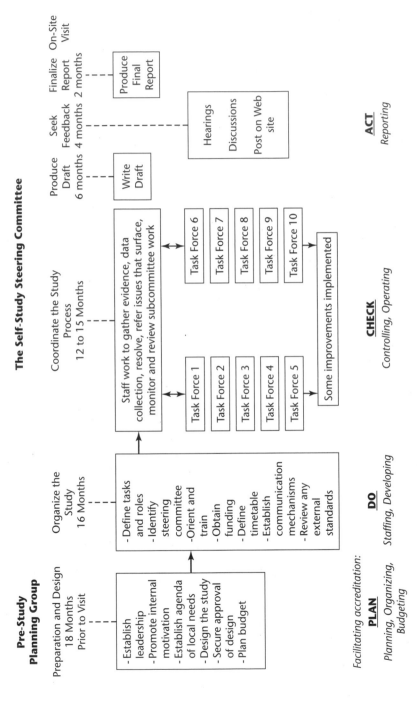

Pre-Study Planning Group

The Self-Study Steering Committee

Preparation and Design
18 Months
Prior to Visit

- Establish leadership
- Promote internal motivation
- Establish agenda of local needs
- Design the study
- Secure approval of design
- Plan budget

Organize the Study
16 Months

- Define tasks and roles
- Identify steering committee
- Orient and train
- Obtain funding
- Define timetable
- Establish communication mechanisms
- Review any external standards

Coordinate the Study Process
12 to 15 Months

Staff work to gather evidence, data collection, resolve, refer issues that surface, monitor and review subcommittee work

Task Force 1	Task Force 6
Task Force 2	Task Force 7
Task Force 3	Task Force 8
Task Force 4	Task Force 9
Task Force 5	Task Force 10

Some improvements implemented

Produce Draft
6 months

Write Draft

Seek Feedback
4 months

Hearings
Discussions
Post on Web site

Finalize Report
2 months

On-Site Visit

Produce Final Report

Facilitating accreditation:

PLAN
Planning, Organizing, Budgeting

DO
Staffing, Developing

CHECK
Controlling, Operating

ACT
Reporting

accreditation self-study often takes place over twelve to eighteen months, during which the study is organized and coordinated, and the draft of a large report is produced. In the organization of the self-study, the tasks and roles of the committee members need to be articulated, steering committee members identified and trained, funding obtained (based on the budget planned in the previous step), timetable established, communication mechanisms set up, and external standards reviewed. During this stage, the staff works to gather evidence for the self-study, collects data, resolves issues, and monitors subcommittees' work.

The checking stage normally begins when an initial draft of the self-study is produced. The chief academic officer or dean is normally in charge of this important step, in which all the voluminous work produced by the steering committee and subcommittees is checked for accuracy of content. Feedback is also solicited from internal and external constituents of the educational community through printed and electronic distribution of the draft report, open meetings, and directives from educational leaders. The final step in the self-study process is to finalize the self-evaluation report and act on some of the findings before the team's visit. This action can be as a result of problems and issues discovered during the self-study, with the actual act being the writing of institutional plans to solve the problems discovered. Some action can be immediately taken on certain issues within the institution, but most accrediting organizations seek to help institutions properly recognize issues and then create action plans for real improvement. These plans should address the important and often challenging findings that will usually result in achievement of recognition by the accrediting agency.

After reporting the self-study findings to the accreditation agency, the final step should be to incorporate the improvement plans and improved cycles of study and planning into the institution's framework. This information will be used as a basis for strategic planning and ongoing institutional research. The lessons learned by institutional leaders and the educational community about self-evaluation and proper planning during the self-study can be as valuable to the institution's development as the reported findings of the self-study report itself.

On-Site Evaluation

In one of the final steps in the accreditation process, the accrediting agency evaluates the self-study report and then decides whether or not to send an evaluation team to the educational institution. This visiting committee of professional academic peers assesses how well the institution meets the standards of the accrediting agency. The written report of the visiting committee helps the institution improve its programs and also provides the basis on which the accrediting agency decides to grant, continue, reaffirm, or withdraw accreditation (Southern Association of Colleges and Schools, 2002).

During a typical visit of several days, committee members examine data and conduct interviews to evaluate the quality and accuracy of the self-study and to ascertain whether the institution is in compliance with the accreditation standard of the regional or specialized association. The committee often offers written advice to the institution, develops a consensus on its findings, and completes a draft report. Finally, the committee usually presents an oral summary in an exit report to the chief executive officer and invited institutional officials on the last day of the visit. The departure of the committee from campus does not mark the end of the accreditation process. The accreditation association reviews the visiting committee's report and the response of the institution to its findings so that a final decision can be made. Members of an evaluation committee function as colleagues as well as critics. The purpose is to produce a committee report that will be useful to the institution and to the agency that must make a decision on accreditation.

An evaluation committee usually has five to fifteen members, with the number depending on the nature of the institution and its programs and the protocol of the accrediting association. Normally, every principal instructional area under consideration by the accrediting agency must be examined. The evaluators are usually assigned from accredited higher education institutions in the accrediting association, appropriate agencies, and possibly other regions or specialties. Many applicants for accreditation seek to have some of the evaluators come from institutions similar to the one to be visited. A majority of the members are often from outside the area or state where the college to be evaluated is located. However, the accrediting association usually has final authority on the makeup of the committee, and experienced evaluators from other regions or from other recognized accrediting bodies are then formally assigned to the evaluation committees. To help ensure objectivity, visitation team members are normally selected who have no prior association with the institution being evaluated and are not considered nearby competitors.

Usually, the committee chair, often a present or former member of the accrediting association, is assigned by the agency more than a year before the evaluation. In selecting evaluators, the association is careful to avoid potential conflict of interest, such as an evaluator who is a former employee of the institution or has other personal bias against the institution. The evaluation committee roster is sent to the institution in advance of the visit, and the chief executive officer or department head is requested to notify the accrediting agency office if it has any question about the composition of the evaluation committee.

The association arranges the dates of the on-site evaluation in conjunction with the institution's president, often up to two years or more in advance (Northwest Association of Schools and of Colleges and Universities, 2002). A determined effort is normally made to arrange dates most suitable to the institution, although compromises on the dates arranged are sometimes necessary for upcoming accreditation meetings within the accrediting association. Most accrediting agencies require a two- to four-day on-site evaluation period. The evaluation may be scheduled for weekdays or a combination of weekdays and weekends, depending on the convenience of the accrediting body and the institution being evaluated (American Association of Museums, 1989). A typical itinerary for an on-site evaluation by a team from a regional accrediting association is shown in Appendix C.

From the institution's perspective, the goal of the visiting team's schedule is not only to present the institution in the most favorable light but also to facilitate communication with as wide an audience as possible for effective data collection by the team. If the self-evaluation is a focused review that concentrates on a particular area the institution has selected, then the visitation team selection as well as the time schedule may be different from traditional evaluations. However, the itineraries for most visits include common elements of data collection through interviews, examination of printed materials provided in a resource room, and a feedback session to the institutional community at the conclusion of the visit.

After the Accreditation Review

Upon completion of the published evaluation, some accreditors may require or encourage educational institutions to prepare a formal written response to the report by the institution (Middle States Association Commission on Higher Education, 2001). Accrediting agencies also may require a follow-up visit to an institution, either after a review of a follow-up report or at the request of staff in light of an institution's changing internal or external environment. For the follow-up report, accreditors usually require an institution to submit this document when the agency needs additional information in a specific area not adequately covered by the institution's periodic self-study report, an initial accreditation self-evaluation, or the response to a recommendation made by the visiting team. The agency also may wish to assist an institution by focusing early attention on a special issue of concern or a need for further information.

The preparation of a follow-up report, like a self-study, can provide opportunities for constructive discussions on a campus involving many members of the academic community and bringing many points of view to the consideration of a particular issue. The report could also serve as a useful planning document for the institution. The follow-up report typically follows no set format, but it should have a functional title, including the institution's name and location, the date it was prepared, and a quotation from the agency's letter requesting the report, excerpted so as to identify the subject of the report.

The scope of the follow-up report depends on the nature of the follow-up activities and issues specified in the agency's letter communicating its accreditation action. If the institution requires clarification of the issues or the agency's concerns, a representative from the educational institutions should contact the agency staff member who serves as liaison to the institution. The text of the report should establish the context for the materials being submitted, and because a year or more usually elapses between the agency's request for a report and the date the report is filed, the report should review sufficient background to make the significance of current developments clear to people who are not involved in the institution's daily affairs. The report could be as brief as a memorandum to the agency, but it should be as explicit and precise as the nature of the materials permits and it should enable readers to assess the situation at the institution.

Where appropriate, it should provide supporting data if they strengthen and clarify the report. Appendices should be limited to those items essential to a reader's understanding of the report. The documentation should be interpreted and presented so that its relevance to the issues being discussed is apparent.

After receipt of the follow-up report, the agency may have a committee on follow-up activities or candidate institutions review each report. In addition, a finance associate may review and interpret reports on financial information. After a thorough discussion of the report and any accompanying materials, the agency typically decides on one of the actions outlined in the range of actions available. In addition, follow-up visits may be made after a specific action of the agency or at the request of an institution. The agency also may require a visit after reviewing a follow-up report or information provided by staff. The areas of coverage in a special follow-up visit usually are limited to specific topics. However, as regional accreditation applies to an entire institution and specialized agencies to an individual area, the follow-up visit implies an evaluation of the specific topic in the context of the institution as a whole or specialized area. The visiting team may be limited in number, and it may include a staff observer and a representative of the appropriate state agency. However, follow-up visits are not the normal response by accrediting agencies for typical regional accrediting periodic reviews. Agencies normally decide the outcome based on a set range of accreditation decisions.

The range of decisions made by accrediting agencies often includes several levels of possible outcomes. For previously accredited institutions following an on-site evaluation by a typical regional accrediting agency in the United States, the agency may take one of several actions, such as reaffirmation without condition, with condition, with a follow-up report, deferment, institutional probation, or a requirement to show cause as to why an institution should have its accreditation removed (Middle States Association Commission on Higher Education, 1997). A more complete list of decisions for initial and renewal of accreditation is shown in Appendix D.

Monitoring by accrediting agencies normally involves periodic review reports requested every few years, and an increasing number of specialized agencies now require annual data reports to be submitted by accredited members for continual review and monitoring. For example, AACSB-International has a Knowledge Services office that provides data and information about the characteristics and practices of business schools and their industry to support accreditation, promote institutional improvement, enrich member services, enhance public understanding, and facilitate informed decisions. Some accredited institutional members find these annual data reports time-consuming and not worthwhile for improving daily operational planning or strategic decision making. The questionnaire provided by AACSB is designed to collect basic data and information that identify and describe member business units. Schools completing the business school questionnaire receive a series of comprehensive statistical reports summarizing the data provided by AACSB-International members, access to custom reports, and an information profile of the school on the AACSB-International Web site. Other accrediting agencies may also be moving toward annual data collection, and there has even been talk of changing structured periodic reviews away from the traditional seven- or ten-year cycles to continual annual reviews with no on-site visits unless needed. This change may be due in part to the increasing power of information technology, the Internet, criticisms of accreditation effectiveness, complaints about the costs of accreditation by institutions, and other factors. Examining whether these changes become reality is not truly important at this time, however, because the accreditation processes must be addressed by educational organizations now, regardless of what the future may hold. Therefore, administrators and faculty in educational organizations should consider all the options for planning the facilitation of the accrediting processes for maximum effectiveness so that the goals and objectives of the organization can be achieved.

Strategies for Achieving Accreditation

S O FAR it has been shown that the world of higher education accreditation is rapidly changing and is very different from the early years of small independent colleges that required little external recognition and rarely renewed themselves. College leaders, administrators, faculty, and staff are now expected to work in partnership with each other and with these quasi-governmental agencies that provide official recognition as well as tremendous opportunities for self-renewal—that is, if the institutions and their leaders choose to take advantage of these opportunities and make the pursuit of and periodic renewal of regional and specialized accreditations more than just a compliance formality. Today, most educational institutions are under powerful pressures to use resources efficiently as market and other factors influenced by global forces play a much greater role in structuring the delivery of educational services. Within this context, those in higher education administration must manage these evolving duties and responsibilities wisely and plan accreditation strategies accordingly. Management of accreditation matters is an important responsibility that should be planned and carried out to meet the demands of these changing markets and global forces. But what is meant by facilitating accreditation matters, and how does it fit into the framework of higher education administration?

The literature on administration and management contains many perspectives on how they are different and where management typically is relegated to a subordinate and specialized part of administration processes (Lynn and Stein, 2003). According to Henry Fayol (1930), it is important to not confuse administration with management. He argued that to manage is to conduct an organization toward the best possible use of all the resources at its disposal and to ensure the smooth working of essential functions, whereas administration is only one of those functions, having been defined as the universal process of efficiently organizing people and directing their activities toward common goals and objectives (Simon, Thompson, and Smithburg, 1991). For educational institutions, administration can therefore be interpreted as the higher-level oversight in the creation, development, and implementation of goals in seeking and renewing regional and specialized accreditations. Management and facilitation of accreditation will be shown to be an effective way in which colleges and universities use all the resources at their disposal to achieve renewal and recognition by accrediting agencies.

Like the recent history of accreditation and higher education in general, the world of management in organizations has also changed rapidly over the years. In the mid-nineteenth century, the phenomenon of management as we know it was unknown (Drucker, 2001). Organizations, businesses, and especially colleges were very small by today's standards. In less than 150 years, management evolved and transformed the social, economic, and even political landscape of the world's developed countries. Well-known management theorists such as Fredrick Taylor, Max Weber, Alfred P. Sloan, Elton Mayo, and W. Edwards Deming developed several approaches to define and understand management from theoretical, descriptive, comparative, and action-based perspectives. The concepts identified, explained, and dispersed by these theorists helped to make improvements in many types of organizations in addition to businesses, including public organizations such as government agencies, non-profit organizations, and postsecondary institutions.

Some of the ways in which businesses, government agencies, and higher education have sought to address these pressures for improvement have been through a variety of popular management systems. These systems include concepts such as planned programming budgeting systems, management by objectives, zero-base budgeting, strategic planning, benchmarking, total quality management, and business process reengineering (Birnbaum, 2000). Some see these management approaches as innovations if they are adapted and retained, others as fads that are part of an expected life cycle of creation, usage, and eventual abandonment. When institutions in higher education adopt a system or are even just exposed to certain concepts and practices, the institutions are likely to discover certain changes in their management processes (Chaffee, 1985a). The research literature and examples from institutions that have successfully achieved accreditation recognition and renewal are good examples to examine.

In recent years, many organizations have been reemerging with smaller, flatter institutional structures organized around a set of generic, value-creating processes and specific competencies (Jones, Thompson, and Zumeta, 2001). The traditional silos or stovepipes of organizational structures within organizations have been replaced by control systems that distribute and decentralize decision making down in the organization to wherever it is needed, such as the point of sale, delivery, or in production (Simons, 1995). In higher education, where decentralized, hierarchical organizational structures coexist with a large flattened component of faculty governance, the movement of administrative and managerial decision making to even lower components may not be possible without strong guidance, personnel retraining, or restructuring. If this change involves management of academic accreditation that spans departments and schools within larger institutions, it is especially important. Therefore, the question remains how accreditation can be facilitated effectively with organizational limitations yet maximize the true potential that modern systems thinking can offer.

One way to frame an answer is to create a taxonomy of accreditation strategies, processes, and best practices within a set of management tasks that can be organized into the common functions or tasks that managers perform in most organizations. Chaffee (1985a) declares that management strategy is multidimensional and based on the situation, and comprises three models that are different but sometimes conflicting: linear strategy, adaptive strategy, and interpretive strategy. The linear approach has been described in much of the research and focuses on the traditional areas of planning and forecasting. The second model is viewed as adaptive and is more closely associated with strategic management, seeking to make the organization and its parts change proactively or reactively based on the environment. The third model, interpretive strategy, is associated with the social and cultural aspects of organizations. This strategy conveys meanings by orienting metaphors or frames of reference that are designed to motivate stakeholders in ways that favor the organization. Chaffee proposes that:

> *Rather than emphasizing* changing with *the environment, as is true of the adaptive model, interpretive strategy mimics linear strategy in its dealing with the environment. There is, however, an important difference. The linear strategist deals with the environment by means of organizational actions that are intended to affect relations instrumentally, but the interpretive strategist deals with the environment through symbolic actions and communication. . . .*
>
> *In interpretive strategy the organization's leaders shape the attitudes of participants and potential participants toward the organization and its outputs. This attitude change seeks to increase credibility for the organization or its output. In this regard, interpretive strategy overlaps with the adaptive model. For example, when an adaptive strategist focuses on marketing to enhance product credibility, the strategist's behavior could be classified as interpretive [Chaffee, 1985b, pp. 93–94].*

Accreditation strategies that educational institutions can consider in using an interpretive approach are seen in several examples (examined subsequently). For the accreditation goals of seeking recognition from external stakeholders and internal institutional renewal in a challenging, decentralized, change-resistant organizational culture, interpretive strategies are the natural outcome that many accreditation plans, processes, and results seem to strive for. These efforts seek to shape the attitudes of participants, both internal and external to the institution (such as accreditors), as well as potential participants (such as prospective students, donors, and institutional partners).

Although many of the examples will indeed be related to self-study, other examples will show how concepts described here can bring together innovative, practical, interesting, intelligent, and useful approaches to facilitating accreditation that many colleges and universities have developed. It will then be up to other educational institutions to look at the interpretive principles for shaping attitudes as applied to facilitating accreditation to adapt best practices, create an overall facilitating accreditation strategy for their organization, and achieve the recognition and renewal that is sought.

In addition, because traditional managerial approaches have been viewed as a bit too inward-looking (Jones, Thompson, and Zumeta, 2001) and have evolved in recent years to include new topics such as diversity, globalization, quality, and organizational learning, the final chapter of this book also includes an overview of leadership in facilitating accreditation and the application of quality initiatives such as the Academic Quality Improvement Project and the Malcolm Baldrige award. Educational leaders who seek to apply interpretive strategies in shaping the attitudes of internal and external participants in accreditation programs will benefit from viewing examples highlighted in that chapter. Commonly debated issues are whether leadership is a different function and activity from management (Capowski, 1994) and whether some formal leaders exercise real leadership and others exercise management (Robbins, 2000). Harvard University's John Kotter has proposed that management is about coping with complexity and that good management brings about order and consistency by creating formal plans, designing organizational structures, and monitoring results against the plans (Kotter 1990a, 1990b). Kotter believes that leaders establish direction by developing a vision for the future, then aligning people by communicating this vision and inspiring them to overcome hurdles. It is seen as necessary for optimum organizational effectiveness in addition to effective facilitation of accreditation strategies.

The need for good management and decisive leadership strategies is especially true for higher education because of the unique organizational structure that has been criticized so often, despite the many successes that have been reported (Birnbaum, 1988; Henninger, 1998). The distinctive feature is the dualism of both administrative and faculty hierarchies through which various decisions are made, and sometimes not made, that all too often results in the status quo. The importance of results, or learning outcomes, has continued to be an important issue for the public, legislators, and accreditors. Judith Eaton, president of the Council for Higher Education Accreditation, states that as accreditors have attempted to tighten the connection between quality and results (or outcomes), these efforts have confronted resistance in the higher education community from discomfort and confusion (Eaton, 1999a). This resistance tends to emerge when students are equated with consumers (as in business) and higher education is treated as a market. The academic culture has a long history and tradition that views colleges and universities as communities of intellectual growth and knowledge development not easily connected with results and a market-driven perspective. In addition, discomfort emerges when the quality discussion turns to outcomes because outcomes are usually attached only to student learning, and many institutions view it as part of their missions along with research and service. Outcomes are also difficult to measure, not easily quantifiable, and many faculty members are already involved with faculty development programs to increase student learning (Alstete, 2000). Confusion can result when the talk is about quality of resources in some circles and quality of results in others. The level of resistance, discomfort, and confusion can be diminished by effectively examining the accreditation process, facilitating the important elements, and communicating the message to the stakeholders of the educational institution.

Facilitating interpretive accreditation strategies should take these factors into consideration as part of an overall institutional schema whereby the accreditation process is coordinated with an institution's organizational internal reviews, strategic planning, and unique organizational issues. Figure 3 illustrates how facilitating interpretive accreditation strategies fits between the general goals of achieving recognition by one or more accreditation agencies and systemic organizational improvement.

Educational institutions have certain responsibilities to make the accreditation process a constructive experience. Facilitating accreditation with an

FIGURE 3
Facilitating Interpretive Accreditation Strategies

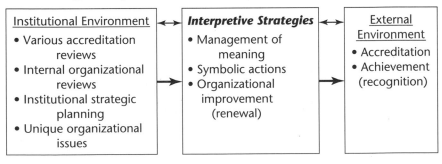

interpretive strategy is a choice that educational leaders can use to help to make accreditation constructive, enlightening to the community, and a properly planned occurrence rather than a reaction to a periodic deadline, as many still perceive it. Twenty years ago, *Understanding Accreditation* proposed several concepts for making accreditation beneficial, including making accreditation a high priority within the educational institutions, properly financing the accreditation function, and facilitating rather than reacting to accreditation (Young, Chambers, and Kells, 1983). Accreditation was viewed then and is still seen by many educators today as a troublesome outside force for periodic contention, a petty annoyance to some, and a dire threat to others. Internal reeducation about the importance and benefits of accreditation and facilitation of the process enable institutions to achieve recognition and renewal less painfully and more effectively than many believe is possible. Today, without facilitating accreditation with interpretive strategies to shape perspectives, defining their own objectives, and creating effective processes for evaluating the outcomes, institutions may run the risk of intrusive imposition of goals, processes, and micromanagement by visiting accreditors. Facilitating accreditation in this manner is not the solution to all the challenges and difficulties related to accreditation, but it is certainly better than having no plan and allowing the educational institution to be impacted by various demands from internal and external forces.

Planning an Interpretive Approach

Planning is the process of determining how the organization, in this case the educational institution, will achieve its objectives (Cerbo, 2003). It can be accomplished by analyzing, evaluating, and selecting among the opportunities available to shape the attitudes of participants, enabling the individuals involved and the institution to see that their accreditation goals can be accomplished. It is common for faculty, administrators, staff, and others to stay focused on the day-to-day operations, challenges, and educational cycles. A sound planning program enhances decision coordination by forcing the institution to look beyond the normal everyday problems to project what situations can be confronted and what objectives can be achieved, such as accreditation. Planning is actually the primary administrative and management function that facilitates the accreditation processes and the one that precedes all others as the basis for organizing, influencing, and controlling.

Broadly stated, planning a three-step process involves (1) determining an organization's mission and goals, (2) formulating a strategy or strategies to achieve these goals, and (3) implementing the strategy (Jones and George, 2003). A good plan builds commitment for the organization's goals, gives the institution a sense of direction and purpose, coordinates the functions and departments, and controls the various individuals and internal groups. Strategic and operational plans differ in their breadth and time frame: strategic plans apply to the entire organization over a longer period, and operational plans specify the details of how the objectives will be achieved (Robbins, 2000). Planning not only gives direction but also can reduce the impact of change in the environment, minimize waste and redundancy, and set the standards that may be much needed in highly decentralized, flat hierarchies, quite common in higher education. Planning is not without criticism, however. Some arguments against it are that it is too rigid, which can lock people and institutional departments into goals when the environment is changing, that it is not a replacement for intuition and creativity (Mintzberg, 1994), and that it can focus too much on competing today rather than tomorrow (Hamel and Prahalad, 1994). In addition, planning can reinforce successful organizations' becoming overly focused on their success, setting up the conditions that can lead to failure (Miller, 1993). Leaders in higher education must keep these points (and other operational and strategic plans for institutions) in mind when crafting plans for facilitating accreditation strategies.

Although strategic planning and accreditation are treated as separate issues in the literature, the two processes share many common elements (Barker and Smith, 1998), including an examination of the college or university's mission, goals, and operational plans to meet the goals and an assessment of how well the goals were met. In an accreditation process, the self-study portion is quite lengthy and requires significant institutional resources. Typically, educational institutions today begin the self-study preparation about two years before the scheduled team visit. When the accreditation goals are included in the institution's long-term and medium-range plans, however, preliminary preparation for the peer review can be accomplished without concentrating all of the institution's efforts, resources, and plans into that two-year period. Therefore, effective accreditation should strive to make accreditation an ongoing process to add unity, make better use of resources, and, most important, help the institution to accomplish the self-study more efficiently and with greater meaning.

The Council for Higher Education Accreditation advises that conduct of accreditation on college and university campuses belongs specifically to the chief academic officer, usually the provost, academic vice president, or academic dean (Eggers, 2000). Whereas faculty members are involved on the self-study teams and often the visiting teams, the operative planning for accreditation is normally the responsibility of the academic administration. It is in the chief academic officer's role that academic institutions could use interpretive strategic planning and seek to integrate regional and specialized accreditation in a single, comprehensive cycle of institutional planning and review. A single process would ultimately be less burdensome on the institution, result in higher quality, and increase the involvement of everyone in the institution. Some institutions have already begun to put this concept into reality by asking accrediting agencies for flexibility and putting their reports and visits onto the calendar for accreditation. In this way, it may be possible one day for increased coordination across the various specialized subject areas as well as the regional accreditations, to share databases and better engage institutional resources in strategic planning.

Figure 4 shows an unplanned time line for various accreditation reviews where the reaffirmation period between reviews may fall over a typical ten-year period. The typical two-year preparation period for each accreditation means that there is virtually no point in a ten-year period when one or more accreditations are under review or in a preparation period. In addition, the strategic planning for the institution overlaps with the accreditations and often involves a two-year review for each five-year strategic institutional plan.

Realistically, it may not be possible to synchronize all the accreditation time lines. Most accreditors, however, are willing to be somewhat flexible, and if several time lines can at least be coordinated, then many of the aforementioned advantages can be achieved, including cost savings, greater effectiveness, and the freeing of people and institutional resources for other pressing needs. Figure 5 shows a more synchronized ten-year time line, with institutional

FIGURE 4
Unplanned Accreditation Time Line

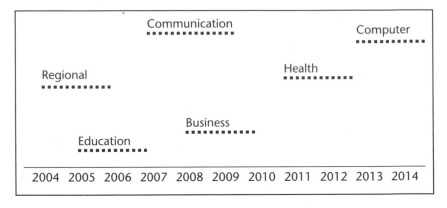

Communication

Computer

Regional

Health

Business

Education

2004 2005 2006 2007 2008 2009 2010 2011 2012 2013 2014

FIGURE 5
Planned Accreditation Time Line Linked to Strategic Plan

Five-year Institution Strategic

Next Five-year Strategic Plan

Regional

Computer

Communications

Health

Education

Business

2004 2005 2006 2007 2008 2009 2010 2011 2012 2013 2014

strategic planning shown in five-year cycles. This approach offers a framework for examining the institution in light of the regional and specialized associations, allows the use of data already available, and can enhance the structure for ongoing institution-wide assessment and decision making. Institutions can perform an environmental assessment to gauge their strengths and weaknesses and determine which accreditation should be pursued, renewed, and perhaps even discontinued if needed.

Although the representation is somewhat idealistic and is more of a goal than might actually be achieved, it does explain the objective of planning an interpretive facilitation of accreditation by working with the various accreditation agencies to move either up or back on the unplanned time line to coordinate institutional planning. Some accreditation cycles are not in ten-year cycles and may fall out of synchronization if the agency is unwilling to be flexible. In addition, institutions may also synchronize internal periodic reviews for academic departments with accreditation review cycles. Good planning processes look into the future and seek to overcome obstacles and ideally can provide regular annual updating for continuous refinement.

To be truly effective, strategic planning for an educational institution needs to recognize a "chief planner," usually the president, and also include a broad-based group of administrators, faculty, and students to assist in developing the strategic plan (Cahoon and Pilon, 1994). The chief academic officer can lead this broad-based group in the area of accreditation goals, and the group could also serve effectively as the steering committee for regional accreditation self-evaluations. This approach can reduce start-up time, help ensure knowledgable personnel, and facilitate access to critical information. The College of St. Scholastica in Duluth, Minnesota, provides an example of how closely the planning process can guide the self-study for a regional accreditation review. Interestingly, this college's planning process was the guiding structure for the self-study process, and the plan was revised annually up until the late 1990s. The planning body that made the annual revisions comprised the president and the senior administrative team, which includes the academic deans, the chair of the faculty assembly, the director of public relations, and student representatives. The annually revised plan, titled *Scholastica Direction,* consisted of four sections:

1. The purpose, process, planning cycle, and overview of the planning document;
2. A review of the mission statement, commentary on the mission statement, and "Mission Statement—Lived Experience," listing the college activities that put flesh on the more idealistic assertions of the mission statement; long-range planning assumptions describing expected external future conditions

over which the College has no control but that will have an impact on the College; institutional characteristics of the College, including societal context, relationships with external agencies, leadership/management, programs, students, student services, staffing/development, physical facilities, equipment, and fiscal resources; a listing of the major strengths and weaknesses of the College;

3. Five-year institutional goals with selected objectives: these include one goal directly tied to enhancing understanding of the College's mission, a series of operational goals, and a goal focused on capital development needs; these goals are set in response to the weaknesses identified in the previous section of the plan;

4. An appendix that usually contains illustrative graphs, particularly supporting statements in the second section [Cahoon and Pilon, 1994, pp. 41–42].

At the College of St. Scholastica, the Plenary Planning Commission met several times during each academic year, collecting input from the college community, reviewing and revising sections of the previous year's plan, and reminding the community of the ongoing planning effort to obtain their agreement. In addition, for those familiar with regional accreditation needs, a clear relationship is seen betweens the college's planning process and the development of the self-study. The plan for the self-study, including the purpose, process, and time lines, can be found in the first section of the college's annual planning document. The self-study also typically included a response to the most recent regional accreditation report and significant changes since the last review team visit. In the second section of the planning document, additional topics related to the self-study were included, such as an examination of the mission and purposes of the college, organization of institutional resources, and assessment processes. The actual self-study report was to be in greater depth than the annual planning efforts, but the self-study teams that were charged with their sections had a much easier start than if there were no planning system in place.

Interestingly, the College of St. Scholastica changed senior leadership in the late 1990s and dissolved the Plenary Planning Commission in favor of an external strategic planning consultant. Although the next ten-year accreditation visit was successful, the accreditation report recommended renewed focus and energy on strategic planning. A reconstituted internal strategic planning committee and a return to updating the annual plan are consequently under way (Cahoon, 2003, personal communication). Assessment of academic achievement and student learning is now a large part of nearly all accreditation standards. The institution's planning strategies need to include these requirements from the very beginning to fully support institution-wide assessment of academic and even the nonacademic programs. If an institution has a long-standing annual planning process such as College of St. Scholastica had, then assessment planning is also strongly supported by a wealth of data that document trends of change and effectiveness within the institution. (Planning the outcomes assessment strategies for facilitating accreditation is examined later.)

The nature of accreditation self-study can easily be confused as a variety of separate tasks rather than part of a planned interpretive strategy of important evaluations linked to the institution's strategic plan. For the chief academic officer or the coordinator of the self-study, the task and activities to accomplish this goal can appear daunting (Giacomelli, 2002). It can be addressed, however, by recognizing at the outset that each task or activity is an integral part of the institution's plan and that the process and the result (accreditation recognition and institutional renewal) are advantageous and critically important. A successful accreditation plan is authentic for each institution, and no one prescription fits all types of missions, cultures, or environments from which the plan should be created. Nevertheless, some preliminary questions should be examined as the first step in the planning process, because their answers will have far-reaching implications in the accreditation and the institution's plans. For example, is the self-study viewed as an opportunity or a threat? Is the institutional self-analysis ongoing and dynamic? Has the institution had a history of difficulties in accreditation? Is the decision-making process centralized or decentralized? (Giacomelli, 2002). In addition, the first steps in the plan should determine whether the institution is data rich or data poor and what current evaluation practices are already in place that can be built on.

In planning the process of accreditation, a suitable work structure is critical to "support the key actions of the self-study, such as communicating, documenting, analyzing, interpreting, synthesizing, evaluating, and prioritizing" (Giacomelli, 2002, p. 284). To accomplish it, the plan should define who will do the work, how it will be done, when, and what the final product should include. The success of the planning process hinges on the principles that guide its design. At Robert Morris College in Chicago, the paradigm of planning, process, and product were recently used in a comprehensive self-study evaluation for regional accreditation renewal. The result was a self-study that achieved many goals of the accreditation, significant institutional change, and improved quality. The plan, process, and product were applied frequently during the recent ten-year period leading up to the periodic review. The institution used them to undertake initiatives such as the addition of new locations, a new degree level, and new degree programs. In addition to the improvements at the institution, the outcome from the regional accrediting agency was a very successful continued accreditation (with the next comprehensive evaluation in ten years), simultaneous approval of three institutional change requests, and no required reports or visits for ten years.

Self-study and strategic planning are a critical combination, and lessons learned from institutions that link these processes can provide useful examples for others. Estrella Mountain Community College, a recently created institution in Arizona, has integrated strategic planning as an integral and ongoing part of life for the campus community (Goodman and Willekens, 2001). Since its inception in 1988, planning at the institution has experienced several distinct stages, the first of which centered on six planning directions: (1) collaborative strategic planning, (2) educational responsibilities to the area communities, (3) comprehensive instructional programs and flexible approaches to instructional delivery, (4) partnerships and collaboration, (5) integration of information technologies across the curriculum, and (6) strong links with public schools. The second stage of the strategic planning focused on divisional planning, with each academic and administrative division required to submit a divisional plan that includes links to the college's strategic plan. The components of each include common items such as the division's mission and objectives (linked to the strategic plan, summary of resources, and a continuous improvement plan). Importantly, the completed plans from the divisions are used as a basis for divisional budget requests and institutional budget decisions. This link and senior-level support, particularly in the budget area, are critical to success for any innovative approach for planning and accreditation that breaks out of the normal operating procedures common at most institutions. The third stage of planning at this particular college integrated the challenges previously addressed during their initial accreditation self-study and were incorporated into the strategic plan. The college's Leadership Council guided development of the strategic plan along with the other plans. The strategic plan is intended to continue to guide all planning and resource allocation.

Institutions too often overlook the link between an accreditation self-study and strategic planning and the ability of the self-study to provide feedback for updating the strategic plan and identifying new or expanded strategic issues. As mentioned previously with regard to the self-study process, strengths, weaknesses, opportunities, and threats can also have a place in accreditation self-studies. The leaders at Estrella Mountain Community College also used SWOT analysis as part of the link between their regional accrediting agency, the North Central Association (NCA), and their institutional strategic planning. NCA's five criteria for accreditation are linked to planning (see Table 1) and demonstrate the potential impact on the strategic planning process.

The 1996 self-study conducted by Estrella Mountain had a large effect on the college's strategic planning process, resulting in a set of six institutional challenges and 36 self-identified recommendations for institutional improvement. After communicating the results of the self-study to the college community, the senior administration then also linked these challenges to the strategic planning process. Table 2 shows the relationships between the college's identified challenge areas and the strategic directions that were the result.

In addition to providing guidance for the college's updated strategic plan, the 1996 self-study also had an effect on several other planning areas. Estrella Mountain made several changes based on findings of the self-study, including updating the college's vision, redeveloping its mission and purposes, creating core values, enhancing institutional effectiveness and academic assessment

TABLE 1
Link Between Accreditation Criteria and Strategic Planning

NCA Criteria	Link to Strategic Planning	Potential Impact on Strategic Planning
Criterion One: The institution has clear and publicly stated purposes consistent with its mission and appropriate to an institution of higher education.	Mission Purposes (Goals) Strategy	Serves as a thorough review and may result in changes to mission and purposes (goals). In extreme cases, changes to mission and purposes may cause the institution to reevaluate the programs and services offered to its publics.
Criterion Two: The institution has effectively organized the human, financial, and physical resources necessary to accomplish its purposes.	SWOT Budget Planning Decision-Making Process Strategy	Identifies the institution's strengths and weaknesses related to all forms of human, physical, and financial resources. Provides an evaluation of the resource allocation process that may result in changes to budgeting and decision-making systems.
Criterion Three: The institution is accomplishing its educational and other purposes.	SWOT Budget Planning Decision-Making Process Strategy Institutional Effectiveness and Assessment	Serves as an internal scan that can identify the institution's strengths and weaknesses related to achievement of the College's Mission Purposes. Identifies program and services that may need special attention in the planning process and require additional resource investment.
Criterion Four: The institution can continue to accomplish its purposes and strengthen its educational effectiveness.	SWOT Budget Planning Decision-Making Process Strategy	Identifies strategic issues that may challenge the institution over time. Provides an evaluation of the planning, budgeting, and decision-making processes that can result in improvement to program and service delivery.
Criterion Five: The institution demonstrates integrity in its practices and relationships.	SWOT Values	Serves as a check on the institution's integrity and values system; may result in changes to an institution's values and/or mission.

SOURCE: Goodman and Willekens, 2001, p. 294. Used with permission.

TABLE 2
Link Between Self-Study Challenge Areas and Strategic Planning

1996 Self-Study Challenge Areas	Current EMCC Strategic Directions
Institutional Planning	Planning and Charting Our Future *Estrella Mountain must fully implement a system of planning and assess progress toward its mission.*
Growth and Development	Growing and Expanding *Estrella Mountain must be proactive in meeting the needs of a growing West Valley population.*
Community Involvement	Creating Partnerships *Estrella Mountain must continue to engage in partnership activities that advance the mission of the College.*
Organizational Governance	Investing in People *Estrella Mountain must continue to develop and invest in systems that support becoming a quality-driven institution.*
Strategies for Information Technologies	Integrating Information Technologies *Estrella Mountain must continue to invest in technologies to support teaching and learning the development of new delivery systems.*

SOURCE: Goodman and Willekens, 2001, p. 295. Used with permission.

processes, and streamlining and clarifying all college planning processes. This last improvement, to the planning process, is critical to successful integration with accreditation planning and overall management of accreditation functions. Estrella Mountain learned several valuable lessons, especially the need for development of continuous planning and review cycles and of strong links to decision making and resource allocation. The importance of a link to assessment efforts and the strong need for collaboration in successful planning should not be minimized. Such interpretive strategic planning is less effective if it is done without collaboration by the institutional stakeholders; a highly participatory process results in increased buy-in and understanding by every-one involved.

Focused Reviews to Influence Communication

When considering an interpretive planning approach for accreditation and institutional strategic planning, educational institutions often have the option to choose from several types of accreditation reviews. Many regional and specialized accrediting agencies offer several models with varying terminology—comprehensive, comprehensive with emphasis focused, special emphases, new models linked to the Baldrige criteria or a quality initiative such as AQIP (Academic Quality Improvement Project, 2002; Middle States Association Commission on Higher Education, 2002; National Council for Accreditation of Teacher Education, 2003). Each type of accreditation model has certain advantages and disadvantages to consider in the planning process for shaping the attitudes of internal and external participants. In choosing which type to pursue, leaders involved in the decision making should examine the capabilities of their institution, challenges to overcome, and benefits that could be received with each model—especially when it is known that interpretive strategies seek to influence communication and meaning. Different accreditation review types can affect both of these features.

The comprehensive self-study is probably the most common type of self-evaluation; it enables an educational institution to examine every aspect of its programs and services, governing and support structures, resources, and educational outcomes in relation to the institution's mission and goals (Middle States Association Commission on Higher Education, 2002). A comprehensive review usually begins with a careful reassessment of the institution's mission, goals, and objectives. This first step lays the foundation for collecting information, analyzing data, structuring priorities, and establishing recommendations for change and improvement in the college or university. The plan for a comprehensive review includes a detailed inquiry into each area of the institution, although some areas may be selected for greater examination.

The criticisms mentioned earlier include perceptions that typical accreditation reviews, which are commonly comprehensive, are not a significant challenge to the vast majority of postsecondary institutions today. Therefore, to address this concern of the public, legislatures, and other internal and external stakeholders, educational leaders should seek to make an interpretively planned accreditation process a method of genuine examination and improvement for their institution. A focused or special-emphasis self-study is an option for accredited, established, well-functioning institutions that are willing to commit serious attention to a select group of critical issues to contribute to institutional improvement and educational excellence (Winona State University, 2003). This option is normally not available to institutions seeking initial accreditation. Because regular comprehensive evaluations have many benefits, a special-emphasis accreditation self-study should be made only after careful consideration by institutional planners and leaders. Whereas a comprehensive evaluation is an excellent opportunity for an institution to submit major issues for examination without singling out specific programs, departments, or issues, a comprehensive evaluation often invites wider involvement from institutional constituencies. But the focused evaluation accreditation process can enable revitalization for some institutions when they seize this opportunity to build their self-study processes around a small number of carefully selected critical areas in which they want to improve or excel. Some institutions may wish to focus on an area that needs improvement such as fundraising, academic affairs, program development, or student services. It can be of great benefit to many institutions when the standard comprehensive evaluation is a "low hurdle" and would add little perceived benefit.

In the planning process, an educational institution can determine whether to exercise the special-emphasis option by examining whether it will have been accredited for several years, including at least one decennial cycle between comprehensive evaluations; demonstrating that it has adequately developed programs of evaluation and institutional research to provide the appropriate data to support the institution's claim that it meets the accreditation agency's criteria; submitting documentation that confirms that there is a strong consensus among various institutional constituencies that the areas of emphasis are appropriate, timely, and among the most critical issues confronting the institution; providing a self-study plan that shows that the work on the areas of emphasis will engage a significant portion of the institution's constituencies;

and testifying to the institution's commitment to respond speedily and positively to the recommendations that result from studying the areas of emphasis and to its willingness to be judged in part on its use of the results of its special-emphasis self-study (Winona State University, 2003).

A steering committee contemplating a self-study built around a limited number of special emphases should contact its agency staff liaison early in the planning process. The institution should submit a self-study plan explaining the selected areas of emphasis, how it will study them in depth, and how it will demonstrate it continues to meet the accreditation standards. The agency staff must review and agree with the appropriateness of the special-emphasis option for the institution. The staff then develops a letter or memorandum that outlines the agency's acceptance of the special emphases. Those documents accompany evaluation team invitations and all accreditation agency materials used throughout the evaluation process.

As mentioned, a focused or special-emphasis self-study may be an opportunity to reconsider and revise the institution's mission, study enrollment trends, initiate a more complex system of assessing student outcomes, assess the impact of a new governance system, work on a long-range plan, and evaluate and revise such a plan. Some additional possibilities might include assessment, community service, cultural diversity, general education, graduate education, undergraduate education, information technology, research, strategic planning, and student development. A special-emphasis self-study should lead to concrete change in the areas covered, as well as help shape attitudes and perceptions about the institution. By the very nature of this self-study process, proposals emerging from the self-study must have the full attention of the administration.

Like comprehensive self-study reports, the special-emphasis self-study report usually includes a table of contents, an introduction, a body, and a summary. In addition to what is normally included in regular self-study reports, the introduction provides the reasons for which the institution undertook a special-emphasis self-study. The first section of the body of the report normally provides solid evidence that the basic accreditation criteria for the accrediting agency are met. Much of this evidence can be provided by interpreting readily available institutional data. Next, the special emphasis or several emphases should be treated, in appropriate depth, in their own section of the body of the report. Finally, the summary should present the institution's argument that it deserves continued accreditation because it satisfies the criteria and because it used the special-emphasis self-study as an effective means to further institutional improvement.

When planning the special-emphasis team's visits to the institution, the institution should make sure that major institutional groups, including the president, recognize the importance of the areas of emphasis and have a stake in the outcomes achieved by the self-study. The plan should expect that the vast majority of those individuals and groups that the evaluation team interviews will be involved directly in the examination of the areas of emphasis or have a clear sense that they have the opportunity to offer input into the examination process. In addition, the plan should anticipate that most critical issues facing the institution will be included in the areas of emphasis and that there will be no unexpected major problems that the self-study failed to confront. As the institution has committed itself to action by undertaking a special-emphasis self-study, the team may recommend more monitoring (especially in the form of gross progress reports) than would be the case in a regular comprehensive evaluation. The accrediting agency staff normally nominates the members of the evaluation team according to the special emphases identified in the written proposal, which should also be considered in the plan. An accreditation evaluation team for a focused visit may be slightly larger than a team for a regular comprehensive evaluation visit.

At least one regional accrediting agency recommends approval of experimentation with the evaluation processes for institutions with certain conditions: that the experiment be done only with strong institutions in low-risk situations, that special training and orientation be provided to the teams involved in these experiments to ensure that they can fulfill the expectations placed on them, that a formal evaluation of the process be integral to each experiment, and that an experiment do the institutions no harm (Winona State University, 2003). In addition, the accreditation agency will ensure that the consultant-evaluators are held harmless, the fee structure covers actual team costs and an administrative fee, and, perhaps most important, an institution interested in developing and conducting an experimental process collaborates with its staff liaison early in its preparations.

The special-emphasis approach is still relatively new and still not known to many leaders in higher education. When considering this approach in planning, several questions should be considered: What is the special-emphasis approach? How does it differ from the traditional self-study? What is the rationale for adopting this method of self-evaluation? How do institutions conduct this type of self-study? (Hutchinson, 1994). Bowling Green State University (BGSU), a Carnegie Category I doctoral-granting institution enrolling nearly 20,000 students in Ohio, used a special-emphasis approach to plan and build a regional accreditation self-study. The associate vice president for academic affairs, Peter M. Hutchinson, described the special-emphasis approach as "more focused" than a traditional comprehensive study (Hutchinson, 1994, p. 79). A more exact description is to view this planning strategy as more "thematic," whereby the college or university defines several specific perspectives through which to examine its progress during the previous accreditation review period. Some find the special-emphasis approach more difficult than planning and performing a traditional comprehensive self-study. For example, all departments and units of the educational institution must conduct their own self-studies, similar to the way that these departments would in a comprehensive study. The findings uncovered from these departmental (both academic and nonacademic) self-evaluations can then form the foundation for the comprehensive section of the report—usually the first section of a typical focused evaluation. Such reports can also provide the basis for the special-emphasis sections of the final report submitted to the accreditation agency.

Some accreditation planners may view this special-emphasis approach as innately more unsure and involving greater risk than a traditional comprehensive accreditation. Senior leaders at BGSU did not believe that this attitude pervaded BGSU's self-study at that time. The main advantage of the thematic approach is that the rewards are greater, which can justify a perceived greater risk by the institution. The special emphasis requires that the educational institution closely examine those issues that are most important, urgent, and needed, and it offers the possibility of significantly greater outcomes from an accreditation review than a comprehensive review. However, the special-emphasis approach may not be the right choice in facilitating accreditation planning for every institution. Colleges that are in the early stages of their development or are seeking initial accreditation should seek a comprehensive review, because they first need to recognize and acknowledge their initial overall quality before addressing specific concerns in a special-emphasis review. Those that seek continued accreditation and have a long history of institutional accreditation could certainly take advantage of this unique, important, and still somewhat innovative approach. Many educational leaders, and especially faculty and midlevel administrators, are still not well aware of the various accreditation types that are often available to choose from. Informing them and obtaining their support for the options that will be planned for in the initial stages of an accreditation review and in the long-term strategic plans of the institution are critical to success. A special-emphasis approach is most appropriate for institutions that have very specific goals and wish to account for their success to date, such as BGSU, or other institutions with a relatively long history of accreditation but with a significant problem to address.

The experience of an institution such as BGSU can show other colleges and universities planning a special-emphasis accreditation review that it is important to consider factors such as the structure, integration, coordination, and potential for duplication in the institutional culture. Although these items may seem obvious, they are important for the planning process, and the institution can address these issues through the appointment of appropriate personnel to the executive committee, steering committee, and support staff (Hutchinson, 1994). A crucial issue that BGSU found in its use of the special-emphasis regional accreditation was the nature of the team visit. The team visit should be structured explicitly for a special emphasis, because the team assigned to this institution did not seem to be attuned to the nuances of the special-emphasis approach that make it truly different from a comprehensive visit. Specifically, the team visit was structured precisely as a comprehensive study, and the team did not meet with the institution's special-emphasis committees. The result was confusion and even some indignation among the special-emphasis committees, whose members believed that they developed some special institutional insights that were not examined by the visiting team. The accrediting agency and the institution probably should have planned it better to gain the full potential benefit of a special-emphasis approach to accreditation.

A positive experience with a focused approach can be seen in the recent regional accreditation review at the University of Michigan–Ann Arbor (North Central Association of Colleges and Schools, 2000). The university arranged a focused visit for its self-study with a special emphasis on new openings for the research university through advancing collaborative, integrative, and interdisciplinary research and learning (p. 3). The evaluation visit to the university was conducted in two parts, with the twelve-person team divided into two teams. The first team of four visitors concentrated on the university's compliance with the general institutional requirements and the criteria for accreditation, which all institutions must address for the association, while the second team of eight evaluators focused all their attention on the special-emphasis initiative. This bifurcated approach enabled an interpretive strategy to present the institution's credibility to outside evaluators in a symbolic (with traditional elements) and favorable light, while also communicating new institutional directions to these important external stakeholders. Both teams visited the university and reported favorable findings, with recommendations to continue accreditation and schedule the next visit in ten years. The interpretive strategy applied at Ann Arbor shows that a well-established research university can convey meanings to internal and external stakeholders in ways that favor the organization, using an approach that has linear elements of planning, organizing, and reporting yet interprets the accreditation differently with a special emphasis.

Staffing and Institutional Culture in Facilitating Accreditation

Proper selection, recruitment, and guidance of the individuals involved on teams in the accreditation process at educational institutions are important parts of effectively facilitating an interpretive strategy. Some keys to successful staffing in accreditation matters can be seen in the example of Eastern Michigan University (EMU), which recently completed a successful self-study that culminated in the award of continued accreditation and the next comprehensive evaluation in ten years (Bennion, Liepa, and Melia, 2002). Although the leaders at that institution know that there are many reasons for success in the self-study effort, they believe that the centerpiece of their success can be attributed to the effective work of a twenty-eight-member self-study steering committee. The selection of the accreditation steering committee is one of the most important decisions that an institution will make when preparing for the accreditation review. Therefore, say the leaders at EMU, the process of selection should not be rushed. At their institution, the selection process lasted an entire semester as the dean's council consulted with the self-study coordinator and sought to select a committee that not only represented all areas of EMU but also was racially diverse and consisted of individuals with good ideas to share who were willing to do the hard work required. The committee consisted of a variety of administrators and faculty, including department heads, deans, academic support unit directors, and two students.

A major concern of the self-study coordinator at EMU was to obtain and keep all committee members actively involved in the self-study process. The coordinator solicited ideas at meetings, asked each member to serve on one or more of the chapter-writing committees, and kept the committee deeply involved in reviewing the drafts of the self-study report, attending public meetings on the report, and reporting back to the committee on any concerns or issues raised by the community. In addition, the coordinator published a monthly newsletter on the accreditation process at the institution, *NCA Self-Study Matters,* which identified the contributions of the various committee members and featured articles written by members. Although no financial rewards were available to committee participants for serving on the team, other inexpensive but symbolic rewards were given to all committee members, including lunches, pins, and tote bags. Other institutions have also published newsletters for staff and faculty; a sample list of newsletter topics is shown in Appendix E. Again, such interpretive strategies, which use images and symbols to communicate meaning, and not necessarily changes in the institution, can be an effective technique for facilitating accreditation. As mentioned previously, a study of the dean's role in change, specifically the implementing of new specialized accrediting standards, was conducted by interviewing faculty at four accredited comprehensive universities in 1996 (Henninger, 1998). This study showed that academic leaders can influence change, but only to a limited extent.

Faculty members in particular are strongly influenced by their disciplinary community and local institutional expectations and constraints. Therefore, the strategy to facilitate accreditation should account for these limitations and consider communicating styles that effectively negotiate these hurdles by supporting, guiding, and nurturing the faculty's desires for recognition and institutional renewal in ways that are amenable to their culture.

The self-study process is often seen as a positive challenge for individuals and institutions involved in seeking accreditation and institutional renewal (Taylor, 2002). Part of the staffing matters that educational leaders and accreditation self-study coordinators should be concerned about is facilitating stress reduction for members of the steering committee. College or university faculty and administrators are usually well aware of the importance of the evaluation process, the high stakes, and the consequences of failure, and many people find the experience somewhat stressful. Even though the institution may have had past successful experiences with accreditation, some may doubt their competence or experience in the area for which they are responsible in the accreditation review. The educational leaders who are overseeing the accreditation strategies at the institution may want to consider seeking some recommendations from the counseling or guidance professionals, who are often on staff at these institutions and may even be on the self-study steering committee. These efforts are part of an inwardly directed interpretive strategy for facilitating the accreditation process effectively. Some of the recommendations may include suggestions about the style of communication by the leaders regarding the accreditation goals, management of self-study related stresses, and a coordinated program of relaxation techniques for members that includes exercise, dietary management, and team-building exercises to create synergy and reduce stress.

A large challenge for facilitation of accreditation processes (and many other processes in postsecondary institutions) is the difference in decision-making conventions, time frames, priorities, and constituents of the two dissimilar cultures: faculty and administrative (Martin, Manning, and Ramaley, 2001). The administrative culture of colleges and universities is characterized by a desire for efficiency, competence, effectiveness, productivity, and accountability, whereas traditional faculty cultures have been described as emphasizing peer review, collegial relationships, self-governance, curriculum preeminence, and a hierarchy of disciplines, among other traits (Clark, 1963; 1989). The differences between the two cultures can cause difficulties in facilitating the accreditation process by interfering with communication and inhibiting institutional change. These cultural barriers to the achievement of clarity and direction in accreditation review can be overcome by:

1. Instilling a discipline of reflection and a culture of evidence that supports honest discussions about the current condition of the institution;
2. Fostering new patterns of conversation and interaction that encourage and support the involvement of a broad spectrum of the campus community in defining the future and assessing institutional progress toward shared goals;
3. Promoting genuine conversation about difficult and controversial subjects as a way to disperse power and leadership throughout the organization;
4. Advancing a philosophy of experimentation, assessment, and management of reasonable risks associated with change;
5. Providing open access to meaningful information about the condition and resource base of the institution; and
6. Approaching planning as a scholarly endeavor that creates a research-based foundation for action [Martin, Manning, and Ramaley, 2001, p. 113].

Development of the campus culture that reflects these principles can help facilitate an interpretive strategic process triggered by an effective accreditation self-study. The result can be an improvement that builds on the strengths of both the administrative and traditional faculty cultures that are a part of most educational institutions. Both faculty and administrators seek recognition and renewal of the institution, albeit in slightly different levels and areas. An effective accreditation strategy that accounts for culture development can help both groups achieve their goals.

Other educational institutions have also discovered that understanding and developing the campus culture is key to success in facilitating accreditation.

For example, North Dakota State College of Science (NDSCS) found that engaging in a purposeful planning process that involved a majority of the people on campus and secured their acceptance was central to the success of a project of the magnitude of a regional self-study (Dohman and Link, 2001). First, the leadership of the institution should be willing to strongly drive the accreditation efforts and become (if they are currently not) intimately familiar with the expectations and requirements of the accrediting agency. NDSCS was fortunate to have a college president who was serving as a regional accrediting association consultant-evaluator and had an excellent working knowledge of the goals and objectives of the accreditation system. If the leader or leaders need refreshment in regard to accreditation expectations, then attending accreditation annual meetings and accreditation workshops, visiting with colleagues who recently completed an accreditation process, and meeting the regional agency's staff liaison are just a few ways to learn what needs to be done.

However, daily coordination and leadership of the accreditation efforts and writing and editing the self-study report are not usually done by a senior administrator of this level because of the amount of time required. Therefore, lead personnel should be selected who are familiar with the institution and are knowledgeable about accreditation and assessment procedures. At NDSCS, the director of assessment and institutional research was selected for this role. The campus culture was then evaluated to determine whether employees are empowered and encouraged to function in a self-directed manner or the majority of leadership comes from a handful of individuals. Once the answer had been determined, an effective strategy that uses the structure and culture was developed to meet the accreditation expectations and requirements. At NDSCS, the goal was to integrate the self-study into the daily routine of the campus and to demonstrate that the processes used to analyze and evaluate the college were continuous and maintainable once the accreditation team's visit was completed.

Buy-in from all constituencies on campus, including the faculty, staff, and students, was secured at NDSCS through both formal and informal discussions between those developing the processes and other key academic leaders. Frequent conversations helped communicate with the campus community about the proposed processes, collect feedback, and even identify strong candidates to serve on the accreditation steering committee. The time line and the strategy for implementation were also developed with the campus culture in mind. The steps to their successful self-study included identifying the steering committee, determining the data-collection process, monitoring the committees' progress, providing a resource area, coordinating the writing of the report, and collecting additional feedback on the report from the college community. The result at NDSCS was a successful accreditation and team visit that involved a majority of the people on campus and was planned within the framework of the institution's culture.

In addition to thoughtful team selection, consideration of the institutional culture, and seeking community buy-in, team building is also an important factor in successful internal interpretive strategies for accreditation processes. Some educational institutions may have difficulty facilitating a cohesive team spirit, while others have a culture that is amenable to this approach. The success of a U.S. Air Force Academy reaccreditation visit in May 1999 can be attributed, in part, to a strong self-study team whose members represented a broad section of the community (Reed and Enger, 2000). The lessons learned by the academy include the importance of the selection of the steering committee, planning an achievable time line, incorporating and integrating data, providing guidance on tackling committee tasks, maintaining focus without stifling creativity, and establishing a single voice in the accreditation review process. Colleges and universities by their nature are staffed by educated, often opinionated, creative, and self-directed individuals who are not afraid to defend divergent opinions or explore additional areas beyond the issues at hand. Therefore, it is up to institutional leaders and self-study coordinators to channel this intelligence and enthusiasm in constructive ways to facilitate the accreditation process without stifling the initiative of the institutional community culture. The Air Force Academy took the time to first agree upon an outline after multiple iterations and then reinforced the agreed-upon agenda to the various subcommittees. In addition, the academy worked to write the self-study report with a single voice by designating one or two authors and asking committees to provide feedback on integrated drafts. This strategy may not work at all institutions, but the goal of integrating perspectives and writing style in the accreditation review is important to help achieve the overall objectives of accreditation recognition and institutional renewal.

As mentioned, a large part of an interpretive strategy is facilitating communication with goals in mind that benefit the institution and seek to change perspectives and garner support. The institutional culture can be communicated by developing an information campaign (McCallin, 1999). The College of Financial Planning, a for-profit educational institution, created a campus-wide campaign to "(1) inform the internal constituency about its self-study process, (2) encourage their participation throughout the process, and (3) teach them about requirements of affiliation with the Commission on Institutions of Higher Education of the North Central Association of Colleges and Schools" (p. 302). This educational institution's information campaign consisted of three components: (1) publicizing the college's recently developed strategic plan and encouraging community feedback; (2) holding open forums with the college president or self-study coordinator to discuss the relationship of the strategic plan to the accreditation criteria and reporting progress of the institution's self-evaluation process; and (3) preparing a weekly newsletter that was distributed during the six-week period immediately preceding the evaluation visit. This newsletter was intended to provide the campus community with a reader-friendly communication piece that covered what the regional accrediting agency is, what the process means, the roles of the self-study report, and members of the evaluation team (see Appendix E). Other institutions' newsletters have been used to communicate accreditation goals to the campus community, prepare for upcoming external visits, and influence the campus culture in a positive way.

Using Symbolic Actions in an Interpretive Strategy for the Accreditation Process

Whether the institution is large or small and seeking accreditation from one or more agencies, the accreditation process is a large undertaking by any institution. It can be effectively controlled and thoughtfully operated using symbolic actions. Controlling issues include monitoring and enforcing rules and procedures of the accreditation agency, encouraging productive and discouraging unproductive behavior within the institution, and rewarding performance that achieves accreditation objectives and institutional improvement.

In a study of the relationship between regional accreditation and institutional improvement, accreditation was shown to have the greatest impact on institutions that were smaller, less selective, and were reviewed by the accrediting agency more frequently than every ten years (Robinson-Weening, 1995). The study also found that the timing of the accreditation in the institutional life cycle was also an important factor on the effect of the accreditation process. These findings are important to consider in controlling the accreditation facilitation strategies for large institutions, which may often need to go beyond the minimal compliance of regional accreditation to achieve effective recognition and renewal. Likewise, smaller institutions should consider the timing of accreditation visits and possibly schedule accreditation studies more often than the usual decennial reviews.

To assist in controlling productive behavior and properly rewarding performance, many institutions have developed systems of operating that include detailed planning and capacity utilization, scheduling of accreditation committees, and information collection.

Institutional research offices can play a critical role in facilitating institutional self-study and the preparation of self-study and supporting documents (Bers and Lindquist, 2002). Professionals in institutional research have strong experience in conducting surveys and special institutional studies, analyzing data from national databases to provide comparative data and information, ensuring validity of data, and creating useful tables and charts for the accreditation self-study. To facilitate effective use of the institutional research, institutions should make sure that the office has access to decision-making discussions about the accreditation process, needed resources, and data.

Many of today's information technology tools offer powerful methods to control and operate accreditation strategies, and their use in controlling and operating the accreditation process should be encouraged, planned, and budgeted for at the institution. These efforts can assist in communicating with the campus community through e-mail, Web pages, and electronic learning systems; communicating with the accreditation agency and self-study team leaders and members; managing the work flow; creating and writing documents; and undertaking research, data collection, and data analysis. Reliable and valid data have moved to center stage in many self-study processes, and consultant-evaluators are arriving on campuses with great expectations not only about what data are available for their consideration but also about what institutions have been doing with the information (Harrington, Reid, and Snider, 2000). The result is that effective management of the gathering, dissemination, and reporting of data is a crucial factor in accreditation processes at educational institutions. It is therefore recommended that a self-study data committee or subcommittee be appointed as one of the first steps in facilitating an accreditation review.

The collection, analysis, and distribution of institutional internal and comparative data are important for controlling and operating accreditation strategies. Normally, data are needed on undergraduate and graduate student enrollment, credit hour production, faculty productivity, student retention, graduate rates, degree production, professional and support staff position histories, room use, facilities planning, library and media use, and budgetary and financial matters (Harrington, Reid, and Snider, 2000). Much of the data required in a self-study may already exist in some form at most institutions, contained in such reports as required annual accreditation updates, state reports, Integrated Postsecondary Education Data System, College and University Professional Association, institutional fact books, and cyclical and ad hoc reports. In addition, as new technologies are becoming more available, many state and national normative and comparative data sets are available on the Internet, and new Web sites are emerging that present new perspectives on the use and application of data. (See http://airweb.org/links/peers.cfm for some Internet-based resources.) In addition, assessment at the program level is becoming increasingly requested in accreditation studies, and professional schools such as AACSB and NCATE that have specialized accrediting agencies often have excellent models of assessment data. As part of an interpretive strategy for the accreditation process, however, an institution may choose to develop a survey in-house. Such surveys often seek to measure campus levels of use and satisfaction with unit programs and their effectiveness. To be most effective, the in-house survey should be well constructed, using the expertise available from academic researchers within the institution.

Software is available to assist with controlling and operating accrediting processes, such as *The Dean's Associate* (Octagram, 2003). This software can be useful for schools that are seeking specialized business school accreditation or as a model for internal software programs that could be developed in house. *The Dean's Associate* is specifically tailored for AACSB-International mission-based accreditation standards and allows business schools flexibility in serving their chosen constituencies. The software was designed with the goal of building a database management system flexible enough to handle many of the management, planning, decision support, and accreditation tasks of business school leaders. Other accreditation management software can be found outside academe, particularly in the health care industry, for example, a product offered by GeoAccess, developer of managed-care software and a popular physician search engine (PR Newswire, 2000). GeoAccess entered into an alliance with CSI Advantage, producer of an integrated, comprehensive tool for National Committee for Quality Assurance (NCQA) accreditation. GeoAccess offers CSI Advantage's accreditation information management system to managed-care organizations that are interested in cutting costs by up to 50 percent by reducing the time and effort required to prepare for NCQA accreditation. The availability of this software may indicate that a potential market exists for accreditation software in education, but for now, controlling and operating the facilitation of accreditation in academe depends on creative use and development of existing structures and institutional information systems.

One such system can be seen at the University of Cincinnati, where a template was used to collect short narrative statements from various departments for their accreditation self-study in 1999 (LeMaster and Johnson, 2001). The institution decided to pursue the special-emphasis option with the goal of using the reaccreditation process as a way to measure the effectiveness of ongoing institutional priorities in the areas of pedagogy and research. The university is large and complex with multiple missions and sixteen colleges. A large degree of autonomy in the various college cultures results in many internal barriers to institutionally driven initiatives such as the facilitation of an accreditation process. The preparation of the self-study required that the institution discover a method to facilitate active participation from all academic and administrative units in an organized and scholarly approach. The system that the university used was to request all academic and administrative units to write a series of short narrative statements based on templates provided on a computer diskette. This simple but effective system included clearly written directions to the department heads informing them that they could include supporting materials and documents and answer only the sections that were applicable to their area. Each issue for pedagogy and research/scholarly work/creative activity included a request for examples of current initiatives, outcomes that demonstrate the impact of the activities on student learning, and documents showing how the examples provided were incorporated to improve practice in the department or institution. In addition, a summary analysis was also collected on the strengths, challenges, emerging issues, and planned initiatives for pedagogy and research in each department or administrative unit. The accreditation self-evaluation team could then use these data in the strategy for proper presentation for recognition and for renewal strategies across the institution.

Large institution-wide strategies and goals established by senior leaders are important not only for providing direction but also for controlling and operating strategies that can be decentralized when possible to be effective. Institutions have the option not only to include data collection systems but also to add functions by linking objectives with performance measures and accreditation criteria. An innovative system that effectively links strategic objectives, including accreditation, to specific action outcomes is seen at Regent University in Virginia (Maher, 2000). This goal is accomplished through a flexible, rolling (annually updated) five-year strategic planning process that is linked to the university's mission and vision but is controlled through operations that tie specific performance measures to budget allocations. This system of accountability and continuous improvement has four components: (1) planning, (2) collecting data regarding the execution of planned actions, (3) comparing and assessing the executed actions, and (4) recommending future actions to improve each planned item.

To facilitate this approach, each academic unit and support department at Regent University has its own computer spreadsheet placed on the institution's network. Inside each strategic planning spreadsheet are columns or computer "fields" that require specific information to track the four components. These fields include various items that give substance and clarity to the planning framework for control of the operation, with titles such as objective number (which relates to the institutional mission), objective statement (which relates to one of the twenty-two institutional objectives), actions to be launched, personnel responsible, completion date, expected results, net profit or cost, and priority as determined by the budgeting guidelines (Maher, 2000). Other fields apply to regional accreditation criteria and require connecting the specific action with the accreditation criteria to be fulfilled. After the data are colleted on the spreadsheets, the plan is linked to the budgeting process in a very controlled manner. Expected results focus on definable ends, not merely on the means or processes. For example, "eighty-five percent of School of Law students will pass the ABA exam" is a programmed result (Maher, 2000, p. 31).

"Controlling" has been defined as a process of measuring performance and taking action to ensure desired results (Schermerhorn, 2002). For interpretive accreditation strategies, it means using symbolic but important methods to keep in touch with internal and external stakeholders, staying informed about operations, using information technology effectively, and keeping the accreditation goals of external recognition and internal renewal continually in mind. These elements of effective facilitation of accreditation are only part of the overall strategy, however. Demonstrating and communicating the results to the accreditation agency and others and proper funding are also very important factors that need to be examined.

Interpretive Approaches to Reporting and Budgeting

Most accrediting agencies offer informative handbooks and guidance for educational institutions that are pursuing accreditation to assist in the self-study process and the preparation of reports and other documents. According to many accrediting agencies, the goal is to link the self-study to the agency's standards, expectations, and external requirements. Whether the educational institution is pursuing a self-study that is comprehensive, focused on special issues, or a collaborative model, the report should be well planned, with strategic interpretive objectives in mind. The standards of many agencies recently have centered on the use of student learning and development as the main gauge of institutional quality but also on faculty and the surrounding learning environment such as the curriculum, social activities, and facilities that encourage students' physical, social, spiritual, and intellectual development (Braskamp and Braskamp, 1997). Barr and Tagg (1995) have identified these criteria as a change from the educational institution's being viewed merely as a place to provide instruction to one that exists to produce learning. Part of the interpretive strategies that educational institutions can use to address these standards is to carefully select the terms and vocabulary applied in the report, insist on standards without standardization, use a variety of evidence, focus on academic quality, and assess the entire spectrum of student learning and development (Braskamp and Braskamp, 1997). Institutions can also be creative in differentiating quality based on students' progress by keeping in mind the overall goals of interpreting the institution for external stakeholders and using symbols of quality as examples. Doing so does not imply disingenuous reporting, merely careful selection of wording, actions reported, and presentation in ways that seek the recognition desired by the accrediting agency while renewing the institution's internal commitment to the restated, or perhaps newly stated, learning objectives and measures. Faculty should be involved in judging the quality, not only to seek their acceptance for this renewal of institutional values but also to communicate the academic nature of the organization to the external reviewers. The judgment of academic quality has significantly more weight than administrative directives or other approaches that do not build on the large wealth of education and expertise available within the institution. Therefore, every effort should be made to ensure that faculty members constitute a large portion of the self-study steering committee and subcommittees.

The written self-study report is probably the most critical element in achieving the recognition sought from the accreditation agency; it is a primary communication vehicle for the interpretive strategy to be implemented. To effectively facilitate the writing of a document that interprets institutional strategies for the accreditation criteria, prepare a report on the committees' findings regarding strengths, weaknesses, and recommendations, and do so in a timely manner is a significant challenge in any accreditation process. Early decisions in planning the report are very important, because they govern the entire process of the self-study during its typical eighteen-month to three-year duration (Reich, 1999). Seeking advice and feedback early during the planning and first draft is extremely valuable, because the importance of this advice compounds by allowing effective editing, rewriting, and further planning. One regional accrediting agency states, "The self-study report is the document that summarizes each institution's self-analysis and future plans. It sets the agenda for the visiting team of peer reviewers. More importantly, it sets the agenda for the institution itself for several years. As a 'living' document, a clear self-study report should serve as a plan and a reference source for all of the institution's constituencies" (Middle States Association Commission on Higher Education, 2002, p. 59).

A large part of facilitating interpretive strategies effectively for the constituencies or participants involves written communication. In accreditation reporting, it is very important to understand that it is not only what is stated but also how it is stated in the documents. As stated earlier, those institutions that invest heavily in conceptual and communication systems that guide and interpret any organizational change for participants are likely to be more resilient when faced with external challenges (Chaffee, 1984).

Many practicalities are relevant to writing the self-study report, interim reports, follow-up letters, responses to visitation teams, and other communications with accrediting agencies. A professor of English and department chair at an institution that recently wrote a successful self-study report and who participated on several site visits as a consultant-evaluator for a regional accrediting agency states that the written tone, grammar, mechanics, punctuation, and presentation are important basic issues that should be carefully addressed (Swanson, 1999). Swanson believes that the tone of the self-study and other communications should be honest, clear, concise, and free of propaganda and jargon. Those involved in accreditation can follow these guidelines while writing and communicating an interpretive strategy that seeks to shape opinions in the environment, increase credibility, and use symbolic actions in creative yet honest ways. It may involve stressing institutional strengths in multiple areas, addressing weaknesses honestly with stated plans for improvement, and writing in such a way that is expected or unexpected from an institutional type of one level to peers in another. Although it may seem obvious, Swanson's recommendation to be diligent in following proper grammar, mechanics, and punctuation is very important for all institutions—particularly in common problems such as sentence fragments, run-on sentences, consistent tense and person, agreement, modifiers, and abbreviation. Such seemingly small details can make the difference between communicating the interpreted message's meaning and allowing the reader to focus on only the format of the message.

Overall, the accreditation report that institutions submit should be clearly written, well organized, focused on the key issues that were determined, and written with the understanding that it will be used to educate various internal and external constituencies (Kells, 1994). In this modern era, the public increasingly expects to see documents such as institutional self-studies available on the Internet for anyone to read, including potential donors, state agencies, and even other accrediting agencies for which the report was not intended. Therefore, content and appearance are important, along with an awareness that the specific agency or agencies to which it was written may not be the only reader(s). Other desired attributes of the self-study report include readability, conciseness (often one hundred back-to-back single-spaced pages are all that is needed), and balanced viewpoints about the institution or program—all written from a seemingly single voice. It is also very important to include a systematic reference to how the institution meets the agency's standards, along with a presentation of the institution appropriate to the interpretive strategic goals of influencing perceptions in a positive way.

A variety of budgetary matters need to be considered when designing accreditation plans and creating short-term and long-term accreditation goals. One of the often cited criticisms of accreditation today is the significant expense that institutions incur for the various regional and specialized accreditations they frequently undergo (Graham, Lyman, and Trow, 1995; Trow, 1996). Although strategies can be implemented to minimize these expenses, the overall goal of budgeting for accreditation should be to thoughtfully plan thorough and complete expenditures to achieve accreditation. In addition, the projected revenues that will be affected by achieving the renewal and recognition that accreditation can help achieve should be budgeted. For most institutions, regional accreditation is a necessary expenditure to maintain student enrollment in light of the link between regional accreditation and approval of federal funds. Specialized accreditation, however, can affect revenues in a variety of ways. Some specialized accreditations may limit an institution's previous faculty use and student admissions, which can result in increased expenses and reduced revenues, while other specialized accreditations may result in increased recognition in certain fields that then can yield more students who generate additional revenue for the institution. In addition, some specialized accreditations are necessary in some states, such as NCATE accreditation for teacher education programs.

Interpretive strategies to consider in budgeting for accreditation to facilitate changes in attitudes and perspectives include not only specific self-study expenditures but also expenditures such as those related to the external team visit, communication, correspondence, travel arrangements, on-site arrangements, and preparation of the institutional community (Palmer, 2002). All members of the college or university community should be well informed about the external team's visit, dates, team composition, the team's expectations, areas of concern, and general information regarding the purpose of the visit and the goals of the accreditation plan. For example, during a regional accreditation visit at a large, urban, multicampus institution that underwent a comprehensive site visit in 1999, the self-study coordinators ensured that the faculty and staff were educated about the site visit by giving presentations and disseminating information to program advisory committees, various divisions and departments, and community groups. To make certain that team members had support for their duties and to demonstrate that the educational institution supported the team, a meeting room with technology was provided at both the hotel and on campus. Additional expenditures were also incurred in the on-site arrangements such as a hospitality room for the team and preparation events for the institutional community. Effective budgeting for accreditation requires thorough and thoughtful planning to help ensure success.

Whether or not existing and new management concepts adapted from the business world become part of the education establishment, the basic tenets of business and public management have been and will remain a part of educational organizations for practical necessity and to meet the ever-increasing challenges that most institutions are now facing. Other concepts can help institutions achieve recognition and renewal through accreditation, such as new quality initiatives and needed leadership, subjects of the last chapter.

Linking Quality Initiatives
with Accreditation

O NE CHARACTERISTIC OF the third generation of academic accreditation is the application of quality initiatives such as the Academic
Quality Improvement Project and the Malcolm Baldrige national quality
awards in education. Such efforts originated in the business world and have
migrated to higher education. Some regional and specialized accrediting agencies are applying these concepts more than others as accrediting bodies, governmental agencies, and the public increasingly call for greater accountability
from colleges and universities. Martin Trow (1996) writes that as long as
accreditation is seen as the means by which higher education polices itself from
alternatives, better methods of improvement may suffer from inattention.
However, improvements and alternatives in accreditation reviews, the subject
of this chapter, are already under way in many agencies and institutions. Trow
recommends a more critical self-evaluation of internal quality control procedures, perhaps looking at the international higher education community for
examples.

Accreditation systems in the United States and elsewhere have begun to
apply quality initiative procedures as an alternative to and improvement in the
system. These procedures are somewhat similar to audits in that rigorous self-
assessment is conducted, but they differ in that a demonstration of higher productivity and quality is also required. These quality initiatives have been
undergoing consideration and adoption by higher education leaders around
the globe as academe is increasingly being bombarded with demands to
demonstrate efficiency and effectiveness (Beanland, 2001; Janosik, Creamer,
and Alexander, 2001). For example, the Australian government recently

created the Australian Universities Quality Agency to promote quality outcomes within the educational institutions that will lead to improvement and development of the educational system (Beanland, 2001). In the United States, several quality initiatives have been implemented, including the Academic Quality Improvement Project and the Malcolm Baldrige awards (North Central Association of Colleges and Schools, 2001; National Institute of Standards and Technology, 2001b). AQIP seeks to offer an "innovative, more challenging alternative process for reaccreditation" (North Central Association of Colleges and Schools, 2001, p. 10), whereas the Baldrige award establishes criteria, with some similarities to accreditation, that are recognized by state and national award programs.

In 2001, the University of Wisconsin–Stout (UW–Stout) became the first postsecondary institution to win the Baldrige award. As stated earlier, the Baldrige criteria are divided into seven categories: leadership; strategic planning; student, stakeholder, and market focus; information and analysis; faculty and staff focus; process management; and organizational performance (Sorenson, Furst-Bowe, and Mooney, 2002). UW–Stout began using the Baldrige education criteria for performance excellence in 1999 as the basis for self-assessment and improvement. In looking at how UW–Stout met the Baldrige criteria, it appears that this achievement was primarily based on clearly articulating existing processes in the institution and providing clear assurances and measurements that demonstrate success. For example, with regard to leadership, UW–Stout's organization is admittedly a set of typical, hierarchical university functions led by a chancellor who is responsible for meeting the goals established by the board of regents. It has a typical system of shared governance with a faculty senate, senate of academic staff, and a student association. This system is intended to encourage responsive two-way communication and essentially flattens the organizational structure by broadly involving all the governed. For the strategic planning factor in the Baldrige criteria, UW–Stout listed its strategic goals, which include excellence in teaching, research, scholarship, and service. Student, stakeholder, and market focus was demonstrated by identifying key elements such as the feeder schools, employers, alumni, and the UW system and its board of regents. Other Baldrige criteria, such as information and analysis, faculty and staff focus, process management, and organizational performance results were similarly met by clearly stating institutional processes and results. These fairly typical processes, relationships, and structures show that because an established institution such as UW–Stout can meet the Baldrige criteria, other respected institutions should also be able to apply and achieve this external and prestigious recognition, or at least benefit from the pursuit.

Both Baldrige and NCA processes are done in preparation for a visit from a team of peers selected to evaluate the institution and recommend whether the institution is worthy to become an affiliated member of the regional accrediting agency or, in the case of the Baldrige award, to earn an award of recognition (Brewer, Trites, Matuska, and Bishop, 1999). As part of a system of total quality management, the Baldrige award is viewed by some as the ultimate recognition that an institution in the United States can achieve. The Baldrige award also has some skeptics, however, who believe that the process is costly in that it creates a contest-like atmosphere and that gaming skills are an important factor in winning the award (George, 1992). Critics also fault the way many companies that pursue Baldrige hire outside consultants to guide the process. Regardless of these concerns, however, many leaders and educational institutions see value in the process and hope to achieve this prestigious recognition.

One institution that used the Baldrige criteria for an accreditation self-study is Mt. San Antonio College, a large southern California community college district with an enrollment of 22,500 full-time equivalent students (Feddersen, 1999). In 1997–98, when the first Baldrige education criteria were published, the college was scheduled to conduct a comprehensive, traditional self-study for reaffirmation of accreditation. The regional accreditation agency, the Western Association, was beginning to encourage special self-studies for institutions. Mt. San Antonio then applied and was given permission to use the Baldrige criteria as the framework for its self-study; it subsequently incorporated the accreditation standards with the Baldrige quality criteria. The college organized the self-study around seven special study teams corresponding to the stated Baldrige criteria, similar to the way that traditional comprehensive self-studies for regional agencies often form teams around accreditation standards.

After beginning application of the quality initiatives, Mt. San Antonio College identified critical systems and critical processes that provide the framework for the operation of the institution. The Baldrige process and approach focus on how customer and critical processes are defined, key customer requirements are determined, key measurement indicators and goals are set, and performance is measured (Feddersen, 1999). The president of the institution stated that the training, guidance, and critique the institution received from a Baldrige consultant were extremely valuable throughout the self-study process, although not all institutions that pursue a Baldrige approach in higher education use a consultant. The president of Mt. San Antonio College identified several lessons learned from this new, complex process:

- *We learned the value of applying a systems perspective.* Accreditation standards are independent variables. Each one stands on its own. The Baldrige asks a set of common and related questions that form a thread that is woven through all criteria. It forces connections and integration and emphasizes how everything contributes to results. By probing deeply, asking many "how" questions, we were led to ask "why". By forcing us to explain things, certain truths were revealed.
- *We learned the critical role played by Key Performance Indicators (KPIs).* We had not clearly identified KPIs, and didn't fully understand them or how they linked operations to results and improvements. Now we can see how performance indicators are related to trends, benchmarking, planning, and goal setting.
- *We learned that measurement and benchmarking are the drivers of change and continuous improvement.* Our Baldrige Self-Study pinpointed our lack of metrics and outcome information. We also learned that we were not very sophisticated about benchmarks and benchmarking.
- *We learned the importance of a leadership system.* While this may seem like an obvious finding, in many institutions leadership is narrowly defined and often misunderstood. The

Baldrige framework taught us to look at shared leadership as a system and how it connects to and drives other parts of a larger system.

- *We learned the importance of training.* Using the Baldrige criteria to assess where an institution is and to drive performance improvement will not happen unless most staff really understand systems thinking. In conducting the Baldrige Self-Study we had to learn how to answer the many similar, but slightly different, "how" questions. We also had to learn how to ask the right questions if we were going to collect useful data.
- *We learned that the Baldrige seems to generate more gaps—more areas for fundamental improvement.* It's not just that the Baldrige raised a lot more questions with fewer items than accreditation; those probing questions appear to generate more fundamental concerns. They really showed us what was missing. For example, we looked at how we do planning and then linked that to results. Baldrige appears to probe deeper, to expose more of the disconnects in the institution. For instance, while accreditation asks whether a certain policy is in place, Baldrige asks how the policy was devised and how the institution evaluates the effectiveness of the policy on student learning [Feddersen, 1999, pp. 14–15].

Although Mt. San Antonio and its president also learned that integrating accreditation standards with Baldrige categories caused a considerable amount of additional work but did not necessarily increase the value of the self-study, they did find that it made the study more meaningful. Overall, the institution found that applying the Baldrige criteria proved to be an excellent institutional assessment and improvement strategy. This approach can be considered an interpretive approach that realigns perceptions of stakeholders and reality in many areas that are important to achievement of accreditation and renewal of the institution.

Setting Baldrige standards for an educational institution does not necessarily mean that an institution will meet those standards. A challenge of using the Baldrige criteria is identifying the skills and abilities necessary for the institution's employees to effectively perform their jobs. It is therefore important to identify the important stakeholder groups within an institution as related to the criteria and then list the skills or competencies needed by these groups. Thorough planning is needed. For example, the regional accreditation self-study at Northwest Technical College in Minnesota incorporated the Baldrige criteria and centered on competencies essential to effective instruction (Swanson, Hedlund, and Neff, 2000). Table 3 shows the stakeholder groups as defined through joint efforts of the college's cabinet, faculty senate, student senate, and the general advisory committee and identifies areas of primary focus for each stakeholder group.

Each stakeholder group at the institution was asked to provide a list of recommendations for improving each performance indicator identified in an assessment. Once the assessment data were established and evaluated, performance indicators deemed critical competencies were included in the assessment along with those for the Baldrige criteria. This exercise was done to provide guidelines for staff development initiatives. The institution found evidence that participating faculty and staff thought the process to be nonthreatening and constructive.

The Baldrige education criteria and the criteria from a typical regional accreditation agency share several similarities. They are both voluntary, have explicit criteria, require written self-studies, have similar goals, and have prestige associated with their achievement (Bishop, Brewer, Ladwig, and Rasch, 2000). Both processes also have several status levels, and both require the collection of data elements. In addition, both regional accreditation and Baldrige have continuous improvement as a goal, and both processes include site visits by appointed evaluators. But there are also several differences, such as the point value system that Baldrige uses, which accreditation reviews do not have. Regional accreditation in the United States has a long history, dating back more than one hundred years, whereas Baldrige is relatively recent. Other differences include the annual review period for Baldrige, compared with the five- or ten-year review for accreditation, and the fact that academic accreditation was developed specifically for higher education, while Baldrige originated in business and industry.

TABLE 3
Stakeholder Groups for Baldrige Criteria

Baldrige Performance Criteria	Primary Focus								
	Administration/ Cabinet	Faculty Senate	Student Senate	Academic Deans	Faculty	Academic Affairs Support Staff	Student Services Support Staff	Maintenance Support Staff	General Advisory Committee
1. Leadership	X			X					
2. Strategic Planning	X	X							X
3. Student and Stakeholder Focus			X		X	X	X	X	
4. Information and Analysis	X	X	X						
5. Faculty and Staff Focus		X	X	X	X	X	X	X	
6. Educational and Support Process Management			X	X	X	X	X	X	
7. School Performance Results	X			X	X	X	X		

SOURCE: Swanson and others, 2000, p. 49. Used with permission.

The most important differences between accreditation criteria and Baldrige criteria, however, relate to what is being evaluated at the institution and who shapes the improvement (Bishop, Brewer, Ladwig, and Raschh, 2000). Whereas a regional accreditation agency such as the North Central Association of Colleges and Schools (NCA) evaluates what is being done and the improvement is shaped by faculty and students at the college or university, a Baldrige review examines how it is done by evaluating the approach, deployment, and results. Table 4, for example, depicts the major and minor correlations between the Baldrige criteria and NCA criteria.

The first Baldrige criterion, for leadership, primarily correlates with NCA Criterion One, which focuses on mission. The second Baldrige criterion, on strategic planning, is closely correlated with NCA's Criterion Four on planning. An educational system that used pioneering efforts to merge the self-study processes of the NCA and the Baldrige award program within an overall context of continuous quality improvement occurred at the Wisconsin

TABLE 4
Baldrige Criteria Compared with NCA Criteria

Baldrige Criteria	NCA Criteria				
	Criterion 1 Mission	Criterion 2 Systems	Criterion 3 Assessment	Criterion 4 Planning	Criterion 5 Integrity
Criterion I Leadership	X	X	X	X	X
Criterion II Strategic Planning	X	X	X	X	
Criterion III Student and Stakeholder Focus	X		X	X	X
Criterion IV Information and Analysis	X	X	X	X	
Criterion V Faculty and Staff Focus		X	X	X	X
Criterion VI Educational and Support Processes	X	X	X	X	X
Criterion VII School Performance Results	X	X	X	X	X

SOURCE: Bishop, Brewer, Ladwig, and Rasch, 2000, p. 42. Used with permission.

Technical College System beginning in 1999 (Bishop, Brewer, Ladwig, and Rasch, 2000). By basing the decision to move forward for this integrated effort on the similarities cited previously, the institution is providing concrete examples of how the NCA reaccreditation process can be used for improvement.

Another quality initiative that is being adapted for accreditation by at least one regional accrediting agency is the Academic Quality Improvement Project, which is based largely on principles from business management (Academic Quality Improvement Project, 2002; Gose, 2002). This approach melds strategic planning with accreditation and features more interaction between the educational institutions and the accrediting agency than a typical comprehensive review. The AQIP approach differs from the Baldrige award in several respects. Specifically, AQIP has nine criteria (Baldrige has seven), AQIP includes results in every criterion (Baldrige aggregates all results), and AQIP has separate criteria for different work processes such as teaching, partnering, administration, or research (Baldrige Criterion Six covers all work processes). In addition, AQIP is focused exclusively on higher education as part of an accreditation review, normally reaccreditation. Baldrige and the state programs in the United States modeled on it are award programs, not accreditation systems. As such, they have different goals and consequently use techniques that may be perceived by some stakeholders as not appropriate for accreditation. The AQIP system strives to stimulate continuous improvement and to ensure the public and funding agents of the quality of higher education providers. The NCA has been implementing the AQIP approach for several years. As part of the program, college and university officials from participating institutions are invited to attend a three-day strategy forum to identify and refine three or four ambitious goals they hope to complete within three years. Institution leaders have reported that AQIP requires more staff time but is worth the additional effort and cost. As of late 2002, approximately seventy institutions, many of them two-year community colleges, were using an alternative accreditation process offered by NCA.

The four steps in an AQIP accreditation include an interest exploration, a comprehensive assessment (both required initially), a strategy forum to refine the action projects, and a systems portfolio. These four steps, repeated every three to five years, are the core of AQIP (Academic Quality Improvement

Project, 2002). The goal of the initial interest exploration is to make sure the institution understands quality improvement and participation in the project and is ready to embark on or continue a quality initiative. The second stage involves a comprehensive self-assessment, whereby the college or university performs a quality-based formative assessment of its systems with an outside perspective. Educational institutions have a choice of methods for conducting their self-assessment. Those new to quality improvement can select an option that will allow them to perform this self-assessment most quickly and effectively, with a relatively modest investment of staff, time, and money. The potential methods include:

- A state quality award application and review (including either a feedback report or a site visit);
- A Malcolm Baldrige National Quality Award application and review (including a feedback report);
- An ISO 9000 registration application and audit;
- A review process (using a quality system framework, such as the Baldrige Criteria, the state quality award criteria, the ISO 9000 standards, or the AQIP Quality Criteria) undertaken internally with the assistance of a consultant or other outsider familiar with quality principles and perspectives;
- A Continuous Quality Improvement NetworkTrailblazer or Pacesetter Review (Academic Quality Improvement Project, 2002).

The strategy forum is a three-day event required of all new AQIP participants and typically held near the NCA's headquarters in Chicago (Gose, 2002). The goal is to refine the action projects that have been developed by the institution, and administrators from several institutions share experiences and query each other about their proposed goals. Institutions are expected to attend a strategy forum every three to five years, which normally coincides with when the college or university is completing the previous projects and establishing new goals. Near the end of the first three years of participation in AQIP, institutions are required to prepare a systems portfolio. This document is typically one hundred or fewer pages and explains the major systems that the institution uses to accomplish its mission. This portfolio, which forms the backbone of the reaccreditation decisions, is reviewed by quality improvement experts, including at least one from outside academe.

Quality approaches to accreditation can provide institutions with the means to accomplish an interpretive strategy for internal organizational transformation as well as improvement of external perceptions about the institution's accountability. However, these approaches should be decided thoughtfully by institutions, and proper support should be garnered before it is begun (Bishop, Ladwig, and Lanser, 2001). Dr. Stephen Spangehl, NCA–AQIP director, recently stated that most institutions he spoke with that have been conducting systematic quality improvement did not invest as much as they should have in the area of cultural shifting—training internal participants to think in new ways, to think in terms of process, and to consider working in cross-institutional teams where a diverse constituency brings various perspectives to bear on a common problem (Browne and Green, 2001). These and other issues are part of the challenges that leaders at academic institutions need to consider as the calls for increased accountability and quality continue by the public, legislatures, and other external groups. In response to the idea that as long as accreditation is seen by some as the only means by which higher education institutions can police themselves, alternative and possibly better means suffer from inattention. The quality initiatives examined in this chapter may contain some hope for new, more critical, perhaps improved self-evaluation mechanisms for institutions to monitor and improve quality.

Conclusion

A S SHOWN THROUGHOUT this examination of accreditation, the recently introduced quality initiatives, interpretive strategies for accreditation, and coordinated accreditation strategic planning all require strong direction from upper-level administrators and senior faculty leaders in educational institutions. Effective leadership of accreditation efforts is needed for enabling institutions to engage in the process of developing accreditation strategies, putting the vision into reality, and continually reminding the internal and external participants of what has been achieved and what the future can hold. An institutional leader's character and integrity are important for properly recruiting and appointing the accreditation team leaders and members and for building up the trust that is necessary for engaging in the process. Leaders of accreditation self-study teams should be selected and assigned who have a vision of where the institution can and should be going in addition to knowing the mission and institutional history. A recent report on academic leadership by Moore and Diamond (2000) states that at its core, leadership is the capacity to engage human potential in the pursuit of common cause. With regard to accreditation, this common cause can be an expansion of the perception by the institution's faculty, staff, administration, students, and board members that an accreditation approach and overall strategy can do more than just receive a stamp of external approval. It can be a method that renews the institution, sets new goals, and changes perceptions. Academic leaders can actively engage faculty and staff with external constituencies in creating and renewing a vision for the institution through engagement, forging necessary partnerships, and driving strategies that turn vision into reality.

Academic leaders face many challenges in striving for accreditation goals and other objectives. A significant planning hurdle in academe is the different cultures of the academy (Newton, 1992). Among these cultures are the corporate community and the community of scholars. These different groups have seemingly divergent goals yet also have a symbiotic relationship because both are needed to be successful. The chief academic officer of the institution should lead the accreditation effort by gathering support from the institution's president and board, the faculty, and subordinate departments. The accreditation efforts need to be thoroughly and thoughtfully planned, coordinated, budgeted, monitored, and reported. Interestingly, many position descriptions in academic leadership areas are increasingly calling for experience in management of accreditation programs. Accreditation leadership and management courses should be included in more higher education graduate programs and professional development programs to help ensure the continuity of this important system of self-regulation and improvement for colleges and universities in the future.

Many reports, private institutions, and legislatures have criticized academic accreditation in recent years (Eaton, 2003). These concerns focus on the supposed lack of information about college performance, inadequate control of quality and costs, and insufficient information on student learning. Educational leaders need to communicate with internal and external constituencies not only about the successful improvements that accreditation has made for their institution but also the changes and improvements that many accreditation agencies have implemented recently. These changes include improvements in standard comprehensive reviews, additional attention to processes and evidence to review student learning outcomes at the undergraduate level, new options for focused evaluations, and coordinated accreditation reviews for cost-effectiveness and efficiency. Leaders should endeavor to change perceptions of participants about the institution and accreditation process to help ensure continuity of the unique regulation of educational systems in the United States.

The system that we know as accreditation was recently at a crossroads: the government informed higher education to monitor institutional performance more effectively through self-regulation and prevention of fraud or face possible additional government oversight and the elimination of the regional system (Glidden, 1996). Increased control of the main responsibility for assuring and improving higher education by the federal government may raise some serious concerns about what impact this change would have on institutional autonomy. Although it is probably not in the context of current law, the government may decide to create another large bureaucracy, similar to a ministry of education in other countries (Eaton, 2003). This additional expense could add increased financial burdens to taxpayers. If the states are delegated the full role of accreditation of colleges and universities, it would mean at least fifty different systems of quality review with varying sets of standards and goals. The system of postsecondary accreditation must be protected by the institutions themselves through internal and external means, because it matters to colleges, universities, and the highly successful system that has evolved over the past century.

What will the next generation of academic accreditation include? Will there be increased accountability and perceived quality through improvements in self-regulation? Scholars and leaders in higher education have stated many reasons and proposed several ideas for the future of accreditation. The shifting context of student learning, the revolution in teaching, including active learning and online formats, and the need for public engagement will motivate the accreditation system to reconsider what is reviewed, how the reviews are conducted, and who participates (Ewell, 1998). The next generation of higher education will need to expand the scope and type of work of accreditation while simultaneously making the accreditation process less time-consuming. In addition, there will continue to be a need to develop additional capacity for quality judgments based on student learning (Eaton, 2001). Some have speculated that the still largely process-oriented accreditation of today is not relevant in this era of increasingly more adult-oriented, nontraditional postsecondary education. There will be a need for highly specialized nontraditional accrediting associations—equivalent in power and prestige to the current regional accrediting agencies in the United States—that should be created to review and accredit nontraditional programs (Hogg, 1993).

More than thirty years ago, Martin Trow articulated the concept and problems of the transition from elite to mass to universal higher education (Trow, 1973). Currently, higher education continues to face "universalization," whereby increasing percentages and numbers of students plan to attend post-secondary education and new commercialization, increasing internationalization, and new technologies not only affect content and instruction but also accentuate the increasing age differential between students and faculty. The next generation of accreditation will have to take into account these factors of change while simultaneously increasing the public's trust. The changes in the future of accreditation may actually impact traditional higher education institutions in surprising and perhaps positive ways by forcing institutions to concentrate on their market niche and mission and not attempt to evolve into areas that are beyond their ability and true market to serve. There are those in higher education who believe that faculty egos sometimes drive program offerings and institutional evolution in an attempt to make colleges more prestigious and to try to be more like the programs and universities where they wish they could teach (Calhoun, 1999). Sometimes these efforts are successful, but many times these institutions are then forced to miss opportunities in enrollment and program development related to their true mission, then resulting in financial problems. In addition, some perceive that institutions offer increasingly too much specialization by discipline, which results in incoherent undergraduate studies in the United States, modularization of courses, and too many elective choices for students (Trow, 1994). Higher education institutions then move away from their mission and reduce their emphasis on good teaching in favor of research, increase already poor student services, and overemphasize nonacademic programs. A new generation of academic accreditation will be needed to ensure that institutions stick to their mission and evolve in an appropriate direction.

In light of the volatile global economy, increased accountability in the business world after recent corporate scandals, increasing costs of college tuition, and government funding cutbacks, the basic principles needed to guide improvements must reinforce internal accountability of educational institutions while enabling institutions to remain free enough to continue success in the areas where they are known to be successful. Accreditation systems should strive to do no harm to institutional autonomy, respect the diversity of institutional types, confirm that academic responsibility is a central objective, and ensure that the processes for accountability are forward looking (Graham,

Lyman, and Trow, 1995). Perhaps one of the most fundamental issues in institutional planning for accreditation, review processes, and accreditation evolution is the essential role of academic freedom (Elman, 1994). The critical role of academic freedom in accreditation criteria and institutional planning complements the important responsibility of accreditation in assuring academic freedom at colleges and universities. This reciprocal relationship benefits educational institutions, faculty roles, student learning, and the public they serve. To substitute increased government regulation for voluntary accreditation could threaten the foundation of academic freedom and diminish the quality of successful higher education institutions that were built on this concept.

This academic freedom has been part of the reason that many faculty and educational leaders have resisted measuring learning outcomes and other performance criteria. The president of the Council of Higher Education Accreditation states that many have perceived accreditation as an affirmation of certain values that are central to the culture and thinking about higher education (Eaton, 1999a). These perceptions and beliefs strongly support collegiality, peer review, self-improvement, and institutional autonomy. Accreditation in the future will need to address these issues and also be able to set high expectations. Active engagement by the institutions in the self-study review processes, similar to active learning that is becoming widely employed in the classroom, can be emphasized to institutional stakeholders such as faculty as a method to change perceptions and gain their acceptance of the process (Ewell, 2001). Accreditation should continue to develop more frequent and meaningful feedback and perhaps help develop institutions into true academic learning organizations that have the capacity for developing and transferring knowledge for continuous improvement (Dill, 2000). The call for internal audit review systems similar to those in other countries will not fully address these needs and the calls for external accountability and institutional and program diversity. But elements of audit systems with real accountability that thoroughly examine systems, perhaps in addition to outcomes, could be part of the future. In the meantime, colleges and universities realize that accreditation does still matter and that there are many new options available for implementation to help all institutions achieve the renewal and recognition they deserve.

Appendix A: CHEA Participating and Recognized Organizations

The following is a list of accrediting organizations in the United States that meet the CHEA eligibility standard as of October 10, 2002, or were recognized by COPA or eligible for recognition by CORPA, or will undergo an upcoming recognition review (Council for Higher Education Accreditation, 2002).

Regional Accrediting Organizations

Middle States Association of Colleges and Schools (MSA), Commission on Higher Education

New England Association of Schools and Colleges, Commission on Institutions of Higher Education (NEASC-CIHE)

New England Association of Schools and Colleges, Commission on Technical and Career Institutions (NEASC-CTCI)

North Central Association of Colleges and Schools (NCA), The Higher Learning Commission

Northwest Association of Schools, Colleges and Universities (NWA), Commission on Colleges and Universities

Southern Association of Colleges and Schools (SACS), Commission on Colleges

Western Association of Schools and Colleges, Accrediting Commission for Community and Junior Colleges (WASC-ACCJC)

Western Association of Schools and Colleges, Accrediting Commission for Senior Colleges and Universities (WASC-ACSCU)

National Accrediting Organizations

Accrediting Association of Bible Colleges (AABC), Commission on Accreditation

Transnational Association of Christian Colleges and Schools Accreditation Commission (TRACS)

Accrediting Commission of the Distance Education and Training Council (DETC)

Independent Colleges and Schools

Accrediting Council for Independent Colleges and Schools (ACICS)

Rabbinical and Talmudic Schools

Association of Advanced Rabbinical and Talmudic Schools (AARTS)

Association of Theological Schools in the United States and Canada (ATS), Commission on Accrediting

Specialized and Professional Accrediting Organizations

Allied Health—Commission on Accreditation of Allied Health Education Programs (CAAHEP)

Art and Design—National Association of Schools of Art and Design (NASAD)

Audiology—American Speech-Language-Hearing Association (ASHA), Council on Academic Accreditation in Audiology and Speech-Language Pathology

Aviation—Council on Aviation Accreditation (CAA)

Business—AACSB International—The Association to Advance Collegiate Schools of Business

Business—Association of Collegiate Business Schools and Programs (ACBSP)

Chiropractic—Council on Chiropractic Education (CCE), Commission on Accreditation

Clinical Laboratory Science—National Accrediting Agency for Clinical Laboratory Sciences (NAACLS)

Computer Science—Accreditation Board for Engineering and Technology, Inc. (ABET)

Construction—American Council for Construction Education (ACCE)

Consumer Sciences—American Association of Family and Consumer Sciences (AAFCS), Council for Accreditation (CFA)

Counseling—Council for Accreditation of Counseling and Related Educational Programs (CACREP)

Culinary—American Culinary Federation, Inc. (ACF)

Dance—National Association of Schools of Dance (NASD)

Dietetics—American Dietetic Association Commission on Accreditation for Dietetics Education (CADE-ADA)

Engineering—Accreditation Board for Engineering and Technology, Inc. (ABET)

Family and Consumer Science—American Association of Family and Consumer Sciences (AAFCS), Council for Accreditation

Forestry—Society of American Foresters (SAF)

Funeral Service Education—American Board of Funeral Service Education (ABFSE)

Health Services Administration—Accrediting Commission on Education for Health Services Administration (ACEHSA)

Industrial Technology—National Association of Industrial Technology (NAIT)

Interior Design—Foundation for Interior Design Education Research (FIDER)

Journalism and Mass Communications—Accrediting Council on Education in Journalism and Mass Communications (ACEJMC)

Laboratory Science—National Accrediting Agency for Clinical Laboratory Sciences (NAACLS)

Landscape Architecture—American Society of Landscape Architects (ASLA), Landscape Architectural Accreditation Board (LAAB)

Library and Information Studies—American Library Association (ALA), Committee on Accreditation (CoA)

Marriage and Family Therapy—American Association for Marriage and Family Therapy (AAMFT/COAMFTE), Commission on Accreditation for Marriage and Family

Medical Education—Liaison Committee on Medical Education (LCME)

Music—National Association of Schools of Music (NASM)

Nuclear Medicine Technology—Joint Review Committee on Educational Programs in Nuclear Medicine Technology (JRCNMT)

Nurse Anesthesia—American Association of Nurse Anesthetists, Council on Accreditation of Nurse Anesthesia Educational Programs (CoA-NA)

Nursing—Commission on Collegiate Nursing Education (CCNE)

Nursing—National League for Nursing Accrediting Commission, Inc. (NLNAC)

Occupational Therapy—American Occupational Therapy Association (AOTA), Accreditation Council for Occupational Therapy Education (ACOTE)

Optometry—American Optometric Association (AOA), Council on Optometric Education (COE)

Osteopathic Medicine—American Osteopathic Association (AOA), Bureau of Professional Education (BPE)

Physical Therapy—Commission on Accreditation in Physical Therapy Education (CAPTE), American Physical Therapy Association (APTA)

Planning—American Institute of Certified Planners/Association of Collegiate Schools of Planning, Planning Accreditation Board (PAB)

Podiatry—American Podiatric Medical Association (APMA), Council on Podiatric Medical Education (CPME)

Psychology—American Psychological Association (APA), Committee on Accreditation (CoA)

Public Affairs and Administration—National Association of Schools of Public Affairs and Administration (NASPAA), Commission on Peer Review and Accreditation (COPRA)

Recreation and Parks—National Recreation & Park Association/American Association for Leisure and Recreation (NRPA/AALR), Council on Accreditation

Rehabilitation Education—Council on Rehabilitation Education (CORE), Commission on Standards and Accreditation

Social Work Education—Council on Social Work Education (CSWE), Division of Standards and Accreditation

Speech-Language-Hearing—American Speech-Language-Hearing Association (ASHA), Council on Academic Accreditation in Audiology and Speech-Language

Teacher Education—National Council for Accreditation of Teacher Education (NCATE)

Teacher Education—Accreditation Council (TEAC)

Technology—Accreditation Board for Engineering and Technology, Inc. (ABET)

Theatre—National Association of Schools of Theatre (NAST)

Veterinary Medicine—American Veterinary Medical Association (AVMA), Division of Education and Research

Appendix B: Accreditation Eligibility Requirements

Essential eligibility requirements that must be met for consideration of Candidacy for Accreditation status for a selected sample of regional accrediting associations in the United States (Northwest Commission on Colleges and Universities, 2002):

1. Authority

   The institution is authorized to operate and award degrees as a higher education institution by the appropriate governmental organization, agency, or controlling board as required by the jurisdiction or state in which it operates. (Standard Six—**Governance and Administration**; Standard 6.A—**Governance System**; Standard Indicator 6.A.1)

2. Mission and Goals

   The institution's mission is clearly defined and adopted by its governing board(s) consistent with its legal authorization, and is appropriate to a degree-granting institution of higher education. The institution's purpose is to serve the educational interests of its students and its principal programs that lead to formal degrees. It devotes all, or substantially all, of its gross income to support its educational mission and goals. (Standard One—**Institutional Mission and Goals, Planning and Effectiveness**)

3. Institutional Integrity

   The institution is governed and administered with respect for the individual in a nondiscriminatory manner while responding to the educational needs and legitimate claims of the constituencies it serves, as determined by its chartered purposes and accredited status. (Standard Nine—**Institutional Integrity**)

4. Governing Board

   The institution has a functioning governing board responsible for the quality and integrity of the institution and for each unit within a multiple-unit institution to ensure that the institution's mission is being achieved. The governing board has at least five voting members, a majority of whom have no contractual, employment, or personal financial interest in the institution. (Standard Six—**Governance and Administration**; Standard 6.B—**Governing Board**)

5. Chief Executive Officer

   The institution employs a chief executive officer who is appointed by the governing board and whose full-time responsibility is to the institution. In the instance of multiple-unit institutions, the governing board may delegate to its chief executive officer the authority to appoint the executive officer of an operationally separate institution. Neither the chief executive officer nor an executive officer may serve as the chair of the institution's governing board. (Standard Six—**Governance and Administration**; Standard 6.C—**Leadership and Management**; Commission Policy B-7 *Evaluation and Accreditation of Multi-Unit Institutions,* page 147)

6. Administration

   The institution provides the administrative and support services necessary to achieve its mission and meet its goals. (Standard Six—**Governance and Administration**; Standard 6.C—**Leadership and Management**)

7. Faculty

   The institution employs a core of full-time, professionally qualified faculty. The faculty is adequate in number and qualifications to meet its obligations toward achievement of the institution's mission and goals. Faculty are involved in the formulation of institutional policy and participate in academic planning, curriculum development and review, student academic advising, [and] institutional governance and are evaluated in a periodic and systematic manner. Faculty workloads reflect the mission and goals of the institution and the talents and competencies of faculty while allowing sufficient time and support for professional growth and renewal. (Standard Four—**Faculty**; Commission Policy 4.1—*Faculty Evaluation*)

8. Educational Program

   The institution offers one or more educational programs leading to the associate degree or higher that are congruent with its mission; are based on a recognized field(s) of study; are of sufficient content and length; are effective in the use of library and information resources; and are conducted at levels of quality and rigor appropriate to the degree(s) offered. It provides a locus or environment in which the learning experience is enriched through faculty and student interaction. If the range of program(s) is so highly specialized that its professional or vocational specialty defines the institution's identity, it must demonstrate that it has candidacy or accreditation status from a specialized or national accrediting body [that] is recognized by the U.S. Department of Education or the Council for Higher Education Accreditation (CHEA). (Standard Two— **Educational Program and Its Effectiveness**)

9. General Education and Related Instruction

   The institution's baccalaureate degree programs and/or academic or transfer associate degree programs require a substantial and coherent component of general education as a prerequisite to or an essential element of the programs offered. All other associate degree programs (e.g., applied, specialized, or technical) and programs of study of either 30 semester or 45 quarter credits or more for which certificates are granted, require at least six semester or nine quarter credits of related instruction or the equivalent. Bachelor and graduate degree programs also require a planned program of major specialization or concentration. (Standard Two—**Educational Program and Its Effectiveness**; Commission Policy 2.1—*General Education/Related Instruction Requirements,* page 36)

10. Library and Learning Resources

    The institution provides library resources, technology, and services for students and faculty appropriate for its mission and for all of its educational programs wherever located and however delivered. (Standard Five— **Library and Information Resources**)

---

11. Academic Freedom

The institution's faculty and students are free to examine and test all knowledge appropriate to their discipline or area of major study as judged by the academic/educational community in general. Regardless of institutional affiliation or sponsorship, the candidate institution maintains an atmosphere in which intellectual freedom and independence exist. (Standard Four—**Faculty**; Commission Policy A-8—*Principles and Practices Regarding Institutional Mission and Goals, Policies and Administration,* c.(2), page 120)

12. Student Achievement

The institution identifies and publishes the expected learning outcomes for each of its degree and certificate programs of 30 semester or 45 quarter credits or more. Through regular and systematic assessment, it demonstrates that students who complete their programs, no matter where or how they are offered, will achieve these outcomes. (Standard Two—**Educational Program and Its Effectiveness**; Standard 2.B—**Educational Program Planning and Evaluation**; Commission Policy 2.2—*Educational Assessment*)

13. Admissions

The institution publishes its student admission policy, which specifies the characteristics and qualifications appropriate for its programs, and it adheres to that policy in its admission procedures and practices. (Standard Three—**Students**)

14. Public Information

The institution publishes in its catalog or in other appropriate publications and/or electronic sources accurate and current information that describes purposes and objectives, admission requirements and procedures, academic rules and regulations directly affecting students, programs and courses, degree(s) offered and the degree(s) requirements, costs and refund policies, student rights and responsibilities including grievance procedures, academic credentials of faculty and administrators, and other items relative to attending the institution and withdrawing from it. (Standard Three—**Students**; Commission Policy 3.1—*Institutional Advertising, Student Recruitment and Representation of Accredited Status,* Item A.3, page 58)

15. Financial Resources

    The institution verifies a funding base, financial resources, and plans for financial development adequate to achieve its mission and meet its goals within an annual balanced operating budget and manageable level of debt. (Standard Seven—**Finance**)

16. Financial Accountability

    The institution's financial records are externally audited annually by an independent certified public accountant or on a regular schedule by a state audit agency. The audit must include an unqualified opinion on the financial statement. (Standard Seven—**Finance**)

17. Institutional Effectiveness

    The institution systematically applies clearly defined evaluation and planning procedures, assesses the extent to which it fulfills its mission and achieves its goals, and periodically publishes the results to its constituencies. (Standard One—**Institutional Mission and Goals, Planning and Effectiveness**)

18. Operational Status

    The institution will have completed at least one year of its principal educational programs and is operational with students actively pursuing its degree programs at the time of the Commission evaluation for Candidate for Accreditation. (Standard Two—**Educational Program and Its Effectiveness**)

19. Disclosure

    The institution discloses to the Commission on Colleges and Universities any and all such information as the Commission may require to carry out its evaluation and accreditation functions. (Standard Nine—**Institutional Integrity**)

20. Relationship with the Accreditation Commission

    The institution accepts the standards and related policies of the Commission on Colleges and Universities of the Northwest Association of Schools and of Colleges and Universities and agrees to comply with these standards and policies as currently stated or as modified in accordance with Commission policy. Further, the institution agrees that the Commission on Colleges and Universities may, at its discretion, make known to any agency or members of the public that may request such information, the nature of any action, positive or negative, regarding its status with the Commission. The Commission treats institutional self-study reports and evaluation committee reports as confidential. The institution, however, may choose to release the documents. (Standard Nine— **Institutional Integrity**)

Approved December 2000

Appendix C: Accreditation Team Visit Schedule

Regional Accrediting Commission on Higher Education
Evaluation Visit to Midsize College, October 27 to 30

SCHEDULE
Sunday, October 27
5:30 pm to 8:00 pm
Reception and Dinner
Evaluation Team, President's Cabinet, and Accreditation Steering Committee
Place: Nearby Country Club

Monday, October 28

9:15 am to 10:15 am
Evaluation Team Orientation
Place: Board Room,
Presidents Hall

10:30 am to 11:15 am
President's Cabinet
Presidents Hall
Director of Libraries
Director of Mission Integration
Place: Board Room, Presidents Hall

Tuesday, October 29

8:30 am to 9:30 am
Members of Legal Board of Trustees
(breakfast)
Place: Board Room, Presidents Hall

9:30 am to 10:45 am
Interviews
Place: Conference Rooms

11:00 am to 12 noon
Students (brunch)
Place: Student Lounge

11:30 am to 12:45 pm
Interviews
Place: Conference Rooms

1:00 pm to 2:00 pm
Steering Committee (lunch)
Place: Board Room, Presidents Hall

2:15 pm to 3:15 pm
Faculty Senate
Place: Faculty Reception Room

3:30 pm to 4:15 pm
Open Walk-In Session
Place: Board Room, Presidents Hall

4:15 pm to 5:30 pm
Interviews
Place: Conference Rooms

12:15 pm to 1:00 pm
Open Walk-In Session
Place: Board Room, Presidents Hall

1:15 pm to 3:00 pm
Interviews
Place: Conference Rooms

3:00 pm to 3:45 pm
Department Chairs, Directors
Place: Board Room, Presidents Hall

Wednesday, October 30

11:00 am to 12:15 pm
Chair's Oral Report to the University
Community
(Students, Faculty, Staff,
Administrators Steering
Committee, President's
Cabinet)
Place: Auditorium

12:30 pm to 1:00 pm
Chair's Debriefing Meeting with
President
Place: President's Office

12:30 pm to 1:30 pm
Optional Lunch for Team with
President's Cabinet
Place: Board Room, President Hall

Appendix D: Potential Decisions by an Accreditation Agency

1. *Reaffirmation accreditation without conditions.* Reaffirmation without conditions indicates that there are no current issues requiring monitoring via reports prior to the Periodic Review Report (filed five years after the evaluation visit).

2. *Reaffirmation accreditation, with a request for a follow-up report on specific issues to be submitted by a specific date.* Reaffirmation with a request for a follow-up report indicates that there are issues where noncompliance with agency standards is possible, if continuing institutional attention and progress are not encouraged. Issues are such (in complexity and seriousness) that the agency sees monitoring prior to the Periodic Review Report as warranted.

3. *Reaffirmation of accreditation, with a request for a follow-up report, to be followed by a special visit.* In such cases, the agency will specify the nature, purpose, and scope of any further information to be submitted by the institution and of the visit to be made. In addition to indicating that there are issues where future noncompliance with agency standards is possible, the special visit requirement signals that the issues are such that a written progress report will not suffice and that an on-site evaluation to validate and supplement information provided by the institution is necessary.

4. *Deferment of a decision on accreditation.* Deferment permits an institution to furnish essential clarifying information or evidence of progress regarding possible noncompliance with agency standards. Submission of the report may be followed by a visit. In such cases, the agency will specify the nature, purpose, and scope of the information to be submitted and of the visit to be made.

5. *Warning an institution that its accreditation may be in jeopardy, unless the agency's serious concerns regarding noncompliance with standards are addressed.* Warning indicates that in the agency judgment, the institution is not in compliance with the standards. This action is usually accompanied by a request for a follow-up progress report, and a special visit may follow.

6. *Placing an institution on probation.* Probation may be used in two sets of circumstances:

    a. Institutions for which a decision on accreditation has been deferred OR institutions already on warning may be placed on probation when, in the agency's judgment, the institution has failed to demonstrate that it has addressed satisfactorily the agency's concerns regarding compliance with the standards, as specified in the prior action of deferment or warning. As such, probation may precede an action of show cause.

    b. Probation will be utilized when an institution previously under show cause has presented substantive evidence of progress in addressing the agency's concerns and has been directed by the agency to prepare a self-study or further progress report and host an evaluation visit.

Alternatively, the accrediting agency may act to reaffirm accreditation when show cause is removed; however, institutions for whom show cause has been lifted will necessarily be placed in a status of probation unless the agency has acted to reaffirm accreditation.

7. *To require an institution to show cause, within a limited period, as to why its accreditation should not be removed,* the agency will specify the nature, purpose, and scope of the information to be submitted and of the evaluation visit to be made. A show cause order requires an institution to present its case for continued accreditation by means of a substantive report and/or an on-site evaluation.

8. Subsequent to a show cause procedure, or in a case where an institution no longer meets the Commission's eligibility requirements, *to remove an institution from the list of accredited institutions holding membership in the accrediting agency membership roster.*

Decisions for initial accreditation of educational institution by a typical regional agency following an on-site evaluation normally include the following possible outcomes (Middle States Commission on Higher Education, 1997) (cited here with permission by Middle States Association):

1. *Accreditation without conditions.* All institutions receiving initial accreditation must be fully evaluated again within a maximum of five years. Accreditation without conditions indicates that there are no current issues requiring monitoring via reports prior to the next evaluation visit.

2. *Accreditation, with a request for a follow-up report* on specific issues to be submitted by a specific date. The agency will specify the nature, purpose, and scope of information to be submitted. Accreditation with a request for a follow-up report indicates that there are issues where noncompliance with agency standards is possible, if continuing institutional attention and progress are not encouraged. Issues are such (in complexity and seriousness) that the agency sees monitoring prior to the next evaluation visit as warranted. All institutions receiving initial accreditation must be fully evaluated again within a maximum of five years.

3. *Accreditation with a request for a follow-up report on specific issues, followed by a special visit.* The agency will specify the nature, purpose, and scope of the information to be submitted and of the visit to be made. In addition to indicating that there are issues where future noncompliance with agency standards is possible, the special visit requirement signals that the issues are such that a written progress report will not suffice and that an on-site evaluation to validate and supplement information provided by the institution is necessary. All institutions receiving initial accreditation must be fully evaluated again within a maximum of five years.

4. *Deferment of a decision on accreditation.* Deferment permits an institution to furnish essential clarifying information or evidence of progress regarding possible noncompliance with agency standards. The report may be followed by a visit. The accrediting agency will specify the nature, purpose, and scope of the information to be submitted and of the visit to be made. The institution retains its candidate status during the period of deferment (cited here with permission by Middle States Association, 2002).

Appendix E: Institutional Newsletter Content Before Accreditation Visit

---

Volume 1, Issue 1. The North Central Association: Who Are They?
    The Five Criteria for NCA Accreditation: A Summary
    Forms of Affiliation
    The Evaluation Process

Volume 1, Issue 2. NCA Accreditation: Frequently Asked Questions
    The Relationships between GIRs and the Criteria

Volume 1, Issue 3. 1997–98 College Self-Study Report: Do You Know?
    NCA Criterion One: Patterns of Evidence
    The College's Request for Institutional Change: Additional Criteria
    What Are Your Questions?

Volume 1, Issue 4. Guidelines for Distance Education: What the NCA Expects
    Criterion Two: Patterns of Evidence
    Distance Education
    Definition
    Curriculum and Instruction
    Evaluation and Assessment
    Library and Learning Resources
    Student Services
    Facilities and Finances
    Question of the Week: What Is the Commission Accrediting?

Source: McCallin, 1999, p. 304.

References

Academic Quality Improvement Project. (2002). Understanding AQIP, the Higher Learning Commission of the North Central Association of and Colleges and Schools. [http://www.aqip.org/doc/UnderstandingAQIP.pdf]. Access date: Jan. 27, 2003.

Alstete, J. (1995). *Benchmarking in higher education.* Washington, DC: Graduate School of Education and Human Development, The George Washington University.

Alstete, J. (1997). The correlates of administrative decentralization. *Journal of Education for Business, 73*(1), 21–28.

Alstete, J. (2000). *Posttenure Faculty Development.* San Francisco: Jossey-Bass.

Alstete, J. (2001). Alternative uses of electronic learning systems for enhancing team performance. *Team Performance Management: An International Journal, 7*(3/4), 48–52.

Amaral, A.M.S.C. (1998). The US accreditation system and the CRE's quality audits: A comparative study. *Quality Assurance in Education, 6*(4), 184–196.

American Association of Museums. (1989). *Accreditation: A Handbook for the Visiting Committee.* Washington, DC: American Association of Museums.

Andersen, C. J. (1987). *Survey of accreditation issues.* Washington, DC: American Council on Education.

Barker, T. S., and Smith, H. W., Jr. (1998). Integrating accreditation into strategic planning. *Community College Journal of Research and Practice, 22*(8), 741–750.

Barr, R. B., and Tagg, J. (1995). From teaching to learning: A new paradigm for undergraduate education. *Change, 27*(6), 13–25.

Bartelt, C., and Mishler, C. (1996). Using quality tools to get started with your self-study. *A collection of papers on self-study and institutional improvement* (pp. 270–273). Chicago: Commission on Institutions of Higher Education, North Central Association of Colleges and Schools.

Beanland, D. (2001). The Australian approach toward quality enhancement. *Society for Research into Higher Education, 46*(1), 4–5.

Benjamin, E. (1994, July–August). From accreditation to regulation: The decline of academic autonomy in higher education. *Academe,* 34–36.

Bennion, D., Liepa, G., and Melia, P. (2002). The selection, care, and feeding of the steering committee: A key to successful self-study. *A collection of papers on self-study and institutional improvement* (pp. 342–344). Chicago: Higher Learning Commission of the North Central Association of Colleges and Schools.

Bers, T., and Lindquist, S. B. (2002). Institutional research: An antidote to accreditation anxiety. *A collection of papers on self-study and institutional improvement* (pp. 367–369). Chicago: Higher Learning Commission of the North Central Association of Colleges and Schools.

Birnbaum, R. (1988). *How colleges work: The cybernetics of academic organization and leadership.* San Francisco: Jossey-Bass.

Birnbaum, R. (2000). *Management fads in higher education: Where they come from, what they do, why they fail.* San Francisco: Jossey-Bass.

Bishop, J., Brewer, J., Ladwig, D., and Rasch, L. (2000). Do we get them? Do we keep them? Do they learn? Applying quality principles to higher education. *A collection of papers on self-study and institutional improvement* (pp. 35–39). Chicago: Commission on Institutions of Higher Education, North Central Association of Colleges and Schools.

Bishop, J. A., Ladwig, D., and Lanser, M. (2001). Preparing your organization for AQIP. *A collection of papers on self-study and institutional improvement* (pp. 135–137). Chicago: Higher Learning Commission of the North Central Association of Colleges and Schools.

Bloland, H. G. (2001). *Creating the Council for Higher Education Accreditation.* Phoenix, AZ: American Council on Education/Oryx Press.

Bonwell, C. C., and Eison, J. A. (1991). Active learning: Creating excitement in the classroom. Washington, DC: ERIC Clearinghouse on Higher Education.

Braskamp, L. A., and Braskamp, D. C. (1997). The pendulum swing of standards and evidence. *CHEA Chronicle, 1*(5), 1–9.

Brewer, J. A., Trites, D., Matuska, R., and Bishop, J. (1999). A partnership worth pursuing: NCA accreditation and the Malcolm Baldrige award. *A collection of papers on self-study and institutional improvement* (pp. 3–11). Chicago: North Central Association of Colleges and Schools.

Browne, L. D., and Green, C. (2001). AQIP as a change agent in higher education: Lessons learned by a charter institution. *A collection of papers on self-study and institutional improvement* (pp. 158–159). Chicago: Higher Learning Commission of the North Central Association of Colleges and Schools.

Cahoon, M. O., and Pilon, D. H. (1994). Linking the NCA self-study to an annual planning process. *A collection of papers on self-study and institutional improvement* (pp. 40–43). Chicago: North Central Association of Colleges and Schools.

Calhoun, C. (1999). The changing character of college: Institutional transformation in American higher education. In B. A. Pescosolido and R. Aminzade (Eds.), *The social worlds of higher education: Handbook for teaching in a new century* (pp. 21–33). Thousand Oaks, CA: Pine Forge Press.

Capen, S. P. (1939). *Seven devils in exchange for one.* Washington, DC: American Council on Education.

Capowski, G. (1994, March). Anatomy of a leader: Where are the leaders of tomorrow? *Management Review,* 12–15.

Casey, R. J., and Harris, J. W. (1979). *Accountability in higher education: Forces, counterforces, and the role of institutional accreditation.* Washington, DC: Council on Postsecondary Accreditation.

Cerbo, S. C. (2003). *Modern management.* Upper Saddle River, NJ: Prentice Hall.

Chaffee, E. E. (1984). Successful strategic management in small private colleges. *Journal of Higher Education, 55*(2), 212–241.

Chaffee, E. E. (1985a). The concept of strategy: From business to higher education. In J. C. Smart (Ed.), *Higher education: Handbook of theory and research* (pp. 133–172). New York: Agathon Press.

Chaffee, E. E. (1985b). Three models of strategy. *Academy of Management Review, 10*(1), 89–98.

Chambers, C. M. (1983). Council on postsecondary education. In A. K. Yeung, C. M. Chambers, and H. R. Kells (Eds.), *Understanding Accreditation* (pp. 289–314). San Francisco: Jossey-Bass.

Clark, B. (1963). Faculty culture. In T. Lunsford (Ed.), *The study of campus cultures.* Boulder, CO: Western Interstate Commission on Higher Education.

Clark, B. (1989). The academic life: Small worlds, different worlds. *Educational Researcher, 18*(5), 4–8.

Continuous Quality Improvement Network. (2003). *Educational excellence.* [http://www.cqin.org/educationalexcellence/pacesetter_award.asp]. Access date: Jan. 14, 2003.

Council for Higher Education Accreditation. (1999). *CHEA almanac of external quality review.* Washington, DC: Council for Higher Education Accreditation.

Council for Higher Education Accreditation. (2002). *Directory of CHEA participating and recognized organizations, 2001–2002.* Washington, DC: Council for Higher Education Accreditation.

Dill, D. D. (2000). Is there an academic audit in your future? *Change, 32,* 1–10.

Dill, D. D., Massy, W. F., and Williams, P. R. (1996). Accreditation and academic quality assurance: Can we get there from here? *Change, 28*(5), 16–24.

Dill, W. R. (1998, July–August). Specialized accreditation: An idea whose time has come? *Change,* 18–25.

Doerr, A. H. (1983). Accreditation: Academic boon or bane? *Contemporary Education, 55*(1), 6–8.

Dohman, G., and Link, H. (2001). Understanding your campus culture is key to self-study process. *A collection of papers on self-study and institutional improvement* (pp. 330–333). Chicago: Commission on Institutions of Higher Education, North Central Association of Colleges and Schools.

Drucker, P. F. (1993). *Post capitalist society.* New York: HarperCollins.

Drucker, P. F. (2001). *The essential Drucker: In one volume the best of sixty years of Peter Drucker's essential writings on management.* New York: HarperBusiness.

Eaton, J. S. (1999a). Advancing quality through additional attention to results. *CHEA Chronicle, 1*(11), 1–8.

Eaton, J. S. (1999b). Letter from the president. Washington, DC: Council for Higher Education Accreditation.

Eaton, J. S. (2001a). Regional accreditation reform. *Change, 33*(2), 39–45.

Eaton, J. S. (2001b). Taking a look at ourselves: Accreditation. CHEA Enhancing Usefulness Conference. Chicago: Council for Higher Education Accreditation.

Eaton, J. S. (2003, Feb. 28). Before you bash accreditation: Consider the alternatives. *Chronicle of Higher Education,* B15.

Eggers, W. (2000). The value of accreditation in planning. *CHEA Chronicle, 3*(1), 1–7.

Elman, S. E. (1994, Winter). Academic freedom and regional accreditation: Guarantors of quality in the academy. In E. Benjamin and D. R. Wagner (Eds.), *Academic freedom: An everyday concern* (pp. 89–100). New Directions for Higher Education, no. 88.

Ewell, P. T. (1994). Accountability and the future of self-regulation: A matter of integrity. *Change, 26*(6), 24–29.

Ewell, P. T. (1998). Examining a brave new world: How accreditation might be different. CHEA Enhancing Usefulness Conference. Washington, DC: Council for Higher Education Accreditation.

Ewell, P. T. (2001). *Toward excellence in learning.* Paper presented at the Annual Conference of the Middle States Commission on Higher Education, Dec. 3–4, Baltimore, MD.

Fayol, H. (1930). *Industrial and general administration.* Geneva: International Management Institute.

Feddersen, B. (1999). Use of Baldrige criteria for an accreditation self-study. *A collection of papers on self-study and institutional improvement* (pp. 12–15). Chicago: North Central Association of Colleges and Schools.

George, S. (1992). *The Baldrige quality system: The do-it-yourself way to transform your business.* New York: Wiley.

Giacomelli, M. A. (2002). Self-study: The proof is in the plan, process, and product. *A collection of papers on self-study and institutional improvement* (pp. 283–285). Chicago: Higher Learning Commission of the North Central Association of Colleges and Schools.

Glidden, R. (1996). Accreditation at the crossroads. *Educational Record, 77*(4), 22–24.

Goncalves, K. (1992). Those persons who do your planning. *Planning for Higher Education, 20*(2), 25–29.

Goodman, G., and Willekens, R. (2001). Self-study and strategic planning: A critical combination. *A collection of papers on self-study and institutional improvement* (pp. 292–297). Chicago: Commission on Institutions of Higher Education, North Central Association of Colleges and Schools.

Goodstein, L. D. (1978). Organization development in bureaucracies: Some caveats and cautions. In W. W. Burke (Ed.), *Cutting edge: Current theory and practice in organization development* (pp. 47–59). La Jolla, CA: Pfeiffer.

Gose, B. (2002, Nov. 1). A radical approach to accreditation: Can the Academic Quality Improvement Project make the process worth the time and money? *Chronicle of Higher Education,* A25.

Graham, P. A., Lyman, R. W., and Trow, M. (1995). Accountability of colleges and universities: An essay. New York: Columbia University Press.

Hamel, G., and Prahalad, C. K. (1994). *Competing for the future.* Boston: Harvard Business School Press.

Hamm, M. S. (1997). *The fundamentals of accreditation.* Washington, DC: American Society of Association Executives.

Harrington, C. F., Reid, R. L., and Snider, K. J. (2000). Developing data resources for facilitating institutional self-study. *A collection of papers on self-study and institutional improvement* (pp. 356–360). Chicago: Commission on Institutions of Higher Education, North Central Association of Colleges and Schools.

Henninger, E. A. (1998). Dean's role in change: The case of professional accreditation in reform of American education collegiate business education. *Journal of Higher Education Policy and Management, 20*(2), 203–213.

Hogg, E. E. (1993). Unraveling the accreditation enigma: A historical approach. Santa Barbara, CA: Fielding Institute.

Hutchinson, P. M. (1994). Building a self-study around special emphasis. *A collection of papers on self-study and institutional improvement* (pp. 78–83). Chicago: North Central Association of Colleges and Schools.

Janosik, S., Creamer, D., and Alexander, M. (2001). *International perspectives on quality in higher education.* Blacksburg, VA: Virginia Tech.

Jones, D., and Schendel, N. (2000). *Fostering employee ownership in the self-study process through committee empowerment.* Paper presented at the 105th Annual Meeting of the North Central Association Commission on Institutions of Higher Education, April 1–4, Chicago.

Jones, G. R., and George, J. M. (2003). *Contemporary management.* New York: McGraw-Hill.

Jones, L. R., Thompson, F., and Zumeta, W. (2001). *Public management for the new millennium: Developing relevant and integrated professional curricula.* International Public Management Network. [http://www.inpuma.net/test2/issue3/PMCURR8.1doc.pdf]. Access date: Dec. 2., 2002.

Kells, H. R. (1994). *Self-study processes: A guide for postsecondary and similar service-oriented institutions and programs.* Phoenix, AZ: Oryx Press.

Kemling, K. (1994). The two elements that made all the difference. *A collection of papers on self-study and institutional improvement* (pp. 26–28). Chicago: North Central Association of Colleges and Schools.

Kezar, A. J. (2000). *Higher education trends.* Washington, DC: ERIC Clearinghouse on Higher Education.

Kotter, J. P. (1990a). *A force for change: How leadership differs from management.* New York: Free Press.

Kotter, J. P. (1990b, May–June). What leaders really do. *Harvard Business Review,* 103–111.

Leef, G. C., and Burris, R. D. (2002). *Can college accreditation live up to its promise?* Washington, DC: American Council of Trustees and Alumni.

LeMaster, B., and Johnson, L. (2001). Electronic data gathering in the preparation of the self-study. *A collection of papers on self-study and institutional improvement* (pp. 369–372). Chicago: Commission on Institutions of Higher Education, North Central Association of Colleges and Schools.

Lynn, L. E., Jr., and Stein, S., Jr. (2003). Public management. In B. G. Peters and J. Pierre (Eds.), *Handbook of public administration* (pp. 14–24). London: Sage.

Maher, J. (2000). *A total quality strategic planning database model linking objectives with performance measures and accreditation criteria.* Virginia Beach, VA: Regent University.

Martin, J. C. (1994). Recent developments concerning accrediting agencies in postsecondary education. *Law and Contemporary Problems, 57*(4), 121–149.

Martin, R. R., Manning, K., and Ramaley, J. A. (2001). The self-study as a chariot for strategic change. In J. L. Ratcliff, E. S. Lubinescu, and M. A. Gaffney (Eds.), *How accreditation influences assessment* (p. 95–115). New Directions for Higher Education, no. 113. Jossey-Bass, San Franscisco.

McCallin, R. C. (1999). The accreditation process: Connecting potential disconnects on campus. *A collection of papers on self-study and institutional improvement* (pp. 302–306). Chicago: Commission on Higher Education of the North Central Association of Colleges and Schools.

Meyer, H. H., Kay, E., and French, J.R.P. Jr. (1965). Split roles in performance appraisal. *Harvard Business Review, 43,* 123–129.

Michels, J. (1998). ARC's corporate accreditation plan is slow out of the blocks. *Travel Agent,* Sept. 5, 1–3.

Middle States Commission on Higher Education. (1997). Range of commission actions on accreditation. Philadelphia: Middle States Commission on Higher Education.

Middle States Commission on Higher Education. (2001). Follow-up reports and visits. Philadelphia: Middle States Commission on Higher Education.

Middle States Commission on Higher Education. (2002). Designs for excellence. Philadelphia: Middle States Commission on Higher Education.

Miller, D. (1993, January). The architecture of simplicity. *Academy of Management Review,* 116–138.

Mintzberg, H. (1994). *The rise and fall of strategic planning.* New York: Free Press.

Moore, M. R., and Diamond, M. A. (2000). *Academic leadership: Turning vision into reality.* Cleveland: Ernst & Young Foundation.

Morgan, R. (2002, Oct. 2). Lawmakers at hearing on college-accreditation system call for more accountability. *Chronicle of Higher Education,* 1–4.

National Council for Accreditation of Teacher Education. (2003). *Focused visits.* Washington, DC: National Council for Accreditation of Teacher Education.

National Institute of Standards and Technology. (1987). *Baldrige national quality program.* Washington, DC: National Institute of Standards and Technology.

National Institute of Standards and Technology. (2001a). *President and commerce secretary announce recipients of nation's highest honor in quality and performance excellence.* Washington, DC: National Institute of Standards and Technology.

National Institute of Standards and Technology. (2001b). *2001 Malcolm Baldrige national quality award education category.* Washington, DC: National Institute for Standards and Technology.

Newton, R. (1992). The two cultures of academe: An overlooked planning hurdle. *Planning for Higher Education, 21*(1), 8–14.

North Central Association of Colleges and Schools. (2000). A report of a focused visit to University of Michigan–Ann Arbor. Chicago: Commission on Institutions of Higher Education of the North Central Association of Colleges and Schools.

North Central Association of Colleges and Schools. (2001). Academic Quality Improvement Project. *Synthesis,* 10–15.

Northwest Association of Schools and of Colleges and Universities. (2002). *Evaluation committee.* Chicago: Commission on Colleges and Universities of the Northwest Association of Schools and of Colleges and Universities.

Northwest Commission on Colleges and Universities. (2002). *Eligibility requirements for candidates for accreditation and accredited institutions of higher education.* Chicago: Commission on Colleges and Universities of the Northwest Association of Schools and of Colleges and Universities.

Octagram. (2003). *The Dean's Associate.* [http://www.octagram.com]. Access date: Jan. 19, 2003.

Palmer, E. (2002). Strategies for a productive team visit. *A collection of papers on self-study and institutional improvement* (pp. 329–332). Chicago: Higher Learning Commission of the North Central Association of Colleges and Schools.

Pfnister, A. O. (1959). Accreditation in the North Central region. *Accreditation in higher education.* Washington, DC: Office of Education, U.S. Department of Health, Education, and Welfare.

PR Newswire. (2000). GeoAccess and CSI Advantage partner to offer accreditation management software. AIMS software reduces NCQA survey preparation time by 50 percent. PR Newswire Association. [http://www.prnewswire.com]. Access date: Jan. 19, 2003.

Raynor, W. I. (1999). Business accreditation: To enhance global labor standards. *Humanist, 59,* 1–3.

Reed, R. D., and Enger, R. C. (2000). Team building: Key to a successful self-study and team visit. *A collection of papers on self-study and institutional improvement* (pp. 313–316). Chicago: Commission on Institutions of Higher Education of the North Central Association of Schools and Colleges.

Reich, M. J. (1999). Question: What worked best? *A collection of papers on self-study and institutional improvement* (pp. 284–285). Chicago: Committee on Institutions of Higher Education of the North Central Association of Schools and Colleges.

Rieves, N. (1999). *A self-study coordinator's responsibility: From campus-wide involvement to community support.* Paper presented at the 104th Annual Meeting of the North

Central Association Commission on Institutions of Higher Education. April 10–13, Chicago.

Robbins, S. P. (2000). *Managing today.* Upper Saddle River, NJ: Prentice Hall.

Robinson-Weening, L. (1995). A study of the relationship between regional accreditation and institutional improvement among New England colleges and universities. Unpublished doctoral dissertation. Graduate School of Education, Boston College.

Rudolph, F. (1977). *Curriculum: A history of the American undergraduate course of study since 1636.* San Francisco: Jossey-Bass.

Safman, P. C. (1998). What accreditors say: Changes in approach to accreditation practice. *CHEA Chronicle, 1*(10), 1–3.

Schermerhorn, J. R. (2002). *Management.* New York: Wiley.

Shaw, R. (1993). A backward glance: To a time before there was accreditation. *NCA Quarterly, 68*(2), 323–335.

Simon, H. A., Thompson, V., and Smithburg, D. W. (1991). *Public administration.* New Brunswick, NJ: Transaction Publishers.

Simons, R. (1995). *Levers of control: How managers use innovative control systems to drive strategic renewal.* Boston: Harvard Business School Press.

Sorenson, C. W., Furst-Bowe, J. A., and Mooney, C. T. (2002). Lessons for higher education planning: Applying the Baldrige criteria. *A collection of papers on self-study and institutional improvement* (pp. 45–50). Chicago: Higher Learning Commission of the North Central Association of Colleges and Schools.

Southern Association of Colleges and Schools. (2002). *General information on the accreditation process.* Atlanta: Commission on Colleges of the Southern Association of Colleges and Schools. [http://www.sacscoc.org/genaccproc.asp]. Access date: Oct. 22, 2002.

Swanson, K. H. (1999). Data ARE . . . Practicalities relevant to writing the self-study. *A collection of papers on self-study and institutional improvement* (pp. 326–330). Chicago: Commission on Higher Education of the North Central Association of Colleges and Schools.

Swanson, R. A., Hedlund, H., and Neff, J. L. (2000). Incorporating the Malcolm Baldrige national quality criteria into your NCA accreditation process. *A collection of papers on self-study and institutional improvement* (pp. 48–51). Chicago: North Central Association of Colleges and Schools.

Taylor, M. (2002). Managing the stress of the self-study process. *A collection of papers on self-study and institutional improvement* (pp. 335–338). Chicago: Higher Learning Commission of the North Central Association of Colleges and Schools.

Tompkins, E., and Gaumnitz, W. H. (1954). *The Carnegie unit: Its origins, status and trends.* Washington, DC: U.S. Government Printing Office.

Trow, M. (1973). *Problems in the transition from elite to mass to university higher education.* Berkeley, CA: Carnegie Commission on Higher Education.

Trow, M. (1994). Managerialism and the academic profession: The case of England. *Higher Education Policy, 7*(2), 11–18.

Trow, M. (1996). Trust, markets, and accountability in higher education: A comparative perspective. *Higher Education Policy, 9*(4), 309–324.

U.S. Office of Postsecondary Education. (2002). *Accreditation in the U.S.* Washington, DC: U.S. Government Printing Office.

Veysey, L. R. (1965). *The emergence of the American university.* Chicago: University of Chicago Press.

Walck, C. (1998). *Organizing and selling the self-study process to the university community.* Paper presented at the 103rd Annual Meeting of the North Central Association of Colleges and Schools, March 28–31, Chicago.

Winona State University. (2003). *The special emphasis study option from the NCA handbook of accreditation.* Winona State University. [http://www.winona.edu/air/nca/New_Folder/ncasproposal.htm]. Access date: Jan. 27, 2003.

Young, K. E., Chambers, C. M., and Kells, H. R. (1983). *Understanding accreditation.* San Francisco: Jossey-Bass.

Name Index

Smithburg, D. W., 46
Snider, K. J., 76
Sorenson, C. W., 86
Spangehl, S., 95
Stein, S. Jr., 45
Swanson, K. H., 81
Swanson, R. A., 90, 91

T

Tagg, J., 80
Taylor, F., 45
Taylor, M., 70
Thompson, V., 46, 47, 49
Tompkins, E., 7, 9
Trites, D., 87
Trow, M., 3, 16, 20, 82, 85, 99–101

V

Veysey, L. R., 7

W

Walck, C., 32, 34
Weber, M., 45
Willekens, R., 58, 60, 61
Williams, P. R., 4, 15

Y

Young, K. E., 2, 6–8, 10, 17, 23, 27, 32, 33, 35, 36, 51

Z

Zumeta, W., 47, 49

Subject Index

About the Author

Jeffrey W. Alstete is associate dean and a tenured faculty member in the management and business administration department in the Hagan School of Business at Iona College, New Rochelle, New York. Alstete earned a doctorate in higher education administration from Seton Hall University and holds an MBA in financial management.

Over the past 15 years, Alstete has held administrative positions at a number of institutions, including director of continuing education at St. Thomas Aquinas College and assistant dean for graduate programs at the Stillman School of Business, Seton Hall University. In these positions, he served on and chaired regional and specialized accreditation task forces and committees, including a recent regional accreditation review by the Middle States Association, and was appointed director of accreditation at Iona College's Hagan School of Business during the final phase of its successful pursuit of initial accreditation. He has also consulted for several national and international higher education professional associations.

Alstete is the author of two previous books, *Benchmarking in Higher Education: Adapting Best Practices to Improve Quality* (Jossey-Bass, 1995), and *Posttenure Faculty Development: Building a System of Improvement and Appreciation* (Jossey-Bass, 2000). He is also an award-winning author of journal articles related to higher education and business. Alstete's primary areas of scholarly research include effective administration, benchmarking, faculty development, distance learning, virtual teams, knowledge management, and organizational improvement.

About the ASHE-ERIC Higher Education Reports Series

Since 1983, the ASHE-ERIC Higher Education Report Series has been providing researchers, scholars, and practitioners with timely and substantive information on the critical issues facing higher education. Each monograph presents a definitive analysis of a higher education problem or issue, based on a thorough synthesis of significant literature and institutional experiences. Topics range from planning to diversity and multiculturalism, to performance indicators, to curricular innovations. The mission of the Series is to link the best of higher education research and practice to inform decision making and policy. The reports connect conventional wisdom with research and are designed to help busy individuals keep up with the higher education literature. Authors are scholars and practitioners in the academic community. Each report includes an executive summary, review of the pertinent literature, descriptions of effective educational practices, and a summary of key issues to keep in mind to improve educational policies and practice.

The Series is one of the most peer reviewed in higher education. A National Advisory Board made up of ASHE members reviews proposals. A National Review Board of ASHE scholars and practitioners reviews completed manuscripts. Six monographs are published each year and they are approximately 120 pages in length. The reports are widely disseminated through Jossey-Bass and John Wiley & Sons, and they are available online to subscribing institutions through Wiley InterScience (http://www.interscience.wiley.com).

Call for Proposals

The ASHE-ERIC Higher Education Report Series is actively looking for proposals. We encourage you to contact the editor, Dr. Adrianna Kezar, at kezar@usc.edu with your ideas. For detailed information about the Series, please visit http://www.eriche.org/publications/writing.html.

Recent Titles

Back Issue/Subscription Order Form

Copy or detach and send to:

Jossey-Bass, A Wiley Imprint, 989 Market Street, San Francisco CA 94103-1741

Call or fax toll-free: Phone 888-378-2537 6:30AM – 3PM PST; Fax 888-481-2665

Back Issues: Please send me the following issues at $24 each
(Important: please include series abbreviation and issue number.
For example AEHE 28:1)

_____

_____

_____

$ _____ Total for single issues

$ _____

SHIPPING CHARGES:	SURFACE	Domestic	Canadian
	First Item	$5.00	$6.00
	Each Add'l Item	$3.00	$1.50

For next-day and second-day delivery rates, call the number listed above.

Subscriptions Please ❑ start ❑ renew my subscription to *ASHE-ERIC Higher Education Reports* for the year 2_____ at the following rate:

U.S.	❑ Individual $165	❑ Institutional $165
Canada	❑ Individual $165	❑ Institutional $225
All Others	❑ Individual $213	❑ Institutional $276
Online Subscription		❑ Institutional $165

**For more information about online subscriptions visit
www.interscience.wiley.com**

$ _____ Total single issues and subscriptions (Add appropriate sales tax for your state for single issue orders. No sales tax for U.S. subscriptions. Canadian residents, add GST for subscriptions and single issues.)

❑ Payment enclosed (U.S. check or money order only)

❑ VISA ❑ MC ❑ AmEx ❑ #_____ Exp. Date _____

Signature _____ Day Phone _____

❑ Bill Me (U.S. institutional orders only. Purchase order required.)

Purchase order # _____
Federal Tax ID13559302   GST 89102 8052

Name _____

Address _____

_____

Phone _____ E-mail _____

For more information about Jossey-Bass, visit our Web site at www.josseybass.com

ASHE-ERIC HIGHER EDUCATION REPORT
IS NOW AVAILABLE ONLINE AT WILEY INTERSCIENCE

What is Wiley InterScience?

Wiley InterScience is the dynamic online content service from John Wiley & Sons delivering the full text of over 300 leading scientific, technical, medical, and professional journals, plus major reference works, the acclaimed Current Protocols laboratory manuals, and even the full text of select Wiley print books online.

What are some special features of Wiley InterScience?

Wiley Interscience Alerts is a service that delivers table of contents via e-mail for any journal available on Wiley InterScience as soon as a new issue is published online.
Early View is Wiley's exclusive service presenting individual articles online as soon as they are ready, even before the release of the compiled print issue. These articles are complete, peer-reviewed, and citable.
CrossRef is the innovative multi-publisher reference linking system enabling readers to move seamlessly from a reference in a journal article to the cited publication, typically located on a different server and published by a different publisher.

How can I access Wiley InterScience?

Visit http://www.interscience.wiley.com.

Guest Users can browse Wiley InterScience for unrestricted access to journal Tables of Contents and Article Abstracts, or use the powerful search engine.
Registered Users are provided with a *Personal Home Page* to store and manage customized alerts, searches, and links to favorite journals and articles. Additionally, Registered Users can view free Online Sample Issues and preview selected material from major reference works.
Licensed Customers are entitled to access full-text journal articles in PDF, with select journals also offering full-text HTML.

How do I become an Authorized User?

Authorized Users are individuals authorized by a paying Customer to have access to the journals in Wiley InterScience. For example, a University that subscribes to Wiley journals is considered to be the Customer.
Faculty, staff and students authorized by the University to have access to those journals in Wiley InterScience are Authorized Users. Users should contact their Library for information on which Wiley journals they have access to in Wiley InterScience.

AWARDS AND PRAISE FOR CAROLYN MACKLER AND *THE EARTH, MY BUTT, AND OTHER BIG ROUND THINGS*

Winner of the Michael L. Printz Honor for Excellence in Young Adult Literature

An American Library Association Best Book for Young Adults

A New York Public Library Book for the Teen Age

A YALSA Teens' Top Ten Selection

"I loved this book. It's funny, sweet, and most of all, hopeful. It should be required reading for all girls, everywhere."
—Sarah Dessen, #1 *New York Times* bestselling author

"Carolyn Mackler is a remarkably astute observer of human frailties and hearts." —E. Lockhart, *New York Times* bestselling author of *We Were Liars*

"No one writes more honestly and empathetically about teenage lives than Carolyn Mackler. She doesn't write teens as adults want them to be; she writes teens as they are." —Gabrielle Zevin, *New York Times* bestselling author of *The Storied Life of A. J. Fikry*

"Mackler writes with such insight and humor . . . that many readers will immediately identify with Virginia's longings as well as her fear and loathing." —*Booklist*

"The heroine's transformation into someone who finds her own style and speaks her own mind is believable—and worthy of applause." —*Publishers Weekly*

"Carolyn Mackler writes with a clarity and impact that lifts her material above the ordinary." —*BCCB*

"Readers will be rooting for Virginia all the way." —*Kirkus Reviews*

Kristen———

THE EARTH, MY BUTT, AND OTHER BIG ROUND THINGS

Embrace the curves!

Carolyn Mackler

Books by Carolyn Mackler

⑥ ⑥ ⑥ ⑥

The Earth, My Butt, and Other Big Round Things
The Universe Is Expanding and So Am I

Infinite in Between
Tangled
Guyaholic
Vegan Virgin Valentine
Love and Other Four-Letter Words

The Future of Us (coauthored with Jay Asher)

Best Friend Next Door (for younger readers)

AUTHOR'S NOTE

Dear Reader,

Fifteen years ago, I wrote *The Earth, My Butt, and Other Big Round Things*. It was a very raw time in my life. I was less than a decade out of my teen years. I was trying to understand my relationship with my parents and my older brother. I was grappling with the fact that I often feel like an outsider in the world. But I'd also recently gotten together with the guy who would become my husband, so my future was starting to emerge— and things looked happy. I created Virginia Shreves because she appeared in my imagination, as characters tend to do, but also because I was trying to figure things out.

Now ready for a crazy history lesson? When I wrote *The Earth, My Butt, and Other Big Round Things*, a lot of people didn't have cell phones. The internet was new and enticing. My main character, fifteen-year-old Virginia, e-mailed her best friend. Netflix only mailed out their movies, and people hadn't even heard of streaming shows. Back then, people flipped through channels on TV and were forced to watch what was on. And forget YouTube. Not even invented.

Well, it wasn't all ancient history. In *The Earth, My Butt, and Other Big Round Things*, Virginia hates her curvy body. She struggles with how she feels about herself and how her family treats her. She's devastated when her older brother is kicked out of college. She wants a boyfriend. She wants to be loved and accepted. Over the years, I've gotten so many letters from readers who have told me how much Virginia meant to them, how her story helped them feel less alone, how Virginia helped them learn to love themselves as they are.

That's why I decided to go in and update some things, make this novel work in today's world. I didn't change Virginia's story, but I rescued her from a slow internet connection and time-traveled her to the present. I gave the girl a phone. I gave her Netflix and YouTube. I let her text instead of e-mail.

Some things change. A lot of things change. But the essentials like trying to understand who we are, working to feel good about ourselves, and figuring out what we want out of life? That stuff stays the same.

Love,

Carolyn Mackler

P.S. Whenever I finish reading a book, I feel sad to leave it. If you're anything like me that way, I have some good news! After a decade and a half, Virginia came back into my imagination, so I decided to write her a sequel. I'm thrilled to announce that Virginia's story continues in *The Universe Is Expanding and So Am I.*

THE EARTH, MY BUTT, AND OTHER BIG ROUND THINGS

CAROLYN MACKLER

BLOOMSBURY

NEW YORK LONDON OXFORD NEW DELHI SYDNEY

First published in the United States of America in 2003 by Candlewick Press
Fifteenth anniversary edition first published in the United States of America in April 2018
by Bloomsbury Children's Books
www.bloomsbury.com

Bloomsbury is a registered trademark of Bloomsbury Publishing Plc

For information about permission to reproduce selections from this book, write to
Permissions, Bloomsbury Children's Books, 1385 Broadway, New York, New York 10018
Bloomsbury books may be purchased for business or promotional use. For information on
bulk purchases, please contact Macmillan Corporate and Premium Sales Department at
specialmarkets@macmillan.com

The Library of Congress has cataloged the original hardcover edition as follows:
Mackler, Carolyn
The earth, my butt, and other big round things / Carolyn Mackler—1st U.S. ed.
p.   cm.
Summary: Feeling like she does not fit in with the other members of her family, who are all
thin, brilliant, and good-looking, fifteen-year-old Virginia tries to deal with her self-image, her
first physical relationship, and her disillusionment with some of the people closest to her.
ISBN 978-0-7636-1958-9 (original hardcover)
[1. Self-perception—Fiction. 2. Assertiveness (Psychology)—Fiction. 3. Family problems—
Fiction. 4. Weight control—Fiction. 5. High schools—Fiction. 6. Schools—Fiction. 7. New
York (N.Y.) —Fiction.] I. Title.
PZ7.M2178 Ear 2003   [Fic]—dc21   2002073921

ISBN 978-1-68119-798-2 (paperback) • ISBN 978-1-68119-799-9 (hardcover)
ISBN 978-1-68119-800-2 (e-book)

Book design by Jeanette Levy
Typeset by Westchester Publishing Services
Printed and bound in the U.S.A. by Berryville Graphics Inc., Berryville, Virginia
2 4 6 8 10 9 7 5 3 1 (paperback)
2 4 6 8 10 9 7 5 3 1 (hardcover)

All papers used by Bloomsbury Publishing, Inc., are natural, recyclable products made
from wood grown in well-managed forests. The manufacturing processes conform to the
environmental regulations of the country of origin.

To Jonas Rideout,
for listening and laughing and loving

THE EARTH, MY BUTT, AND OTHER BIG ROUND THINGS

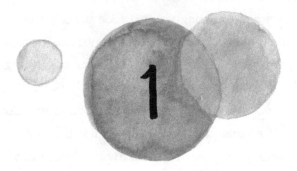

Froggy Welsh the Fourth is trying to get up my shirt.

This is the third Monday that he's come over to my apartment after school. Every week we go a little farther, and today, on September twenty-fifth at 3:17 p.m., he's begun inching his fingers across my stomach and toward my bra.

"Virginia?"

I'm not sure whether Froggy is saying my name as a prelude to a question or whether he's uttering it in ecstasy. As much as I wish it were the latter, I conclude that it's the former. We're only fifteen, after all.

"Yeah?" I ask.

"Is it okay if I . . . ?" Froggy rubs his nose a few times. He's always tweaking his nose. I think it's an anxiety thing. "Would you mind if I . . . ?"

"I . . . er," I say. "I mean . . . um . . . yeah."

Not exactly the sensuous dialogue you conjure up when you imagine your first time reaching second base. But Froggy and I don't score high on the communication front. Especially once we've stuck our tongues into each other's mouths.

I think it's because we're not boyfriend and girlfriend or even *friends,* for that matter. Until the beginning of tenth grade, Froggy and I just passed each other in the halls at school, sometimes waving, sometimes saying hi, sometimes doing nothing at all. Which is pretty much how it still is, except for this kissing aspect. I can't say it's what I want, but I know this is all it can ever be.

It's not like Froggy Welsh the Fourth is a huge catch. First of all, there's his name. Not a nickname for Frank or Frederick or even *Frog.* I'm still shocked that his great-great-grandparents named a son Froggy. But what astounds me to no end is that three subsequent generations decided to follow suit.

Froggy is medium height and slender. His ruffled blond hair crests into a cowlick. His dollop of a nose reminds me of a lamb's snout. Especially since it's always pinkish, probably from so much tweaking. Whenever his pubescent voice cracks, he sounds like a screeching chicken. Put his name and traits together and you've got a farm.

But he's here.

And he's a halfway decent kisser.

Maybe it's all the trombone lessons.

Trombone is the reason we've been fooling around since the beginning of the school year. Froggy takes Monday-afternoon trombone lessons from a student at Juilliard. That's this prestigious music school on the West Side of Manhattan, about fifteen blocks from my apartment. Brewster, our small private school, is on the East Side. Every Monday we ride the crosstown bus together.

On the first Monday of the school year, Froggy slid into a seat next to me on the bus. We chatted the whole way across the park, comparing our summer breaks and complaining about Mademoiselle Kiefer, our evil French teacher. When we got off on Broadway, Froggy said he had an hour to kill before his trombone lesson. I suggested we head over to my apartment and hang out.

I sounded innocent, but I have to admit I had ulterior motives with Froggy. Simply put, I was tired of being the only teenager in America—if not the world—who had yet to French-kiss. And along came Froggy, a halfway decent male specimen, with an hour to kill. The only trick was figuring out how to steer him from platonic-friend-who-hangs-out-and-watches-shows to lusty-guy-deflowering-my-virginal-kissing-status.

Opportunity knocked when we stepped into the elevator of my building. As I pushed the PH button, Froggy said, "So . . . you live in the penthouse."

I shot Froggy a coy glance. "Yep, and no one's home."

It was an early September afternoon, particularly muggy in the elevator. Froggy grinned as he wiped the perspiration from his forehead. I felt a tremor deep in my gut, in that region south of my belly button.

As soon as we got into the apartment, I poured us both a tall glass of Diet Coke and we retreated to my bedroom. From there, it didn't take long—fourteen minutes, to be exact—until Froggy and I were making out.

Here's how it happened:

I said that the soda was making my braces cold. I've heard that women should always call attention to their mouths, as in licking a lollipop or sliding on lip gloss.

Froggy bought it hook, line, and sinker—going so far as to reach over and touch my brackets.

Once our faces were in such close proximity, we had no choice but to giggle and nuzzle noses and kiss.

At first, it was nice. Nibbly and soft and not too spitty. I liked the way Froggy smelled up close, sort of sweet and musky and boyish.

But then I started worrying. *Does my inexperience show? What do I do with my tongue once it's in his mouth? Am I suctioning my lips too tightly? Should I keep my eyes open? Too weird! Or closed? Maybe. But what if HIS eyes are open and mine are closed and I make a freaky face and he sees it and laughs so hard that he bites off my tongue?*

I tried to recall make-out tips I've read, and then I remembered a quiz I once took where you rate your kissability on a scale of one to ten. I decided that I ranked about a two, maybe two and a half.

Froggy and I kissed for the next few minutes, until he glanced at the time on his phone and dashed into the hallway to retrieve his trombone case.

Which brings us to today, two Mondays later, sprawled on my bedroom floor yet again. Froggy has spent the past several minutes fumbling around my shoulder blades. I don't have the guts to inform him that this particular bra unhooks in the front.

I'm doing my best imitation of a lover seized by passion. Eyelids heavy, faint upward curve to lips—just like women in movies who always look so orgasmic. But, truth be told, I'm having a panic attack. I'm worried that Froggy is going to attempt to take off my shirt. It's okay for his hands to be rummaging *inside* it, but there's no way I'm letting him see my upper arms and stomach. I don't know where *"love* handles" got their name, but I have a feeling Froggy wouldn't find mine all that endearing.

I'm also double-checking and triple-checking whether I've locked my bedroom door. My workaholic parents rarely leave their offices before seven, and most nights they eat dinner out or grab something on the run. But I'd hate this to be the day they come home early, only to discover their youngest child going at it with a guy named after an amphibian.

I'm also trying to figure out why the droopy-eyed, faintly smiling movie stars never mention rug burn. I have a plush pink rug, but it's chafing my back every time my shirt slides up. I clutch both hands to the bottom of my shirt, anchoring it down. That serves the double purpose of not exposing any flabby body parts.

"Don't you want to . . . ?" Froggy's voice cracks as he gestures in the direction of my boobs.

"That's not it." I point to my phone. "It's just, you know, your trombone lesson."

Froggy tries to smooth back his hair, but it flops messily over his forehead. I'm tempted to run my fingers through his cowlick, but I know I shouldn't. No affectionate girlfriend-isms, especially once the make-out session has ended.

I escort Froggy to the front door, where he collects his backpack and trombone case from our foyer. I make a mental note to be more careful next time, to suggest that Froggy stash his stuff in my bedroom, just in case Mom or Dad or even my big brother makes a surprise visit. If there *is* a next time. I can never tell for sure.

Froggy stands in the doorway, rubbing his nose and pivoting his leg from side to side, like he's trying to burrow through the floor with his heel.

"Well, thanks," he says. "See you at school."

"Yeah." I smile weakly and my lower lip gets snagged on my braces.

"Yeah," Froggy mumbles.

I try to muster the courage to suggest we sit together at lunch sometime, but then I wimp out, say one final *yeah,* and close the door.

2

About a year ago, before my sister joined the Peace Corps and moved to Africa, she sat me down and had a sex talk.

"Look," Anaïs said, flopping next to me on the couch. "I know Mom's not going to discuss this with you, and I'd shudder to think what Dad would say, so I propose we have a little sex talk."

It was a quiet Saturday afternoon. Mom, Dad, and our brother, Byron, were at Yankee Stadium. I'd begged to go with them since they had four field-level seats, which would have offered prime views of players' butts in tight uniforms. But Byron made a case to bring his girlfriend du jour, a Parisian student who'd never seen a ball game before. Byron, a top debater in college, won out. Especially since my only argument was that I wanted to salivate over a certain sexy shortstop.

After they left, I spent an hour sulking—scrolling through

my phone and trolling through the cupboards—and basically feeling sorry for myself. Then I headed out to the street and bought some Doritos and a Snickers bar. When I got back to the apartment, I parked on the couch, watched shows, and devoured my munchies until my sister interrupted me with the sex-talk business.

I wiped my Dorito-orange fingers on a paper towel and rolled my eyes. "I know about sex, if that's what you're wondering," I told Anaïs. "I've known for years."

"But do you know about guys?"

I stared at my sister.

"Right," she said. Then she launched into one of her rants, something she'd been doing ever since she discovered the feminist rocker Ani DiFranco and stopped shaving her legs. "Let me guess. On your thirteenth birthday, Mom left *It's Perfectly Normal* on your bed with a note that said"—Anaïs crooked her fingers like quotation marks—"'Come to me with questions.' But then, of course, she never has a spare minute to talk because she's too busy helping other teenagers figure things out and, anyway, who wants sex advice from someone who considers *Dad* an ideal mate?"

My jaw dropped to the floor. Mom is an adolescent psychologist. She has a booming therapy practice and often speaks at conferences on teenagers. Dad is a high-powered software executive. He goes on business trips to Europe and California. One time he got written up in *Wired* for the streaming software that his company invented.

Even though they're in their early fifties, my parents are

youngish-looking and active. Mom is a workout fiend, and Dad goes to the gym a lot, too. On warm weekends they golf together at their country club in Connecticut. That's where Mom and Dad spend practically every weekend. We have a house in southwestern Connecticut. I used to go more when I was younger, but there's nothing to do out there—no phone reception, no Wi-Fi, no town within walking distance—so I usually stay in the city on weekends.

"How did you know about *It's Perfectly Normal*?" I asked. That's the sexual health book that Mom gave me when I turned thirteen.

"She did the same for me." Anaïs twisted her curly dark hair into a knot on the top of her head. "But by the time she gave me *It's Perfectly Normal*, I'd already gotten my period, been felt up by two boys, and read every sexuality book in her office, all of which went typically"—Anaïs made the quotation marks again—" 'unnoticed' by Mom."

"Well, you know how hard Mom works," I said. "She's totally overwhelmed by her—"

"Her patients? Her spin classes? Her social engagements?" Anaïs paused for a second and then sourly added, "Then again, when you're Dr. Phyllis Shreves, you don't have to worry about your *own* children because they're obviously going to turn out perfect *and* normal."

Dr. Phyllis Shreves. That's what Anaïs calls Mom whenever she's pissed at her. They argued a lot during my sister's senior year in college, about her decision to join the Peace Corps rather than go right to medical school. It always made me uncomfortable when they battled it out. I love my sister, but Mom usually knows what she's talking about when it comes to life plans.

I hugged a couch pillow to my stomach and attempted to change the subject. "Do you think Mom gave that book to Byron, too?"

Anaïs snorted. Anaïs snorts about anything related to our brother, who is four years older than me, four years younger than her. Anaïs is the only person I know who snorts in reference to Byron. The rest of the world worships him, myself included. He's incredibly handsome—supposedly the spitting image of Dad when he was in college—with tousled brown hair, maple-syrup-colored eyes, and a confident Shreves jaw. At that point, last summer, he was about to start Columbia, the Ivy League university here in New York City. Now he's in his sophomore year, where he's a star of the debate team, a rugby god, a total Don Juan loverboy, and a straight-A student. Byron happens to think a lot of himself, but if I were even a smidgen like him, I'd have an ego the size of Brazil.

"I think she left Byron up to Dad. Can't you picture it?" Anaïs lowered her voice and scratched her chin mannishly. "You need sex ed, son? Here's a pack of condoms. Go out and get some."

I cracked up at my sister's imitation of Dad, which made me start choking on the sharp point of a Dorito. Anaïs shook her hair around her bare shoulders. She always wears skimpy tank tops and short shorts, things I could *never* imagine wearing, not even on the hottest days of summer. The best way to garb my heavier-than-average body is to hide it beneath layers of loose clothing. When the time comes for college, I'm considering checking out campuses in the Arctic Circle, where floor-length puffy coats are probably all the rage.

"Anyway, where were we?" Anaïs asked.

"The sex talk," I said, clearing my throat.

"Right."

Anaïs scooped up a handful of Doritos and briefed me on lust and crushes. She emphasized the importance of knowing your body, knowing what you like, because horny teenage guys aren't going to try to figure that out. She explained that, contrary to everything you see in movies, losing your virginity is sloppy and painful and about as fun as getting your toe amputated, so it should definitely happen with someone you care about.

We chatted on the couch until Mom, Dad, Byron, and the French girl returned from the ball game, giddy from beer, sunburns, and a Yankee victory. Mom's always nagging me about junk food, so I stashed the Doritos bag behind a couch cushion and buried my face in my phone. Anaïs retreated to her room, closed her door, and pumped an Ani album.

Three weeks later my sister began her two-year Peace Corps stint in Burkina Faso, where she's administering medication to rural West Africans.

And now, over a year later, as I stand in the hallway and stare at the door through which Froggy has just disappeared, I remember what Anaïs told me that afternoon.

"If you can't talk about something with a guy, you have no business doing it with him."

"You mean sex?" I asked.

"I mean anything. Making out. Second base. Third base. And, yes, home runs."

It made sense at the time. But now it dawns on me that it's easy for Anaïs to give that kind of advice when she's waify and gorgeous and people have stopped her on the sidewalk to tell her she should be a model.

When it comes to me, however, Anaïs failed to factor in one crucial thing. She forgot about the Fat Girl Code of Conduct.

3

I hear the elevator doors close, transporting Froggy down to the lobby. I head into the kitchen and splash my face with cool water. My cheeks feel feverish, so I lean into the spray for a long time. I use this sink as much as possible because the kitchen is the only room in the apartment besides mine that doesn't have a mirror. I hate mirrors. That's why I limit my reflection-gazing to twelve seconds in the morning when I deal with my shoulder-length layered hair.

I've been mulling over the Fat Girl Code of Conduct a lot recently. Ever since I heard this joke on a creepy video that was going around. Here's how it went:

Question: What do a fat girl and a moped have in common?

Answer: They're both fun to ride, as long as your friends don't see you.

Really hilarious. So hilarious that it made me want to throw myself down our garbage chute, if only I could squeeze through the hole.

The strange thing is, as cruel as it was, that joke actually got me thinking. Basically, I can't resolve two contradictory facts of life.

Fact of Life #1: Fat girls don't get much action.

Fact of Life #2: I want to increase my kissability.

It's probably time to write a list. That's what I do whenever I'm overwhelmed and confused. It's not like I figure out any huge answers, but I always feel better after my thoughts are in writing.

I dry my face with a paper towel and grab a handful of animal crackers. Once I'm in my bedroom, I open my computer, munch on two lions, and start writing.

THE FAT GIRL CODE OF CONDUCT
by Virginia Shreves

1. Any sexual activity is a secret. No public displays of affection. No air-kisses blown across the cafeteria. No carefully folded notes passed in the hall. No riding the moped in public.
2. Don't discuss your weight with him. Let's face it. You both know it's there, so don't start bemoaning your body

and pressure him into lying, i.e., "What are you talking about? You don't look fat at all."

3. Go farther than skinny girls. Find ways to alert him to this, such as slutty comments peppered into the conversation. If you can't sell him on your body, you'd better overcompensate with sexual perks.

4. Never, ever, ever, ever push the relationship thing. Everybody knows that guys hate discussing relationships, so make it easy on him. Same goes for dates to movies and school dances. Bottom line: let him get the milk without having to buy the cow.

I don't candy-coat my lists, so they tend toward the brutally honest. That's why I've never shown them to anyone, not even my best friend, Shannon. But I keep everything under password on my computer, just in case my family decides to poke around in my personal files.

To be honest, it's probably not necessary. I don't get the sense they're that interested in what's going on in my life, much less my head. Sometimes it feels like they don't think anything's going on at all.

☙ ☙ ☙ ☙

I have this theory that I was switched at birth.

It doesn't happen much, but every once in a while you hear about a demented hospital worker who swaps ID bracelets on two wailing infants.

I just know there's a stout, blond family out there wondering how they wound up with a beautiful, slim, brown-haired daughter. What they don't realize is that she was meant to bear the name Virginia Shreves and live with her beautiful, slim, brown-haired family in a roomy apartment on Riverside Drive.

And I know that my beautiful, slim, brown-haired family wonders how they wound up with a daughter who has dishwater-blond hair, pale-blue eyes, a roundish face, and a larger-than-average body.

Okay, fat.

Not *fat* fat. More like chubby fat.

Enough so I'm picked last in gym if the activity has anything to do with running, climbing ropes, or propelling oneself over a horse. Enough so I've heard people refer to me as plump, as if being likened to a vine-ripe tomato is some kind of compliment. Enough so family friends, upon comparing me to my skinny siblings, raise their eyebrows as high as McDonald's golden arches.

That's the most frustrating thing. I can't even blame it on genetics. Byron and Anaïs can eat whatever they want and still maintain their long, lanky bodies, just like Dad. If I so much as *smell* a bucket of fried chicken, I gain five pounds. I have more of Mom's metabolism. She used to be heavy when she was younger. She doesn't talk much about that time in her life. It's just occasional mentions of an awful childhood, a crazy family, how lucky we have it, how far she's come from Ozark, Arkansas. Mom slimmed down by the time she went to Dartmouth and met Dad because in early pictures of them together, she looks about the same size as she is now.

Even so, she's always obsessing about not gaining weight. She eats lettuce at every meal and spends half her life at the gym. I don't know what she's worried about because she's totally thin. Maybe it's Dad. He's the first to admit that he likes women skinny.

They say that people become therapists to figure out their lives. That's probably the case with Mom. As soon as she hit college, she began studying adolescent psychology and didn't stop until she had a PhD. I think it would be interesting to do what Mom does, sit there all day and listen to teenagers spill their secrets. Dad shudders at the idea, but he's not happy unless he's managing dozens of people—phones ringing, texts dinging, constant chaos. Byron and Anaïs are more like Dad that way. I'm more like Mom, craving plenty of peace and quiet.

That's probably why Mom reads so much. Whenever she's not working or working out, she's reading a book. She named us after famous authors—Anaïs Nin, Lord Byron, Virginia Woolf— with the hope that we'd achieve greatness someday.

Except for my sister going into the Peace Corps, Anaïs and Byron have fulfilled all of Mom's dreams for her children. They are athletic and attractive. They love golfing at the country club in Connecticut. Our storage space in the basement is a treasure trove of their trophies and plaques and awards. They are both fluent in French, like my parents. Sometimes the four of them carry on an entire conversation in French. Anaïs also speaks Spanish, and Byron is currently learning Japanese.

They all love artsy films. And jazz clubs. And museum exhibits. When she was in college, Anaïs brought home boyfriends with whom Dad talked about gaming gadgets and fantasy football. Byron's girlfriends always bond with Mom, chatting it up about anything from handbags to hundred-dollar eye serums.

Sometimes I wonder if my parents wish they'd stopped at two kids. No one's ever spelled it out, but I think I was a mistake. They had me when they were in their late thirties, once they already had the ideal nuclear setup. And along came me, blemishing the image of a picture-perfect family.

I'm not saying I'm a huge loser. It's just that I'm not exceptional like the rest of them. I'm obsessed with celebrity gossip. I love taking online quizzes and watching viral videos. I hate cardiovascular exercise. I can't see the point in hitting a golf ball from here to eternity. I suck at French, but other than that I'm a good student. I love sitcoms and reality shows and cheesy blockbuster movies. I'm not crazy about artsy films (they don't star anyone cute!) or jazz (no lyrics!) or museum exhibits (all the artists are dead!). Needless to say, a guy will probably never like me enough to want to meet my parents.

I'm definitely the weakest link in the Shreves clan.

I know I'm lucky to have been switched into such a stellar family. I just wish I made them feel more fortunate to have wound up with me.

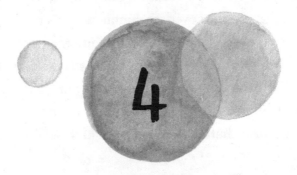

4

I'm standing at the entrance to the lunchroom, balancing a tray in my hands. The odor of burned chicken nuggets and sour milk penetrates my nostrils. I feel like I'm going to puke, but I'm not sure if it's from the cafeteria stench or the anxiety in my stomach.

This is the moment I most dread every day. Back when Shannon was here, lunch was no big deal. We'd grab a table in the back and talk and laugh like we were the only people on the planet. But so far this year, it's been a panicky occasion. I never know who I'm going to sit with—or if I'll sit with anyone. Usually, I can locate some nice quiet types from one of my classes. But it's never consistent. And if one of my standby tables is full, I don't have a backup plan.

No, actually, here's my backup plan:

I spend lunch period locked in a stall in the second-floor bathroom, thumbing through my phone and eating potato chips. It sounds gross, but it's actually okay. Especially since they installed toilet-seat lids over the summer, so it's not like I'm sitting over the open hole. No one comes into that bathroom during lunch, so it's pretty peaceful. And they clean it on a regular basis, so it either smells like lemon-lime or bubble gum, depending on which cleanser the nighttime janitor used.

It's not ideal. But no one ever said high school is a bed of roses.

My number-one objective in the lunchroom scenario is to not spend too much time hovering with my tray, gawking at my sea of classmates. It's essential to appear as if I know exactly where I'm sitting, which requires split-second scanning skills as I emerge from the food line and enter the cafeteria.

I hate calling attention to myself. A lot of it has to do with being heavy at a school where nearly every other girl weighs two pounds. Also, the cliques at Brewster are divided into popular, regular, and dorky—as kids refer to the various crowds. There's an unspoken rule that if you're not on the popular side of things, you shouldn't take up too much space. Just go with the flow and people will pretty much leave you alone.

If I had to chart it, I probably fall somewhere between regular and dorky.

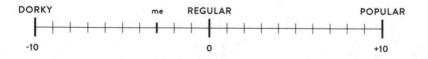

I figure everyone starts with a zero and points are added or subtracted according to coolness/dorkiness.

I gain points because
- Byron went to school here and he was popular, so his legacy gives me some mileage (+5).
- I have decent hair that requires little work (+2).
- I'm smart, except in French (+2.5).

I lose points because
- I'm overweight (–6.5).
- I wear neutral colors, loose T-shirts, baggy khakis, and oversized sweatshirts (–4).
- I'm smart, which works against you if you're smarter than a popular kid (–2).

On the far end of the cafeteria, I spot an available seat at a table of girls from my chemistry lab. The only problem is, Froggy Welsh the Fourth and his friends are at a neighboring table. Froggy and I haven't spoken since he was at my apartment two days ago, so I don't want to give him the wrong idea, like I'm stalking him.

I hear someone calling my name. I look over to see Ms. Crowley waving and heading my way.

"Virginia!" She squeezes my shoulder. "I've been hoping to run into you since the beginning of school."

Eileen Crowley was my ninth-grade language arts teacher. She's in her thirties, a published poet, and moderately overweight. Some of the popular kids used to call her *Ms. Cowley* behind her back, which made me so angry I would dig my fingernails into the palms of my hands. In my end-of-year evaluation letter, Ms. Crowley wrote: *It's rare to encounter a student like Virginia Shreves. What a talented writer! She'll go far.* I tucked that letter into the small cedar box that I keep in the back of my undies drawer. The only other things I have in that box are a strip of pictures Byron and I once took in a photo booth, a receipt I saw a cute boy drop on Broadway, and a snippet of Shannon's red hair.

Ms. Crowley must have read my mind. "I've been wondering how you're surviving without your spiritual twin."

"Shannon?" I ask, readjusting the tray in my hands.

Ms. Crowley nods.

"It's definitely different with her away," I say.

I guess I'd call Shannon my spiritual twin. She's my best friend. Her full name is Shannon Iris Malloy-Newman. I've heard people describe her as mousy, but I firmly believe she was a cat in a former life. She's small and graceful, with pumpkin-colored hair, masses of freckles, and felinelike eyes. She's incredibly funny, but most people don't give her the chance to show it. Shannon has a stutter, so it can take her several tries to complete a sentence. She rarely stutters around me. Only with strangers or during a class presentation or if she's trying to say something quickly. Sometimes I think our deficits (me = heavy; Shannon = stutter) are what initially brought us together, back in sixth grade. From there, we totally connected.

Shannon is away for the school year. In Walla Walla,

Washington. I once joked that Walla Walla is a haven for stutterers because it's one of the only geographic locations where you're *supposed* to say the name twice.

"Great, Virginia," Shannon had responded. "A town full of stutterers with bad breath. *Just perfect.*"

Walla Walla is the hometown of the Walla Walla onion. That's what brought Shannon's family to Walla Walla. Shannon's dad is writing a book on onions. Liam Newman always writes about obscure topics, like the role of the shoelace throughout history, which was a bestseller in New Zealand.

But onions. Onions are the clincher.

Appropriate topic, actually, because whenever I think about facing the next ten months without Shannon, I burst into tears.

Ms. Crowley must sense something on my face. "Virginia, are you ever free during lunch period?"

"Sure . . . why?"

"I'm swamped with grading my freshman vocabulary tests. Remember how many I gave you last year?"

I nod.

"I'd love your help," she says.

"Really?"

"My office is still on the second floor. Come up anytime. I'm always there this period."

As soon as Ms. Crowley is out of sight, I glance down at my tray. The side dish of corn has congealed, so little blobs of butter are mingling with the bloated kernels. I grab the salt and vinegar chips and toss the rest of my lunch into the trash bin. As I do, I notice Froggy looking my way. I think he's smiling.

I offer a brief smile back. Enough so he'll see it, but not so much that I'll look like a freak grinning into thin air.

Then I hurry out of the cafeteria and head up the stairs to spend the rest of the period in peace.

Ten minutes later I'm locked in a stall, watching a video on mute on my phone, when I hear the bathroom door open and some pairs of shoes click in.

I breathe a sigh of relief that I'm far from the mirrors, where the feet are remaining. But as I peek through the crack between the doorway and stall, I groan to myself.

It's Brie Newhart, Brinna Livingston, and Briar Schwartz. The Queen Bee Popular Girls of the tenth grade. Major requirements: be bony, be bitchy, and begin your name with "Bri." Brinna and Briar are Ladies in Waiting, actually. Brie is the head honcho. Never mind that she's named after a fattening French cheese, she's as skinny as an eight-year-old boy. She's also gorgeous, with wide blue eyes, sandy-brown curls, and Neutrogena-model skin. Supposedly her family is loaded, so she can have anything she wants. Even so, she wears the same high-heeled magenta boots every day. I overheard her say she got them in Paris over the summer. To top it off, Brie has a sweet voice and a toothpaste-model smile. Teachers go gaga over her.

Brie and her friends are in a completely different stratosphere than I am, so it's not like I ever talk to them. But sometimes I watch Brie across a classroom and wonder how one single person can be endowed with so many gifts. I inch my legs up, so I'm sitting cross-legged on the toilet seat, make sure my phone is on silent, and breathe as quietly as humanly possible.

I can see them through the crack. They're clustered around the wide mirror, unclasping their little black bags and producing various lip and eye products. I half listen to them discussing makeup, shopping, body, hair, body, shopping, makeup.

Brinna brags about how little she's eaten today, something about one peeled cucumber and a bag of baby carrots.

Briar boasts about spending two hours at the gym last night.

Brie, of course, tops them both.

"I was at Brandy yesterday, and I didn't even fit into their denim skirts." She pauses before adding, *"Trop grande."* I think Brie is saying "too big" in French.

"Oh my God!" squeals Brinna.

"I'm so jealous!" says Briar.

Then they start talking about guys. Brinna and Briar go back and forth about which seniors are hot. Brie *cluck-clucks* at their choices, saying that she finds any guy under eighteen completely *booo-ring.*

"Speaking of older men," Brie says, "guess who I ran into on the subway last weekend?"

"Who?" Brinna and Briar ask.

"Remember Byron Shreves? He was a senior when we were in eighth grade."

I can't believe this! I hold my breath and wait to hear what the others say.

"Oh my God!" squeals Brinna.

"He was *so* sexy!" says Briar.

"Well, you should see him now," says Brie. *"Ooh la la!*

He's a sophomore at Columbia and totally filled out. We flirted for four stops on the local train."

As Briar and Brinna *ooh* and *aah* and *Oh my God,* I begin to relax. But then I hear something that makes my stomach lurch.

"Doesn't his sister go to Brewster?" Brinna asks.

"Yeah," says Briar. "Virginia."

"Virginia *who?*" asks Brie.

Ouch. I know Brie and I reside in different universes, but still. We've been going to Brewster since sixth grade. And we're in three classes together, for God's sake.

"Virginia Shreves," says Briar, cracking up. "That chubby girl."

"No way!" Brie shrieks. "I never knew they were related."

"Of course they are," says Briar. "It's not like Shreves is a common name."

I bite down on the flesh inside my cheeks. *That chubby girl.*

After a moment Brie says, "All I can say is, if I were that fat, I'd kill myself."

"Totally," murmur Briar and Brinna in unison.

When the bell rings a few minutes later, the Bri-girls—who'd long since changed the subject—file out of the bathroom. I remain locked in my stall, gnawing at my cheeks. My spit tastes salty from the swirls of blood. I can feel loose flaps of skin with my tongue.

I can't get those words out of my head.

Brie and Brinna and Briar would rather be dead than be me.

5

I'm still feeling crappy on the bus ride home from school. I can't stop thinking about what Brie said. I've been teased a lot in my life, especially in junior high, when kids oinked at me in the halls or asked if I was pregnant when I was wearing a loose dress. But there's something particularly dreadful about *overhearing* people trash you.

As I trudge through the lobby, the doorman hands me a package wrapped in brown paper and covered with stickers. I glance at the return address. *Shannon Iris Malloy-Newman.* I love presents, especially ones from my best friend, so it lifts my spirits a little.

When I arrive in our apartment, I go right to the freezer and pull out a Popsicle. The ice soothes the insides of my cheeks, which are raw and sore. Mom's always insisting we only have healthy foods in the kitchen, but Dad has a sweet tooth, so he manages to smuggle home the good stuff.

As soon as I'm in my bedroom, I tear open Shannon's package. Underneath the brown-bag exterior is a smaller parcel wrapped in tissue paper. I rip off the paper and crack up. Shannon has sent me a green sweatshirt that says Walla Walla is for Lovers on the front. It's fuzzy on the inside and extra-extra-large, just the way I like it.

I'm slipping the sweatshirt over my head when the door opens and Byron steps into my room. I've told him a million times to knock first, but he never seems to remember.

I'm not surprised to see Byron. His dorm is only forty blocks from our apartment, so he often drops by to do laundry or loot the cupboards. But today he's wearing a starched white shirt and tuxedo pants. He's still barefoot, though. I notice patches of hair sprouting up from his big toes.

"Hey, Gin," Byron says. "Would you help me with these cuff links?"

"Sure."

As I fasten on the silver cuff links, I can't stop thinking about how he flirted with Brie Newhart on the subway a few days ago. I'm tempted to tell him what a bitch she is and that the next time he sees her he should shove her in front of an oncoming train. But I can't. Because then I'd have to tell him what she said, and I can't tell anyone that. Not ever.

"Why are you all dressed up?" I ask.

"Mom invited me to some fancy dinner. Lots of big-time psychologists will be there. Should be interesting."

Dad hates wearing tuxedos, so Mom is always bringing Byron to black-tie events. She used to do the same with Anaïs. I keep hoping Mom will invite me one of these days, but she hasn't so far.

As soon as I've finished with his cuff links, Byron runs his fingers through his wet hair. "Does your big brother clean up nicely or what?"

"You look great," I say. I quickly glance at his chest, to see if it's true what Brie said. He looks a little bigger, more filled out. He spent all summer lifting weights, so I guess it's starting to pay off.

"After shorts and T-shirts on campus every day," Byron says, "it feels so civilized to dress up."

"Speaking of sweatshirts, what do you think? Shannon just mailed it to me."

Byron studies my sweatshirt. "I don't get it."

"What's there to get?"

"It's a little silly. I mean, *Paris* is for lovers, not Walla Walla."

I roll my eyes. "That's the irony, stupid."

"Couldn't she have gotten a smaller size?" Byron asks.

"What do you mean?"

"That one's just so . . ." Byron searches for the right word. "Extra-large."

Extra-large. I can feel the tears coming on. *Virginia who? That chubby girl.* I choke out a quick laugh and tell Byron I have homework to do.

Once he's gone, I yank off the sweatshirt and kick it under

my bed, so it's mingling with the dust balls and candy wrappers that the vacuum cleaner never seems to reach. Then I grab my phone and text Shannon.

VIRGINIA: I got your sweatshirt. I'd vowed to wear it every single day until you return home, but then Byron told me it looks extra-large. Which means, of course, that he's talking about ME and the fact that I LOOK extra-large in it. Which is probably true. No, I bet I look FAT. Because I am. I'm fat and repulsive and should live among the blind for the remainder of my days.

VIRGINIA: Hang on. You're probably still at school. Time change and all. I'm sorry to sound so down.

VIRGINIA: I love the sweatshirt.

VIRGINIA: It's just me that I hate.

ⓖ ⓖ ⓖ ⓖ

"Don't you look handsome!" I hear Mom exclaim.

"I can't get my bow tie straight," says Byron. "Can you help me with it?"

"Sure, honey. Just let me set down my . . ."

As their voices fade, I stretch out across my comforter. I'm on my bed reading *People* on my phone and trying to clear my mind. Mom thinks celebrity gossip is a waste of time, but hearing about famous people divorcing and having break-downs and going to rehab always helps me forget my own problems.

There's a knock on my door.

I shove my phone under my pillow and stick my nose in *The Scarlet Letter*. That's what we're reading for language arts right now. We're doing a unit this fall called "Ostracism and Oppression." I actually like *The Scarlet Letter*. It's about a woman in colonial New England who committed adultery, so the Puritanical townspeople force her to wear an embroidered red "A" on her chest as a punishment for her sin.

"Yeah?" I ask.

Mom peeks inside.

"You're home early," I say.

"I rescheduled some patients so I could get ready for tonight." Mom twirls around the center of my room. "What do you think?"

"About what?"

"My hair. I just got the color touched up."

Mom's hair is naturally dirty blond, like mine, but she always has her colorist add highlights and lowlights.

I shrug. "It looks nice."

"Well, it's a professional expense."

That's how Mom justifies treating herself to facials, expensive shoes, silk scarves. She gives the receipts to her accountant, who writes them off as professional expenses. Dad frequently tells her that we're doing fine and Mom doesn't have to justify her luxury items. But Mom grew up on the verge of poverty, so it's difficult for her to spend money without major guilt.

Mom is so together that it's hard to imagine she used to be Phyllis Nutford, Fat Girl from Ozark, Arkansas. Her classmates used to call her Phyllis *Nutcase*. I only know this because I once discovered her yearbooks stashed in our storage space in the basement. I also learned that her high school's mascot was the hillbilly. No joke. Barefoot, overalls, a corncob pipe, the whole bit. Mom would murder me if she knew I looked through her yearbooks. She wants to put as much distance as possible between her Ozark past and her Manhattan present. She barely even stays in touch with the Nutty Nutfords. I've only met that side of the family once, when I was nine and they were in town for a dog competition. I have to say, they were definitely up there with cashews and pistachios.

"Mom?"

"Yes?"

"Why can't I ever go to these events with you?"

Mom clicks her manicured fingers up and down my dresser. "You will."

I sit up. "Really?"

"Sure."

"Do you have any idea when?"

"I can't give you an exact date, Virginia," Mom says. Then she pauses and adds, "I just wanted to tell you that I made an appointment for you with a new doctor. It's next Monday afternoon. I'll meet you here and we can take a cab up there together."

"Why do I need a new doctor?" I ask. "What's wrong with Dr. Nakamura?"

Dr. Nakamura is my pediatrician. I've been going to her since I was three.

"This guy specializes in adolescent medicine," Mom says. "I heard about him through colleagues. He's all the way up in Washington Heights, but I think it'll be worth it for you to see him."

"Why?" I ask. "I feel fine."

Mom gets an uncomfortable look on her face. I know what's coming next. It's about my weight. Mom has a hard time talking about my body. Her therapist side wants to reassure me that I'm fine the way I am, accept myself, all that self-esteem stuff. But her mom side wants me to be thin and perfect, like the rest of the Shreveses. The end result is that she can barely say the word "fat" around me. She uses euphemisms such as "heavy" and "like I used to be."

After a moment Mom says, "I want to discuss your nutrition with the new doctor."

"My nutrition?" I ask. "Why can't I see Nan again?"

Nan Grossman is a friend of Mom's from the gym. I privately call her Nan the Neurotic Nutritionist because she's always freaking out about additives and preservatives and caloric content.

Mom sighs impatiently. "Look, I've got to start getting ready for tonight. Just remember . . . Monday at four thirty."

"Fine," I say. I lean against my pillow and pick up *The Scarlet Letter.*

I know Mom's intentions are good, like she wants to help me feel better and look better and be a better person. But I can't help wishing she'd accept me the way I am. And I can't help wondering whether if I were thin, I'd get invited to these fancy dinners as well.

As soon as Mom is gone, I grab my phone out from under my pillow and immerse myself in a scintillating story about botched Botox.

ⓖ ⓖ ⓖ ⓖ

Mom said that Dad would be home around seven, but I don't get a call until after eight.

"I'm picking up Chinese food," he says. "What would you like?"

"Nothing."

"Aren't you hungry?"

"Not really," I say. I don't mention that I've already eaten a heaping bowl of pasta, the leftover Vietnamese food from last night, and a container of cherry yogurt.

"Do you want an egg roll?"

"No thanks."

"Okay. I'll be home in ten minutes. Has the game started?"

"Just singing the national anthem."

When Dad comes through the door, he's toting two plastic bags. I'm stretched on the couch, wrapped in a blanket and watching the ball game.

"Score?" he shouts as he heads into the kitchen.

"One to nothing, Yankees."

"Inning?"

"Top of the second."

When Dad joins me a few minutes later, he's carrying a glass of wine and a plate overflowing with shrimp, asparagus, and rice. He sits on the ottoman and spreads a checkered dishtowel across his lap.

"They're going to beat Boston, Ginny," Dad says as he sips his wine. "I can feel it in my bones."

"Me too."

Dad and I both love the Yankees, though for different reasons. He wants to see them make it to the World Series. I want to bear their children. Whenever Dad is home, we watch the games together.

During a commercial Dad carries his dishes into the kitchen and returns with a plate heaped with pastries.

"I stopped by the bakery," Dad says, handing me a napkin. "Thought I'd pick up some treats."

I prop myself onto my elbows and eye a plump slice of apple strudel.

Dad drops two cookies onto his napkin. "Let's consider it a precelebration."

I sink my teeth into the strudel.

We've polished off all the pastries when a beer commercial comes on. A woman in microscopic shorts and a bikini top parades around the baseball diamond.

Dad whistles. "Now *there's* an attractive woman."

Typical Dad. He's constantly praising thin women's bodies. It used to drive Anaïs crazy. Whenever Dad complimented her figure, she would yell at him and spout feminist theory about how men shouldn't judge women by their body type. Even though I've heard the skinny-women-are-more-attractive spiel a million times in my life, it strikes a sore nerve tonight.

I feel my stomach tightening up.

Nine hours ago, Brie Newhart said that if she were as fat as me, she'd kill herself.

Five hours ago, Byron called me extra-large.

Four hours ago, Mom announced that I have to see a special doctor about my "nutrition."

And here I am, wolfing down Popsicles and pasta and pastries like they're going out of style.

ⓖ ⓖ ⓖ ⓖ

SHANNON: Sorry it took me so long to get back to you. What a dumb thing for Byron to say! Why can't he be nice to you for a change?

VIRGINIA: Byron was just being honest. How's Walla Walla?

SHANNON: Not much to report. Liam and Nina are currently having a love affair with onions. It's all they talk about. And cook. French onion soup. Sausage and onions. They even baked an onion pie the other day. No wonder I'm not making any friends.

VIRGINIA: It sucks here, too. At least we can be comforted by the fact that we are in sucky solidarity.

SHANNON: I'm counting the days until I return to NYC.

VIRGINIA: Me too. 298.

VIRGINIA: Better go. I have to study for Friday's French quiz. Did you know that "fat" in French is "gros"? If I didn't hate French enough already, I hate it even more now.

*C*arry me back to old Virginny," Mr. Moony sings as I approach his desk.

I hear a few kids in the study hall chuckling. I hug my notebooks to my chest and pray that my cheeks aren't too flushed or my butt doesn't look too big.

"*There's where the cotton and the corn and taters grow,*" Mr. Moony warbles, tapping his worn leather shoe as he sings the old hymn about the state of Virginia.

Clive Moony is my geometry teacher and the oldest living person. He probably taught math back when the abacus was the latest technology. He's so ancient that he's senile. He can never remember any mathematical formulas. But he's managed to retain a database of songs in his head, songs that have our first names in them, songs that he delights in singing to mortified students.

I generally try to avoid Mr. Moony. I never raise my hand in his class for fear of being serenaded. He's also my study hall teacher, so I rarely ask for a pass to the bathroom or the water fountain. But I've been languishing in study hall for the past twenty minutes. I've finished my homework and chewed off nine fingernails. If I have to listen to the buzz of the fluorescent lights for one more second, I'm going to gnaw off my left arm.

I finally reach Mr. Moony's desk. I hurriedly explain how I *must* go to the computer cluster to finish up a Global Studies assignment. Instead of simply filling out a hall pass, Mr. Moony responds with another song.

"Almost heaven, West Virginiaaah . . ."

He pauses to suck in a raspy breath, so I quickly interject. "Could you *please* give me a pass to the computer cluster?"

Mr. Moony closes his eyes, sways his liver-splotched head from side to side, and continues crooning "Country Roads."

"TODAY!" I shout, surprising even myself.

Mr. Moony flaps open his droopy eyelids. "What did you want?"

"A pass." I gnaw off my final fingernail.

"Where?"

"To the computer cluster."

"Oh, sure," says Mr. Moony. "Why didn't you say so in the first place?"

⊚ ⊚ ⊚ ⊚

The computer cluster is one of Brewster's favorite bragging points. It's a well-lit room on the ground floor. The school's promotional literature drones on about "state-of-the-art equipment that will situate every student on the cutting edge of contemporary technology." Translation: twenty computers, twenty ergonomic chairs, and a lot of game-playing during free periods.

The room is more populated than usual. I hand my pass to Krishna. He's the NYU student who works part-time overseeing the computer cluster. He's a nice guy if you can look beyond his pock-marked skin and thrasher band T-shirts.

"Your favorite computer is still available," says Krishna, pointing to a white desktop in the back.

I glance at a group of guys clustered around a new computer. "What's going on?"

"They're fooling around with a graphic design program," says Krishna.

I study the jumble of baseball caps and T-shirts and scuffed sneakers. I recognize several of the kids, fellow sophomores. And then, in the center of the action, there's Froggy Welsh the Fourth. He's leaning toward the monitor, one hand on the keyboard, the other gripping the mouse.

Oh God. Now Froggy's *totally* going to think I'm stalking him.

Krishna continues. "It's mostly the guy with the blond hair. What's his name? Frog?"

"Froggy," I say in a hushed voice.

"Yeah, Froggy. Supposedly, he's a huge graphic design whiz."

"Really?"

"They say he'll be a millionaire before he's twenty."

I peek over at Froggy. I wonder what he could ever see in me. He has his group of friends. He has his trombone. And now he's this budding design genius. The last thing I want to do is park my big butt at a neighboring computer, which would present two miserable, pathetic options:

Miserable, Pathetic Option #1: *Froggy would feel sorry for me and give me a pity wave.*

Miserable, Pathetic Option #2: *Froggy would ignore me, making me feel like a loser with a capital "L."*

I know about the Fat Girl Code of Conduct, but this whole ride-moped-in-private arrangement makes me feel awful sometimes. In movies people fool around without giving it a second thought, so I always thought it would be easy. But with Froggy, I'm getting a little attached. I mean, I can still feel his lips on my lips, his fingers stroking my cheeks. So how can it be that four days later we barely say hello to each other? And, come Monday, we'll most likely be rolling on my rug again?

I need to get out of here. Normally I'd hide out in the second-floor bathroom, but I've been avoiding it ever since the Bri-girls episode. Then I remember Ms. Crowley's offer to help grade freshman vocabulary tests.

"Krishna?"

"Yeah?"

"Can you give me a pass to Ms. Crowley's office?"

I take the back staircase. Less chance of running into anyone as I huff to the second floor.

This is one of the many things I hate about Brewster. The thousands of stairs we must mount on a daily basis. There's actually a creaky elevator, but it's only used for carting desks and chairs and Mr. Moony. Students are expected to ascend multiple flights on an hourly basis without so much as leaking a drop of sweat. Because the Model Brewster Student is a lean, mean, stair-climbing machine.

That's another thing I hate about Brewster. The Model Brewster Student. They're always talking about the MBS at assemblies. They even give out MBS awards every fall. The MBS is "worldly and active and humanitarian," so they say. They also like to ramble on about how the MBS is "generous and kind, embodying the qualities of our esteemed founder, Theodore Brewster." The truth is, if you want to be an MBS, you have to dress a certain way (expensive/urban/chic) and look a certain way (skinny/flawless skin). Recently Brewster has been going for diversity with their MBS choices so they give a lot of awards to students who are black/Asian/Latino/Indian/biracial, but still skinny and without a zit in sight.

It's all such a crock. First of all, Brie Newhart won an MBS award last year, and she's definitely not "generous and kind," at least not to the regular or dorky kids. But what's really ironic is that Theo Brewster was a tough-talking rumrunner during the Prohibition era of the 1920s. That's how he made his fortune. He smuggled rum from sugar cane plantations in the Caribbean to booze-thirsty ports in the Northeast.

That's why every spring, on Brewster Day, they serve us piña coladas and strawberry daiquiris, just without the alcohol. The seniors sneak in miniature bottles of rum, spike their drinks, and spend the rest of Brewster Day singing pirate songs.

At least that's what Byron told me happened when he went to school here.

⟨ ⟨ ⟨ ⟨

Ms. Crowley is standing behind her desk. Her wavy hair is secured into a bun with two yellow pencils. The wisps around her face are held back by paper clips.

"Hello there," she says, smiling.

My heart is still thumping from taking the stairs two at a time. "I was just wondering if you needed help grading tests, like you said the other day."

Ms. Crowley glances at her watch. "I'm running out to a meeting, so I don't have time to get you started." She studies my face for a second before adding, "You can hang out here for the rest of the period, if you'd like."

I step into her office. "Are you sure?"

Ms. Crowley maneuvers around me. "Make yourself comfortable. Read whatever you want."

"Thanks, Ms. Crowley." I set my notebooks on her desk.

"My pleasure." She hoists a tote bag onto her shoulder. "Let's do the tests another time."

As soon as she's gone, I sink into her chair and survey the small room. Ms. Crowley's office is cluttered with books and coffee mugs and photographs of her husband and their two

Great Danes. The only other chair is piled high with literary journals. I think a few of them have published Ms. Crowley's poems. An entire section of her bookshelf is dedicated to poetry compilations by Maya Angelou, E. E. Cummings, Allen Ginsberg, Pablo Neruda.

On a top shelf, I spot *A Room of One's Own* by Virginia Woolf. I've tried reading several books by Virginia Woolf, since Mom named me after her and everything. But I always get lost after a few pages. Her writing is so dense and enigmatic. Exactly what you'd expect from someone who committed suicide by filling her pockets with stones and walking into a river.

I open my notebook to a new page and scribble *Froggy + Virginia*. It's strange to see it on paper. It makes me wish I could write it on my locker or with a highlighter on my hand, like other girls do with their crushes. I tear out the page, rip it to shreds, and sprinkle it into the trash can.

That's when I notice that Ms. Crowley's office overlooks the small courtyard behind the school. I've never actually set foot in there, since that's where the popular kids sneak out to smoke cigarettes.

There are mostly juniors and seniors in the courtyard. And then I see Brie Newhart weaving through the crowd, sucking at a cigarette and flaunting her Parisian boots.

I turn away from the window, pull out my phone, and text Shannon. I haven't heard from her in a few days. I hope she's not too miserable out there in Walla Walla.

I mention that there are only 296 days until our lives begin again.

I don't mention that it's lucky I'm not near a pile of stones and the Hudson River.

Because I can't guarantee that, if given the opportunity, I wouldn't take Brie's advice and go the way of my namesake.

On Saturday I sleep in until 11 a.m. Mom and Dad are long gone by the time I wake up. They usually leave for Connecticut at the crack of dawn, so they can beat traffic and hit the golfing green early. Most weekends they don't return until Sunday evening. They call and check in a few times, but basically I have two solid days to myself.

When Anaïs was in college and Byron was fifteen or sixteen, weekends were great. As soon as Mom and Dad took off, my brother and I would take over the apartment. We'd keep the TV going for thirty-six hours. We didn't pick up our wet towels. We'd make kooky food creations. We wouldn't do a single dish until 5 p.m. on Sunday.

But then Byron got into girls and going out, so I began spending weekends at Shannon's apartment down in Greenwich

Village. But with Shannon in Walla Walla, weekends have been a drag recently.

Dad's always saying, "Give Ginny a phone, some books, and a Netflix account and she's set for life."

I guess that's true. But even I get a little lonely sometimes.

I pour myself a bowl of Rice Krispies, plop onto the couch, and browse through Netflix. Nothing is jumping out at me, not even *Beauty and the Beast*, which I watched twice last weekend.

I know some families are all *rah-rah* about having nightly sit-down dinners. Believe me, it would be nice to have a Shreves family meal every once in a while, but I've basically come to accept that that's not what my family is about. Besides, Byron and I used to have a blast creating our own dishes. They were much better than stir-fry or spaghetti or whatever normal families eat every night.

Sometimes we'd make run-of-the-mill things like Rice Krispie treats, except we'd eat them for dinner, which rendered them exotic. One time, when I was sick, Byron made me a waffle sundae. He toasted a frozen waffle and topped it with vanilla ice cream and chocolate syrup. Making food together became our special ritual. On a Saturday evening or a Sunday afternoon, as we were plugging away in the kitchen, I'd get a warm feeling inside, wishing we could freeze the moment forever. Other times, I would have the craziest notions, like hoping Mom and Dad would move full-time to Connecticut and Byron and I could live together, just the two of us.

But everything changed once my brother got popular. "In demand" is what Mom used to call it. He had parties to go to on weekend nights. And during the day he hung out with his friends, playing soccer or football in Riverside Park. That's around the time I started blimping out, so I think Byron got embarrassed to be seen with me in public. He never said as much, but sometimes it felt like he was walking a few strides ahead of me on the sidewalk.

I choke up as that thought crosses my mind.

I miss spending time with the old Byron. Maybe he misses it, too. Maybe he wants our closeness back, but he's too busy with school and life to do anything about it.

As I set my empty cereal bowl on the coffee table, I come up with a great idea. I race into the kitchen and tear through the cupboards to see what ingredients we have and what I need to go out and buy.

🌀 🌀 🌀 🌀

Two hours later I'm riding the subway up to Columbia, toting a warm batch of Rice Krispie treats topped with a layer of melted chocolate morsels. I'm hoping the goodies will jump-start Byron's memory of the old days. If nothing else, it'll soften the shock of my showing up, unannounced, at his dorm on a Saturday afternoon.

I've never dropped in on Byron at college before. I visited his old room a few times last year with Mom and Dad. And then, in late August, we helped him move into his new suite. That was after my parents' Biannual Byron Brunch. At the beginning of

48

every new semester, they put out a bagel and fruit spread and invite the whole world—from downstairs neighbors to Connecticut friends to Byron's preschool teacher. Everyone toasts Byron and, wired on coffee, the guests' speeches commending him last longer than the president's State of the Union address.

Byron's dorm is called Wallach. I thought I remembered where it was, but as I step through Columbia's entranceway, all the buildings look identical—stately, stone, draped in ivy. I stop a professor type on the path and ask him about Wallach. He gestures to a dorm off in the distance.

It's a balmy fall afternoon, so the grassy expanses in front of the majestic library are overflowing with students. Everyone is tossing Frisbees, stretched out on blankets, laughing, eating chips, writing in notebooks. I scan the crowd for Byron. I hadn't considered the fact that he might not be in his room. If he's not there, I guess I could hang out in his hallway for a while. Either that or leave the treats at his door with a note to call me.

Once I get to Wallach, I spot a security guard at the front desk. She's scanning everyone's student ID cards. I linger on the front steps until a gaggle of students filters into the dorm. As they hand their IDs to the guard, I slip past them and dash up the narrow staircase.

I mount three flights of stairs, catch my breath, and study doors until I find Byron's suite. That's just a fancy way of saying he's in a single room with several other singles, a shared bathroom, and a common room.

I cross the empty common room and knock on Byron's door.

"Door's open," he says.

I try the knob. It's locked, so I knock again.

"Door's open."

"It's not," I say. "I just tried it."

Silence.

"Virginia?" Byron asks.

"Yeah?"

Byron swings open the door. His hair is kind of messy, and he's wearing shorts and a T-shirt that says Columbia Rugby.

"Hey," I say.

He looks like he doesn't know what to make of all this. "What are you doing here?"

I'm quiet for a second. This isn't how I imagined it. Not that I pictured us throwing our arms around each other, but I thought maybe "what a nice surprise" might be in order.

"I made you these." I open the Tupperware container and reveal the contents. "Thought you'd like them."

"Well," he says, rubbing his cheeks. "Well, well."

"Can I come in?"

Byron opens his door wider, and I step into his room. The first thing I notice is that he's replaced the bed with a futon mattress directly on the gray industrial carpet. On the windowsill, there are three candles with frozen waterfalls of wax.

I kick off my shoes and sit on the futon. Byron settles into his chair. I offer him a Rice Krispie treat, but he shakes his head.

"What are you up to today?" I ask.

"Not much," Byron says. "Getting reading done for a paper."

"Oh." I nibble some chocolate off a treat.

"How's Brewster?" Byron asks after a moment.

"Fine," I say. "Same as usual."

"Is Old Moony still there?"

"Yep," I say. "Still singing his crazy songs."

"He used to sing some to me," says Byron, "but they were always about *Brian*, and I didn't have the heart to correct him."

We both laugh.

I polish off the rest of my treat.

There's a knock on the door.

"Come on in," Byron calls out.

The door opens to reveal a smallish guy with closely shorn hair and a pointy nose. He smiles as he eyes me on Byron's bed. Actually, not a smile. More of a male-bonding grin. If there could be a facial expression that conveyed a thumbs-up sign, this would be it.

"Never a surprise to see a lovely young woman hanging out in Lord Byron's room," he says. "Who have we got here?"

As much as I think incest is the grossest thing in the world, I'm flattered that someone would think Byron and I are enough in the same league to be "hanging out." Also, do I need my hearing checked or did this guy just call me "a lovely young woman"?

I'm totally basking in the praise, but Byron doesn't seem thrilled about the mix-up. "It's my little sister," he says, shooting the guy a scolding look. Then he nods in my direction. "This is Shawn. He lives in our suite."

"Hi, Little Sister," Shawn says. "Do you have a name?"

"Virginia." I pull one of Byron's pillows onto my lap. I always feel safer that way, like my body is more concealed.

"Virginia." Shawn lifts up a stapler and sets it down again. His jerky movements remind me of a hamster. As he gives me the once-over, I hug the pillow tighter around my middle. "Are you *really* Byron's sister?"

"Yeah," I say.

Shawn glances from my brother to me and back again. "You're serious, man?" he asks Byron. "You two look nothing alike."

There's a long silence in which I can't help but wonder: Is it our hair color? I have a Yankee cap on. Our height? I'm sitting on the bed. Our weight? *Aha!*

Byron types something on his phone. "So, what's up?" he asks Shawn.

"Not much." Shawn picks some wax off one of the candles. "Just letting you know we're tapping the pre-party keg in the common room around ten."

"Sounds great," Byron says.

Shawn rolls the wax between his finger and thumb. "You're coming to Bros and Hos, aren't you?"

"Yep," says Byron.

"Are you still bringing Annie Mills?"

"Yep."

"Lord Byron strikes again," sings Shawn. "She's cute,

man." Shawn rubs his knuckles up and down his chest. "For a math major."

As soon as Shawn is gone, I ask, "What's Bros and Hos?"

Byron checks his phone. "That's a party that a bunch of us are going to tonight."

"Why's it called Bros and Hos? Isn't that sort of . . ."

Byron takes a deep breath. "It's just a joke. It doesn't actually mean anything. The theme is 'the more you bare, the less the fare.' The cover charge is ten bucks, but there's a sliding scale depending on how much skin you reveal."

"Who's Annie Mills?"

"Just a girl."

I scratch at a pimple on my arm. "Do you know what she's going to wear?"

Byron laughs. "She says she's wearing a black leather bustier and fishnets, but I'll believe it when I see it."

"What about you?"

"I don't know. Probably just boxers."

I examine my arm. A tiny dot of blood has cropped up, so I rub it off with my thumb.

We chat for a few more minutes. I eat a Rice Krispie treat and then another and then another, until I realize there are only five left in the Tupperware. Byron hasn't even had one, which strikes me as a little strange. This is the boy who used to consume an entire panful during the course of a half-hour show.

After a while Byron stretches his arms over his head and yawns loudly. "I'd better get started on this paper," he says. "Fifteen pages. Due Wednesday."

"I hope you have fun tonight," I say.

I give Byron a meaningful stare. I guess on some small level, I'm hoping he'll invite me to hang out for the rest of the afternoon, maybe go with him and that girl to the Bros and Hos thing. I've heard of kids who visit their older siblings at college and go to parties and get totally wasted.

But Byron doesn't nibble. Not even close.

"Do you know your way out of here?" he asks.

"I think so," I say, slipping my feet into my shoes.

Byron hands me the Tupperware. "Thanks for the treats."

"You're welcome. I thought maybe it would . . ." I trail off.

"What?"

"Nothing."

Byron opens the door. "Look, Gin, the next time you want to come up here, can you text first?"

I stare at my feet. "But I wanted to surprise you with the . . ." I hold up the container.

"Even so," Byron says.

As I head across campus, I feel a lump lodging in my throat. What I wanted to say a few minutes ago was *I thought maybe it would remind you how much you love me, how close we used to be.*

By the time I reach the subway station, tears are trickling down my cheeks. I keep wiping them away, but every time I do, more slide out to replace them.

ⓖ ⓖ ⓖ ⓖ

When I arrive home, I have a headache. It feels like there's a thick band stretched around my forehead. I go into the kitchen and splash my face with water. Mom always leaves a few twenties on the counter in case I need anything. I don't feel like going out for food, so I hop onto Seamless and order mu shu pork and fried veggie dumplings.

I head into my room and open my computer.

THE MORE I BARE, THE MORE I SCARE
by Virginia Shreves

1. The Bri-girls would rather commit suicide than look like me.
2. No one ever believes Byron and I are related because he's cool and attractive and I'm, well, not.
3. If they filmed another *Beauty in the Beast,* I'd get cast in a leading role. And not as Beauty.
4. If I eat a slice of pizza on the sidewalk, strangers give me nasty looks, like I'm supposed to live on lettuce until I've whittled down to the size of a chopstick.
5. Relatives don't send me clothes because they're scared to guess my size, so I have more gift boxes of nail polish than a cosmetics factory.
6. Whenever I picture myself squeezed into a black leather bustier and fishnets, I get violently ill.
7. If I were thin, maybe Byron would have invited me to Bros and Hos—or at least been happier to see me at his dorm.

By the time I've finished writing, my headache has subsided. I reach for my phone. I haven't heard from Shannon since Wednesday, so I'm starting to worry that the onion fumes are depressing her.

VIRGINIA: What's up? You've been MIA. Are you okay?

SHANNON: Sorry! Yes! I'm running out the door, but I have to tell you that I think I'm making real, live friends in Walla Walla! Stay tuned . . .

VIRGINIA: ?????

VIRGINIA: Who, what, when, where, and why?

VIRGINIA: YOU CAN'T LEAVE ME HANGING LIKE THIS.

No word back. I collapse on my bed. My forehead is tightening again. I must be an evil person, but I'm not thrilled that Shannon is making new friends. What if she forgets about me? Also, our bicoastal boo-hoo fest has offered me a certain degree of comfort, like I'm not alone in my misery.

I roll over and stare out my window. I can see a narrow stretch of Riverside Park and the Hudson River. I've watched the most amazing sunsets from my bed, especially during late fall when the air is cool and clear.

The intercom rings. It must be the Chinese food. As I'm heading to the front door, it crosses my mind that if I don't go out tomorrow, the delivery guy is going to be the only human I'll see for the next twenty-four hours.

Froggy Welsh the Fourth has made it up my shirt!

Every star and planet must be perfectly aligned today. As Froggy and I rode the crosstown bus, we chatted more than usual. He described a citywide graphic design competition he's just entered. We also discovered that we've both memorized the theme song to nearly every sitcom from the past three decades.

As we walked toward my building, we knocked our hips against each other and sang a few verses from *Friends*.

The only glitch arose when we were in the elevator. As we got on in the lobby, we were joined by Mrs. Myers. She's an elderly woman who lives on the ninth floor. Whenever she goes to Miami to visit her grandnephew, I feed her Siamese cats.

As soon as we stepped into the elevator, I noticed Mrs. Myers eyeing Froggy.

"Anaïs"—she tapped her metal cane on my sneaker—"why don't you introduce me to your boyfriend?"

I wasn't sure whether to be more taken aback that Mrs. Myers confused me with my gorgeous sister or that she called Froggy my boyfriend.

"I'm Virginia."

"I *know* who you are." Mrs. Myers prodded her cane toward Froggy. "But who is *he*?"

"He's . . . he's . . ." I desperately searched for a way to inform her that Froggy and I aren't boyfriend and girlfriend. "He's Froggy."

"*Froggy?*" Mrs. Myers looked puzzled.

The elevator arrived at the ninth floor. As she hobbled out, I heard her muttering, "What kind of name is *Froggy* for a handsome young boy?"

The door closed. I glanced fearfully at Froggy, but to my relief, he cracked up. I started laughing, too. By the time the elevator arrived at my apartment, we were both in hysterics.

We headed straight to my bedroom rather than stopping off for our usual snack. Froggy unlaced his sneakers and kicked them off. We flopped onto my bed and started making out. The kissing was intense from the start. Our lips were open. Our tongues took turns exploring the insides of each other's mouths. For a moment, I imagined myself as Emma Stone kissing Ryan Gosling in *La La Land. That's* how good it felt.

When we finally came up for air, I planted a row of soft kisses along Froggy's earlobe. He moaned from deep in the back of his throat. The next thing I knew, his hands were inside my shirt.

I'd carefully selected my bra this morning. It's tan-colored, hardly as sexy as my black one, but easy to undo, with a simple hook in the back. Froggy got it on the first try. He eased my bra onto my collarbone, leaving my breasts bare under my shirt.

And now, for the first time in my life, a nonmedical person is touching my chest. He's stroking my breasts, gently pulling at my nipples. It feels so good that I'm getting wet between my legs.

After a few minutes, Froggy rolls onto his back, so we're lying shoulder to shoulder. "Virginia?" he whispers.

"Yeah?"

"That felt good."

"I know."

"I've never done that before," Froggy says quietly.

"Me neither."

As Froggy caresses my hair, I snuggle into the crook of his neck. We're silent for a few minutes. I'm just thinking that this is the nicest moment in my entire life when I hear the front door unlock. Froggy's body tenses up. We pull away from each other.

"Virginia?" Mom calls out. "Virginia?"

Froggy and I go into panic mode. We fly off my bed. I yank my bra around my boobs and hook it into place. As Mom knocks on my door, I gesture toward my bed.

Froggy flattens himself to the floor and slides awkwardly under the frame.

"Virginia?" Mom asks, turning my knob.

I thank my lucky stars that I always lock the door when Froggy's over.

"I'm here, Mom," I say.

My heart is racing. I make sure none of Froggy's appendages are exposed as I cross the room, attempt a calming breath, and open my door.

"Are you okay?" Mom asks. "Your face is flushed."

"I'm fine. I just fell asleep." I glance covertly at Froggy's backpack and trombone case. "Why are you home early?"

"Don't you remember? We have your doctor's appointment at four thirty."

"What doctor's appointment?"

"I told you last week. That new doctor who specializes in adolescent medicine."

"I guess."

"Well, I'm glad you're home."

"Yeah," I say.

"I wanted to remind you that I'm planning to discuss your weight with the new doctor." Mom pauses and adds, "Just so it doesn't come out of the blue."

I'm sure Froggy heard that.

I'm going to drop dead.

How could Froggy not have heard that?

I'm going to get a shovel, dig a huge hole in Central Park, and crawl into it. I'll pay someone to cover me up with dirt and put a stone on my grave that says: *Virginia Shreves, 15, died from utter humiliation.*

Mom looks like she's waiting for a response. Did she ask me a question?

"I guess," I say, shrugging my shoulders.

"Let's leave in ten minutes. I'll be in my office if you need me."

As soon as Mom is gone, I close the door.

"Coast clear?" Froggy whispers.

"I think so." I touch my flushed cheeks. It's all I can do to remember to breathe.

Froggy slides out from under my bed. As he brushes the dust balls off his clothes and laces up his sneakers, I can't look him in the eye.

We don't say a word to each other as we tiptoe through the apartment. I nudge him into the foyer. He waves good-bye, but I quietly close the front door.

I will never, ever, ever be able to face Froggy again.

ⓖ ⓖ ⓖ ⓖ

I don't say anything for the entire cab ride up Broadway. The new doctor's office is past Columbia, way up in Washington Heights. That's almost eighty blocks from our apartment. Mom is on her phone the whole time, so she doesn't notice my silence.

As the cab pulls up to the corner nearest the hospital, Mom hangs up and turns to me. "Are you sure you're feeling okay?"

"Yeah."

"You still look flushed." Mom enters a tip on the touch screen of the cab and then inserts her credit card. "Maybe you should ask Dr. Love to take your temperature."

"Dr. Love?"

The driver gives Mom a receipt. She tucks it in her wallet and says, "Your new doctor."

I slide out of the cab. Someone named Dr. Love should sing lead vocals in a punk band. Or be a porn star. But my *doctor*? I picture a smarmy, fake-tanned doctor from a show about emergency rooms.

Fortunately, Dr. Love turns out to be nothing like I expected. He's young for a doctor, probably in his early thirties, with cappuccino-colored skin, dark eyelashes, and pencil-thin dreads poking out all over his head.

I'm sitting on the examining table when he walks in. Mom is out in the waiting room. I'm bemoaning the fact that the paper robe the nurse gave me is smaller than a cocktail napkin. I'm also wondering whether she groaned when she weighed me. It sounded like she did, but I never look at the scale, so I'm not sure whether it was bad news or *extremely* bad news.

Dr. Love sits on the revolving stool and extends his hand. "I'm Benjamin Love," he says. His voice is warm and soothing, like a bubble bath.

I shake his hand. "I'm Virginia."

We chat for a few minutes, and then Dr. Love pulls out his stethoscope and wheels toward me. He listens to my lungs and heart, feels my nodes, and presses my appendix. Throughout the examination, he keeps murmuring "very healthy" and "excellent." When he takes a blood sample, he talks to me the whole time, so the needle barely hurts.

Once the exam is over, Dr. Love swivels around on his stool, writes something in my chart, and turns to face me again.

"When your mom made this appointment," he says, "she mentioned that she wanted the three of us to discuss your weight."

I stare at my bare feet dangling over the side of the examination table.

Dr. Love frowns. "This isn't something I usually like to do. You are my patient. I want you to feel you can be candid with me, that whatever you tell me won't get back to your mom." Dr. Love searches my face. "I'm only going to invite her in here if you're comfortable with it."

I tug at the robe. Why doesn't it cover more of my body? I should write to the company that manufactures medical gowns and suggest they make them in a size other than extra-small.

"So?" Dr. Love asks.

I don't know what to say. I'm sure Mom is just trying to be helpful. But sometimes it feels like I'm beyond help, beyond hope.

"I guess it's okay," I say.

"You guess or you're sure?"

"I'm sure."

He stands up to leave. "I'll give you a few minutes to change back into your clothes."

"Thanks."

When they return, I'm sitting on the examination table, one knee over the other, my arms tight across my chest. Dr. Love settles onto his stool. Mom sits in the hard plastic chair.

Dr. Love rotates so he's facing Mom. "You wanted us all to talk, Dr. Shreves?"

Mom's mouth twitches. "I'm concerned about Virginia's weight."

Dr. Love raises his eyebrows.

Mom continues. "I was heavy as a child, but I slimmed down by the time I was fifteen or sixteen. I always assumed that's how it would be for Virginia, but it just doesn't seem to be happening."

I feel my cheeks flushing, and my underarms are moist with sweat.

"May I ask why you've decided to address this now?" Dr. Love asks.

Mom fiddles with the clasp on her purse. She's much better at listening to other people's problems than discussing her own. "It's so hard being overweight. I want to do everything I can to make life easier for Virginia."

Dr. Love is quiet for a moment. When he finally speaks, he addresses me directly. "Let me start by saying that I prefer to look at things in terms of *health* instead of *weight*." He glances over at Mom, who shifts in her chair. "Until I get your blood work back, I can't give a comprehensive report on your health. But from the initial examination, you're very healthy, on par with most teenagers."

Dr. Love pauses before adding, "I want to be frank with you, however. While you're not in the range we classify as obese, you're heavier than average. If you continue to gain weight into adulthood, you'll be at risk for heart disease, hypertension, even diabetes. So while there's no reason to panic, it would be beneficial to start thinking about the long term."

I glance at Mom. She points her chin toward Dr. Love, as if to say, *Listen up.*

"I'd like you to reevaluate your diet," he says. "Cut down on carbs and greasy foods, exercise at least three times a week. Do you get much exercise?"

"I'm always encouraging Virginia to come to the gym with me," says Mom. "Exercise is how I keep my weight down, but she says she finds it boring."

Dr. Love frowns. "With all due respect, Dr. Shreves, I prefer not to focus on weight or body size. It's about fitness and nutrition and feeling good. Once those things fall into place, Virginia will become her natural body type"—Dr. Love gives Mom a long look—"which is different for every person."

Mom mashes her lips together.

"So?" Dr. Love asks.

"I'm not a jock, if that's what you're asking."

"You don't have to be a jock to get exercise." Dr. Love sets down my chart. "I'd be happy to help you figure this out, as long as you're up for the challenge. Is this what you want?"

Is this what I want? I want to not be embarrassed around Froggy. I don't want Brie to trash me behind my back. I don't want to get any more of those looks from Mom, like she feels sorry for me or she's ashamed of me. I want to be more like Anaïs and Byron. I want my parents to consider me Shreves-worthy.

Mom and Dr. Love are waiting for my response. I raise and lower my shoulders. "I want to be healthier."

For the next several minutes, Dr. Love talks about nutrition and non-jock ways to get a decent workout. I sit there, listening and nodding. Every once in a while, I glance over at Mom. I think I detect a tinge of pride on her face.

ⓖ ⓖ ⓖ ⓖ

Mom drops me off on our corner and tells the cabdriver to continue to her office. As soon as I get upstairs, I won't allow myself to go into the kitchen, like I usually do. Instead, I read over my old texts. I haven't heard back from Shannon since Saturday, when I demanded the scoop on her friends. There's no word from Walla Walla, but there's a voicemail from Dad.

"Ginny," he says, "I've got two tickets to a Yankees playoff game later in October, assuming they make it that far, which you and I both know they will. Mom and I have a golf tournament in Connecticut that day, so I was thinking you and Byron might like to go."

A Yankees playoff game with my brother! I text Byron, telling him to call me as soon as possible.

A few hours later, I'm hunched over the dining room table, attempting to finish *The Scarlet Letter*. Dad walks into the room, munching a handful of cashews.

"Any word from Byron?"

I shake my head. "Not yet."

"I just got off the phone with Mom." Dad tosses back a few nuts. "Sounds like you had a productive appointment with that doctor."

"Yeah," I say, flipping to the next page in my book.

"It's a good thing." Dad picks a bit of cashew out of his teeth. "You've got a great face, Ginny. Think how much prettier you could be if you lost twenty or thirty pounds."

I feel like I've been punched in the stomach. I've always known that Dad was absent on the day they handed out tact. And I've always known that Dad is a fan of thin women. But he's never said it so bluntly—that I'm not that attractive the way I am.

I can't speak. I can't look up. If I do, I'll burst into tears.

If I lived in Nathaniel Hawthorne's time, I bet I'd have to wear a scarlet letter on my chest, just like Hester Prynne. Except in my case, it would be an "F" instead of an "A."

9

It's official. I'm on a diet.

In the four days since my appointment with Dr. Love, my entire life has changed. I can already fit two fingers into my normally snug waistband. Before long I'll be sticking an entire fist in there.

My goal is to lose as much as I can as quickly as possible. I'm not putting a number on it because I refuse to step on a scale unless I'm in a medical establishment. But all I know is that I want to get thin. And fast.

I've tried other diets before. Like in eighth grade when I decided to work out at Mom's gym. I stumbled along the treadmill every afternoon for a week. But after five days, I was bored to tears. I couldn't see the point in walking and walking and never getting anywhere. Or there was that time last year when

Mom set up an appointment for me with Nan the Neurotic Nutritionist. Nan presented me with a food regimen that consisted of protein powders and low-carb bars. It made me parched just thinking about it. As soon as I left her office, I stopped by Starbucks and downed a venti caramel Frappuccino just to get some moisture into my mouth.

But not this time. This time I'm taking it seriously.

All week long I didn't eat a real breakfast. I just grabbed a banana as I headed off to school. On Thursday I took a stalk of celery instead. *Big mistake.* I had to spend ten minutes in the bathroom at school extracting pale-green celery strings from my braces.

By lunchtime every day I was famished. Sometimes I even had a hunger headache. But rather than surrendering to my appetite, I'd close my eyes and play a Thin Virginia fantasy in my head. I'd visualize myself partying up at Columbia. *See how sexy I look in a bra and thongs and hip-hugger jeans! How much will you charge ME to get into Bros and Hos?* I had tamer variations as well. Sometimes I'd be laughing with Byron as we jumped for foul balls at a Yankees game. Other times I'd suck in my stomach as Mom proudly introduced me to her colleagues at black-tie events. I even imagined Dad complimenting my body, like he used to with Anaïs. Except I wouldn't get angry at him and launch into a feminist tirade the way my sister did.

These visions were enough to make me skip lunch on Tuesday, Wednesday, Thursday, and Friday. I steered clear of the cafeteria to avoid being beckoned by Tostitos or a tray of tater tots. Also, it eliminated the stress of finding tablemates, which

I couldn't handle on such a light head/empty stomach. Hiding out in the second-floor bathroom was out of the question, too. If I overheard another comment from the Bri-girls, I'd probably flush myself down a toilet.

My solution was to go to Ms. Crowley's office. She always welcomed me warmly. We'd chat for a few minutes, low-key stuff, like what I'm reading for "Ostracism and Oppression." Then she'd put me to work grading quizzes or suggesting pop songs that could get kids excited about reading *The Grapes of Wrath*. Ms. Crowley is cool that way, trying to reach students on their level rather than just shoving dead authors down their throats all the time.

When she didn't have any work for me, I reviewed my notes from various classes. It was hard to concentrate during class all week, with my abdomen cramping and my brain pulsing from hunger. Sometimes I'd have to put my head on my desk for a few seconds and close my eyes. No one seemed to notice any difference in my behavior, though Ms. Crowley *did* observe that I was drinking a lot of water.

Diet Tip #1: Whenever you're hungry, chug a bottle of water to fill your stomach.

I'm spending my days in a constant state of peeing or starvation. But I know this will all be worth it.

Besides, it's not like I have any alternative.

ⓖ ⓖ ⓖ ⓖ

Friday night. My parents and I have a rare sit-down dinner. Dad cooks himself a steak, and Mom and I have salads sprinkled with pomegranate seeds.

Diet Tip #2: Allow each bite to linger in your mouth for as long as humanly possible.

I slowly chew my plate of mixed greens and hungrily gaze at Dad's meat.

Dad catches my eye. "I have a proposition for you," he says.

"What?" I ask.

"How would you like me to take you on a shopping spree, to celebrate your new diet?"

Silence.

I glance at Mom. When Anaïs was in high school, Dad used to take her on sprees and they'd come home with great outfits. But my shopping always happens with Mom. She's good at picking out clothes with lots of strategic layers and camouflaging colors.

"Mike," Mom says, setting down her fork, "maybe we should hold off on that for a while."

"I thought it would be fun for Ginny," Dad says. "A reward."

Mom looks at me. I shrug, as if to say, *Don't ask me . . . I don't make the decisions around here.*

"It would be wonderful to take Virginia shopping once she's slimmed down," Mom says. "But if she buys things now, they'll be a few sizes too big before long. I think we should wait until she reaches some kind of weight goal. Besides, it can be an incentive for her to keep it up. Then it'll be a *real* reward."

"Do you have a weight goal?" Dad asks.

I shake my head.

Dad carves off a generous bite of steak. "Maybe you should make one."

"I don't do scales," I mumble, thinking how Dr. Love said he doesn't like to focus on weight.

Mom cuts in. "Why don't we call it a 'body goal' instead?"

Dad raises his wineglass. "Once you've reached your body goal, we'll hit the stores."

"Great," says Mom. "It's all set."

Mom and Dad look over at me. Did I even want to go on a shopping spree? Do I have a body goal? Sometimes my parents are so sure of what's best for me that I don't stop to think about what I really want.

I push aside my plate of lettuce.

ⓖ ⓖ ⓖ ⓖ

Saturday morning. I'm sitting on my bedroom floor, flipping through *Fitness*. Mom brought home a stack of magazines from her gym. All week long I've been sifting through *Fitness* and *Women's Health*, scouring for diet tips. Whenever I find a valuable one, I clip it out and add it to a pile on my dresser. Mom and Dad are in Connecticut, so I'm blasting music and humming along.

I turn the page and stare down at a picture of a waify young model. Her upper arms have the circumference of my pinky.

I tear out the page. Then I thumb through the rest of the magazine, ripping out the skinniest girls, the ones I'm most aiming to resemble.

These models will be my Food Police. They'll be my thinspiration. They'll help me reach my body goal.

I carry the magazine scraps to the kitchen and stick them to the refrigerator door with magnets.

For the rest of the day, whenever I reach into the fridge for a hunk of cheddar cheese or some salami, I'll catch sight of the Food Police.

Don't do it, they'll chant. *Not if you want to be thin like us.*

So I'll chug a gallon of water and find something more low-fat to do.

☽ ☽ ☽ ☽

Sunday morning. My parents return from Connecticut early because Dad has to leave for a business trip to Chicago this afternoon. I'm sitting on the couch, watching TV and chewing my fat-free nails. They say hi to me and then Mom goes into the kitchen to make herself a protein shake.

A moment later she appears in the living room again.

"Virginia, I'm so proud of you," she says.

I mute the volume. It's not every day I hear "Virginia" and "proud" in the same sentence.

"Why?"

"I just saw those pictures you stuck on the fridge."

Mom, meet the Food Police.

Mom continues. "You want to hear something funny?"

I nod.

"Back when I was"—Mom pauses—"a teenager, I put images of models on *my* family's fridge to keep me from eating too much."

"Really?"

Mom nods. "Like mother, like daughter."

As she heads back into the kitchen, I pump the volume on the TV again.

Since when did Mom become Ms. Observant Parent? A few weeks ago, I got an A-plus on a language arts paper about *One Hundred Years of Solitude* by Gabriel García Márquez. I even managed to include two mentions of "ostracism" and three of "oppression," so my teacher gobbled it up. I stuck it to the fridge with a few magnets, hoping Mom—a big Márquez fan—would say something, but she never seemed to notice.

So how is it that she's in the apartment seven minutes and already spots the Food Police?

Oh well. I should probably look on the bright side of things. Mom has never said *like mother, like daughter* to me before. And that in itself is worth one hundred years of hunger.

⟲ ⟲ ⟲ ⟲

Sunday afternoon. Mom is taking a CrossFit class at her gym. Dad is picking up some toiletries so he can pack for Chicago. I'm stretched on the couch, painting my nails and reviewing my chemistry notes.

Diet Tip #3: *If you feel the need to feed, grab some polish; by the time your nails have dried, the craving will have subsided.*

The front door unlocks. Dad comes in, toting several plastic bags.

I'm about to greet him when I notice he's not alone. Two men are hauling an oblong object wrapped in brown paper into our apartment. They set it down in the hallway. Dad hands them some money.

"What's that?" I call out as soon as they're gone.

"It's yours!" Dad exclaims.

"Mine? What is it?"

"Come in here and find out for yourself."

Once I'm in the hallway, Dad says, "Open it up."

I stare at the object. I'm usually a sucker for presents, but I have a funny feeling about this one. As I sit on the ground and tear away the brown paper, my heart sinks.

It's a mirror. A tell-all, show-all, full-length mirror.

"What do you think?" Dad is hovering expectantly above me.

"It's a mirror," I say glumly.

"I noticed you didn't have a mirror in your bedroom," Dad says. "I thought if you could watch yourself losing weight, it might help you reach your body goal."

Since when did Dad become Mr. Observant Parent? This past spring my computer was constantly crashing, shutting down in the middle of tasks, losing files. Whenever I asked Dad to help me with it, he always said things like, *I'm so busy . . . I'll look at it this weekend . . . Sorry, I'll make an appointment at the Genius Bar next week.* I finally brought it to Shannon's mom and she straightened it out.

So how is it that he suddenly has time to take a complete inventory of my bedroom *and* fill in all the gaps?

Dad glances at his phone. "I'd better start packing for my flight. Will you help me carry this into your room?"

I remain on the floor, staring at the mirror.

Dad wraps his arms around the mirror and grunts as he lifts it by himself. "Come on, Ginny, give me a hand."

I've barely eaten anything today, so my head feels light. I slowly stand up and help him carry the mirror into my room.

ⓖ ⓖ ⓖ ⓖ

Later Sunday afternoon. Dad is on his way to the airport. Mom just called from the gym to say she's staying longer to do weights. I'm slumped on the couch watching *Friends*. Whenever I've seen *Friends* these past few days, I've gotten a pang inside as I remember how Froggy and I sang the theme song together last Monday.

Ever since last week, I've been too humiliated to look him in the eye. I mean, he knows I saw a doctor about my weight. What could be more embarrassing than that?

Froggy and I are only in French class together, so it hasn't been hard to avoid him. Whenever I see him in the halls, I pretend to be fascinated by the cover of my notebook or an imaginary insect whizzing through the air. I've steered clear of the cafeteria and the computer cluster. And we sit two rows apart in French, so I'm careful not to glance in his direction. I still haven't figured out what I'll do tomorrow, when we usually have our Monday tryst at my apartment.

Once *Friends* is over, I glance at my phone. The battery is almost dead. I haven't heard from Shannon in eight days. Last night I broke down and called her in Walla Walla, but her voice sounded weird as she rushed off, promising I'd be hearing from her soon.

When I stand up, my head feels fuzzy, like I'm blacking out. My energy is so low. I collapse back onto the couch, sink my head between my knees, and take several deep breaths. After a few minutes I rise again, but slower this time.

I promised myself I'd only stay in my bedroom long enough to grab my charger. But after I plug in my phone I can't stop glancing at the mirror leaning against the wall between my desk and bookshelf.

I go over to my dresser, scoop up the pile of diet tips I've been collecting, and wedge them into the mirror's frame. That way, whenever I glimpse my reflection, at least I'll be comforted by the fact that I'm doing something about it.

I take a few steps backward to admire my work. That's when I catch sight of myself. I'm wearing baggy sweats and an oversized T-shirt, so it's hard to get a good reading on my body. I have to admit I'm curious to see how six days of starvation has left me. I know I'm not about to appear on the cover of *Fitness,* but maybe I'll have a little bit of a waist or something.

I sit on the edge of my bed and pull down my sweats. I yank my shirt over my head. I pause before unhooking my bra and wriggling out of my undies, but if I'm going to do this, I'm going to go full throttle.

As I walk toward the center of my room, my heart is thumping against my chest. I *never, ever, ever* look at myself in the mirror naked. When I get into the shower, I always turn the other way as I'm passing the mirror. Obviously I've seen myself as I'm lathering up or getting undressed, but that's different. That's just a little skin here and there. Not the complete and honest picture.

I take a few shallow breaths before reaching the mirror. This probably isn't the best idea. Not yet, anyway. But there's some force pulling me to the mirror, the same kind that makes me finish a jumbo bag of M&Ms when I know I should stop after a few handfuls.

One more step and . . .

Oh no.

This is why Mom dragged me to Dr. Love.

This is why Dad bought me a full-length mirror.

This is why Brie would rather kill herself than be me.

This is why Froggy won't be seen with me in public.

As I stare at my naked body, I remember an article I once read about a sorority in California. The girls all had to strip down and stand in a line. Then the sorority president went down the row with a big black marker. As she stopped at each girl, she circled onto her skin wherever she needed to lose weight or tone up.

I direct my eyes to my stomach. This'll be the first to go. I grab a fold of my tummy and squeeze. It hurts, but a good pain, like I'm showing my body who's boss. I squeeze it once more, so hard that I suck in my breath.

Next, I zero in on my outer thighs. They're dimpled with cellulite, resembling cottage cheese. I pinch the flesh on my thighs between my fingers and thumb.

I rotate around and check out my butt.

What's the opposite of buns of steel? Buns of dough. Buns of butter.

I pinch and squeeze all over my butt cheeks, so hard that it leaves red marks. I'm choking back tears, but I keep telling myself that I deserve this. I got myself this way.

I proceed to pinch every unsightly part of my body—my inner thighs, my upper arms, my breasts, my hips. It happens in a colorless blur, like a pinwheel spinning too fast. I'm pinching and crying, crying and pinching. Snot is running down my nose and dripping saltily into my mouth, but I keep grabbing at my skin, harder every time.

I sink onto the floor and curl up into the fetal position. I sob and shake and hug my knees and suck my knuckles.

Sometimes I wish I could just disappear from this earth, float away, like an old plastic bag that gets caught in a gust and carried over the Manhattan skyline.

It's a drizzly, cold Monday morning. The spots where I pinched myself are now eggplant-colored bruises. Most are located on regions of my body that are easy to conceal, but the big trick today is to avoid gym. I always change in a bathroom stall, so the locker room isn't a problem. But flouncing around in shorts and a T-shirt definitely puts me at high risk for bruise exposure—especially the ones on my thighs and upper arms.

It won't break my heart to skip gym. We've just started a unit called "Shoots and Ladders." Typical gym-teacher glorification of tumbling on mats, climbing ropes, and hanging precariously from clammy rings. I hate it. I loathe it. I detest, despise, and abhor it. There aren't enough words to express how much I dislike clutching a gnarled rope as our pint-sized instructor, also known as Teri the Tiny Gym Teacher, barks, "Come on, Shreves! At least give it a try!" If it's not bad enough that there's no way in hell I have the upper-body strength to hoist myself from the ground, factor in Brie Newhart, Brinna Livingston, and Briar Schwartz perpetually smirking at me from the mats.

As the second-period bell rings, summoning me to gym, I head to Paul the School Nurse's office. Paul the School Nurse is my secret weapon at Brewster. He's monumentally trying to overcompensate for his male-nurse status. Utter a syllable about cramps or PMS and he's bemoaning the woes of woman-hood, feeling your menstrual pain.

Along with ditching gym, I also have to dodge Froggy. Even if he hadn't overheard that weight comment, there's no way I could fool around with him today. Let's say he lifted up my shirt and saw the welts on my stomach and hips. That would be a fun one to explain. *Oh, didn't I tell you? In my spare time, I like to pinch myself.*

We usually meet on the front steps of school and walk to the crosstown bus together. I've decided that I'm simply not going to show up. It's not like we've ever made a verbal agree-ment to both be there, so what's keeping me from being other-wise occupied? I know I should probably tell him, but I'm too chicken for that. Like, what if he asks for an explanation? *Because you know I'm seeing a Fat Doctor. Because I'm cov-ered in bruises.* Or worse, what if he says something like, *Why are you telling me this? I thought we were just going to keep it casual. I hope you're not starting to think we're boyfriend and girlfriend or anything.*

No, no, no. That would put me at risk of breaking the Fat

Girl Code of Conduct, rule #4. Never make him discuss your relationship. Better to avoid the situation altogether.

My last class of the day is math. Mr. Moony's heart must be acting up because he's panting like a golden retriever as he hands out worksheets on the Pythagorean theorem. I attempt to concentrate on $a^2 + b^2 = c^2$, but I'm growing increasingly anxious about a potential Froggy encounter.

The bell rings. Rather than heading down the front stairwell with the other kids, I slink down a rear flight to the second floor and peek into Ms. Crowley's office. She's working at her computer, so I slip inside, remove the stack of books from her extra chair, and sit down. Ms. Crowley holds up a finger to signal that she'll be with me soon.

After a moment she says, "How's it going?"

"Okay, I guess."

"Is everything all right?"

"What do you mean?"

"You seem a little distracted recently. Your eyes don't have their usual sparkle."

"I'm fine," I say. "I'm just trying to lose some weight."

Ms. Crowley frowns. "Is a doctor helping you?"

"Sort of."

Ms. Crowley pulls a rubber band out of her hair and rolls it over her wrist. "I think it's great that you want to take control of your weight and I hope you're doing it in a healthy manner, but I have to warn you that dieting is a slippery slope."

I pick up a paper clip from her desk. "A slippery slope?"

"I know how difficult it is to be a large woman in this society," Ms. Crowley says. "Do you think I don't know that students call me Ms. *Cowley* behind my back?"

I wonder if Ms. Crowley overheard them the way I overheard the Bri-girls in the bathroom that day. I wonder if it made her gnaw on her cheeks until they were raw.

"I've heard everything," Ms. Crowley says. "You name it, I've been called it. When I was younger, it affected me so strongly that I had some close calls with crash dieting, one where I spent a week in the hospital with a tube in my arm, feeding me nutrients."

"Are you serious?" I unbend the paper clip until it's a straight line.

"I was in my early twenties. I'm not telling you this to scare you. I'm just asking you to be careful. Don't try to change everything overnight."

I jab the paper clip wire into the palm of my hand, not hard enough to break skin, but enough to leave tiny indentations. I understand what Ms. Crowley is saying. But that doesn't take away Workout Fiend Mom and Naturally Thin Dad and Beautiful Anaïs and Built-Like-a-Greek-God Byron.

ⓖ ⓖ ⓖ ⓖ

I stayed in Ms. Crowley's office long enough to avoid Froggy after school on Monday. But that means I have to face him in French this morning. As I head down the language corridor, I hug my books to my chest.

There are a million reasons why I hate French. First of all, I suck at it, which is so frustrating because it pulls down my otherwise high-A grade point average. I can spend an entire evening memorizing irregular verbs, but when I wake up the next morning, it's like they've leaked out of my brain and onto my pillow.

I really wanted to take Chinese. I thought it would be fun to be able to tell people off in Chinese. Unless you're in Chinatown, no one will know what you're saying. But Mom insisted that I have to take French because every other Shreves converses fluently in it. She says I can only take Chinese after I've finished my three-year language requirement.

I also hate French because my teacher is evil. Mademoiselle Kiefer—born and bred in Erie, Pennsylvania, but a total French wannabe—wears black all the time and has long spidery legs. I've nicknamed them baguette legs because it looks like her torso is propped atop two narrow loaves of French bread. Mademoiselle Kiefer is always swearing at us in French. The only people she's nice to are the popular kids. There are several in my class, including Brie Newhart and Brinna Livingston. Brie is her pet, probably because she's named after a French cheese. Last week she let Brie go into the hallway to make a call even though phones are prohibited during school hours.

When I arrive in class, most kids are already seated. Brie and Brinna are milling around Mademoiselle Kiefer's desk, comparing notes on their favorite Left Bank bistros. Brie twirls her sandy curls into a French twist and says how she knows Paris like the back of her hand. Brinna murmurs and nods. I don't think Brinna's family is as wealthy as Brie's, but she's always acting like they are.

As I slide into my seat, I force myself not to look in Froggy's direction.

The bell rings.

Brie and Brinna head to their desks. Brie's high-heeled Parisian boots click down the aisle as she takes her seat, one row to my left. I make a special attempt to turn my eyes away from Brie, but I have to admit it's hard. She flirted with my brother on the subway, for God's sake! She now knows exactly who I am. So how can she still sit three feet from me and act like I'm a non-person?

Mademoiselle Kiefer slams a hole-punch onto her desk to get everyone's attention. *"Bienvenue,"* she barks, welcoming us to class.

Mademoiselle Kiefer writes *Weather Expressions* on the chalkboard. I copy it into my notebook. Then she rattles off various ways to describe the elements. Oddly, she only seems to be teaching us foul-weather phrases such as "It's cold" and "It's windy."

I feel a sharp jab in my arm. I glance to my left. I'm shocked to see Brie holding a folded piece of paper with my name on it. As I grab it, I attempt to offer her a smile of thanks, but she won't make eye contact with me. Oh yeah, I might contaminate her perfectly popular reputation. Or maybe she thinks my cellulite is contagious.

It's an expertly folded note, with five different edges poking into various flaps. I carefully unfold it. The first thing I notice is

Froggy's handwriting. He writes with scrupulous block letters—
very neat, very consistent.

VIRGINIA—
WHERE WERE YOU YESTERDAY?
I WAITED ON THE STOOP FOR FORTY-FIVE MINUTES.
IS EVERYTHING OKAY?
FROGGY WELSH THE QUATRIÈME

I am shocked.

I am stunned.

Froggy knows I'm going to a Fat Doctor and he still wants
to fool around!

I'm about to climb on top of my desk and whoop for joy
when it hits me that I actually have to answer Froggy's question
about why I stood him up.

I chew my lower lip for a second. A white lie will have to do.

F—
I was feeling sick so I went home early.
Sorry.
V

I refold the paper, cross out my name, and print *Froggy* on
the outside.

Ordinarily I wouldn't ask anything of Brie.

Iron Rule of the High School Way of Life: *Only address a*

popular kid if they address you first. Don't just approach
them and strike up a conversation, unless it's a matter of life
and death—and even then, it should be a matter of the popu-
lar person's life or death.

This isn't life and death, but it's pretty important.

I work up my nerve before lightly tapping Brie's bony forearm.

I can see her flinch, but she pretends to be enraptured by Mademoiselle Kiefer's lecture on crappy weather.

I poke Brie again.

"Humph!" she snorts.

Mademoiselle Kiefer spins around and glares at me. I cower like an abused puppy. As soon as she turns back to the board, Brie snatches the note out of my hands and tosses it at Froggy's feet.

"*Il fait mauvais* means it's stormy," Mademoiselle Kiefer says. "*Il pleut.* That's what you say when it's raining."

I can see Froggy writing on a fresh page, tearing it from his spiral notebook, and folding it up.

Brie flings a new note onto the floor near my desk. I slide out of my chair and swipe up the paper.

VIRGINIA—
MAYBE WE SHOULD TAKE A TRIP TO WALLA WALLA
TOGETHER.
WOULD THAT MAKE YOU FEEL BETTER?
FW4

I'm puzzled.

I've never talked to Froggy about Shannon, so how does he know about Walla Walla? And why a vacation there?

I turn to Froggy, scrunch my eyebrows together, and mouth, *Walla Walla?*

Froggy pantomimes a swimming/crawling gesture and tugs at his sweatshirt. At that same moment, someone's phone starts playing an instrumental version of the French national anthem. Mademoiselle Kiefer spins around in time to catch Froggy while he's still in action.

"That's it, *ma petite grenouille*," she snarls. "Into the hallway."

I can see Brie glancing at her phone inside her bag. An uncomfortable laughter ripples through the classroom. Mademoiselle Kiefer has just called Froggy her "little frog." I only know that because I recently looked up "frog" in my French-English dictionary.

"Excusez-moi?" Froggy asks as he rubs his nose. He's definitely not the type of kid who's ever sent into the hallway. He plays *trombone*, after all.

Mademoiselle Kiefer angrily extends her arm in the direction of the hallway, as if to say, *Don't doubt the magnitude of my evil.*

Froggy gathers together his folders. As he stands up, he turns to me and yanks his sweatshirt one more time.

"Maintenant!" growls Mademoiselle Kiefer.

Once Froggy is in the hallway, I turn it over and over in my head. *Crawling. Tugging at sweatshirt. Swimming. Crawling.*

That's it! When Froggy crawled under my bed last week, he must have seen my Walla Walla is for Lovers sweatshirt that I kicked under there a few weeks ago. I'd almost forgotten about that sweatshirt from Shannon. I smile as I ponder the romantic implications of Froggy suggesting we go to Walla Walla together. Walla Walla is for *lovers,* after all.

Mademoiselle Kiefer stomps toward me.

"Is there some joke you want to share with the rest of us, *La Vierge?*"

The class cracks up. I can hear Brie's high, hiccupy laugh above everyone else's.

"No," I say.

Mademoiselle Kiefer marches back to the board. I flip through my French-English dictionary. When I come to *vierge,* I feel my cheeks heating up. I have just been called "The Virgin" in front of the entire class. If there's ever a self-prophesying name, mine's the one. At least *la grenouille* was out of earshot.

11

$\mathbf{S}$hannon and I rarely e-mail, which is why I'm surprised to see a message from her at my school account. I happen to be checking because I needed to ask Mr. Vandenhausler about a Global Studies review sheet and there it is.

To: Virginia.Shreves
From: Shannon.Malloy.Newman
Date: Tuesday, October 10, 9:38 p.m.
Subject: HA is not funny

Virginia—

I'm soooooo sorry for my absence. I hope you're not mad at me. I've been on House Arrest. For the past nine days, Liam and Nina have taken away my phone and I'm only allowed to use my computer for homework. That's how I'm sneaking in this quick e-mail.

It's all because of my new friends. There are three of them—two guys, Evan and Hunter, and a girl named Sabrina. Most people at Walla Walla High School think they're freaks. Hunter has aquamarine hair, and Sabrina has "Mom" tattooed on her arm. But I don't care. They were the only people who treated me like something other than a stuttering misfit.

Last Saturday night, the four of us decided to meet at a playground near my house. It was just going to be some after-dinner hanging out, but we started talking and walking and talking and talking. GUESS WHAT? I didn't stutter around them, not even once.

The next thing I knew it was one thirty. IN THE MORNING.

I sprinted all the way home, but when I got there, Liam and Nina were livid. They thought I'd been squished by farm machinery. They yelled at me. I called them "onion-loving fuckers" and locked myself in the bathroom. That's when I was slapped with HA. Liam and Nina say they're happy I'm making friends, but that still doesn't mean I can stay out all night. Whatever.

Love,

Shannon

P.S. Sabrina, Evan, Hunter, and I have been sitting together at lunch all week. Evan eats tofu in peanut sauce.

To: Shannon.Malloy.Newman
From: Virginia.Shreves
Date: Wednesday, October 11, 6:17 p.m.
Subject: HA is DEFINITELY not funny

Shan—

Good to hear from you. I was about to file a Missing Persons report. I'm not mad, but I wish you'd found a way to tell me what was up, like snail mail or carrier pigeon.

Congrats on your new friends. They sound interesting. Are you sure Sabrina's tattoo is real?

Shan, may I admit something? I'm a little worried that you're going to forget your boring old best friend now that you've found these exciting new people. Well, I hope you know I won't let you escape that easily. Even if I have to start eating tofu.

Love,

Gin

P.S. Speaking of eating, have I told you I'm on a diet? For real this time.

P.P.S. Things on the Froggy front are starting to improve.

P.P.P.S. Just thought I'd remind you that you never stutter around me either.

ⓖ ⓖ ⓖ ⓖ

I'm sitting on my bed, struggling to conjugate verbs in the *passé composé*. Mademoiselle Kiefer gave us a worksheet of verbs that we have to transform into the past tense. I've heard that in Chinese you don't have to make verb forms change for tenses. What a far superior language.

There's a knock on my door.

"Come in," I shout.

Mom peeks into my room. "How was school?"

"Fine."

"Anything interesting happen?"

"Not really."

"Would you like to go out to dinner?"

I drop my pencil. "Just you and me?"

Mom nods.

I can't remember the last time Mom and I went to a restaurant, just the two of us. She's always so busy with her patients and her exercise and everything. Besides, she usually has dinner with Nan the Neurotic Nutritionist on Wednesday nights.

"What about Nan?"

"Nan's out of town," Mom says, "so I thought it would be nice to have a little mother-daughter time."

Mom gives Dad a quick call in Chicago, and then we walk down to an elegant Mexicany-Japanesey restaurant on Amsterdam Avenue. It's a mild fall night, the last gasps of summer. The sidewalks are buzzing with people and strollers and dogs straining at their leashes. With each step, I squeeze my butt cheeks together.

Diet Tip #4: Find creative ways to exercise undesirable body parts.

Mom orders a glass of chardonnay. I get a Diet Sprite. When the waiter brings our drinks, he plops a basket of multicolored tortilla chips and a bowl of salsa onto the table. I'm zooming in for a chip when I catch Mom's eye.

Diet Tip #5: *Utilize something other than a grease-drenched chip to eat salsa.*

I scoop up some salsa with my spoon. Mom smiles approvingly.

As I drink my Diet Sprite through a straw, Mom starts talking about her patients. She never calls them by name, so she won't break their confidentiality. It's more like the Girl Who Swallows Pocket Change When She's Upset or the Boy Who Shoplifts Even Though His Parents Are Millionaires. Mom's stories often shock me. I can't believe how screwed up some people are.

I'm tempted to tell Mom about Shannon's e-mail. I'm curious to see if she thinks I'm in danger of being replaced by the Walla Walla friends. But I decide not to mention anything. After listening to problems all day, Mom's tolerance for hearing mine is usually pretty low. Sometimes at night, as she's making a mug of tea or curling up with a novel, she'll sigh and say, *I'm glad my children have turned out so healthy.* Having a stable family is important to Mom, probably because her own childhood was so rocky.

I spoon up some more salsa and study the menu. Whenever we've been to this restaurant before, I've gotten the cheesy fajita platter. But this time around, I'm determined to order something light, like mango sushi. Maybe that will score me another approving maternal smile.

Shannon hasn't been the only Missing Person. I haven't spoken with Byron since the day I brought him the Rice Krispie treats. I've texted a bunch of times about that Yankees game to which Dad is offering us tickets. New York beat Oakland in the Division Series, so if they can hang on in the playoffs, it looks like this game will happen. It's a big-deal game to any Yankees fan, especially one who aspires to bear the offspring of several players.

Unfortunately, no one's heard a peep from Byron, not even my parents.

That's what Dad and I are arguing about now. It's Thursday evening. Mom is doing her group-therapy night. Dad has just returned from his business trip. He's reclining on the ottoman and watching the news. I'm sitting on the floor, removing my nail polish with a cotton ball. This afternoon, while in the throes of munchie-mania, I painted each finger a different color. After applying Strobe, Zippy, Sizzle, Tidal Wave, and Firecracker, I decided the rainbow thing was too flashy for someone like me.

Every time there's a commercial, Dad and I start arguing again.

"If Byron can't give you definite word by tonight," Dad says, "I'll have to give the tickets to one of my colleagues."

"Dad, you can't! It's a playoff game, and you said I could go." I attempt to throw a cotton ball at him, but it lands an inch in front of me.

"I'm afraid I have no other choice, Ginny. The game is next Saturday, so I've got to get something figured out. Mom and I will be in Connecticut all weekend, and I can't let you go to Yankee Stadium alone."

I unscrew a bottle of mauve and polish my middle finger. I'm almost angry enough to flip Dad a big pink bird. "Who says I'd go alone?"

"Is there another person you had in mind?"

Sometimes Dad can be as sensitive as a cement block. I search my brain for an answer. Normally I would say Shannon and that would be that. Who can I bring now? Froggy? We've actually been talking in school a little more recently. Like in French class today, he asked to be my partner for "Everyday Conversation." That's what Mademoiselle Kiefer has us do whenever she wants to go chase after the sexy male physics teacher. But I'm not about to ask Froggy on a date. That's in total violation of the Fat Girl Code of Conduct, rule #1. No riding the moped in public. Besides, Froggy is a Red Sox fan. He has a bunch of their stickers on his trombone case.

The news comes on. Dad pumps the volume. I've just finished my left hand when the home phone rings.

"Would you get that?" Dad asks.

As I stomp into the hallway, I suspend my hand in the air so I won't smudge my nails. My only hope at this point is that it's Byron, finally calling back to say he can come to the game.

I pick up the phone. "Hello?"

"I'm calling for Dr. or Mr. Shreves," a man says. His voice sounds deep and official.

"May I ask who's calling?"

"This is Maxwell Briggs." He pauses before adding, "The dean of students at Columbia University."

"Hold on, please."

I carry the phone into the living room and tap Dad's shoulder.

"It's for you," I whisper. "Sounds important."

Dad mutes the volume on the TV, clears his throat, and lifts the phone to his ear. "This is Mike Shreves," he says.

I flounce onto the couch and blow at my fingertips. I'm half watching the news and half listening to Dad's side of the conversation. He's not saying much, just an occasional "I see" and "of course."

My ears only perk up when I hear Dad ask, "Are you sure there hasn't been a mistake, sir?"

I don't think I've heard Dad use the word "sir" since a

doctor called from a Phoenix hospital three years ago to report that his father had a stroke.

"What was that about?" I ask as Dad hangs up the phone.

Dad is staring blankly at the television. The color has leaked from his face, leaving him a sickly greenish hue. The last time Dad looked this bad was the day he got the phone call about Grandpa Shreves.

ⓖ ⓖ ⓖ ⓖ

I don't know how much time has passed.

I'm sitting on my bed. I've just devoured an entire box of contraband Frosted Flakes, handful by handful. I hear my parents' voices rising and falling in the living room. Mom's voice is high and squeaky. Dad's sounds drained, devoid of emotion.

Mom's phone rings. I hear her scamper to get it. I hear shrill sobs. I hear someone go to the liquor cabinet and pour a drink.

I concentrate on numbing myself. That's what I've been doing ever since the call from Dean Briggs. I've started with my heart and am expanding outward to the rest of my body. Now I am numbing my arms and legs, elbows, and knees.

There's a knock on my door.

I don't answer.

Another knock.

I don't answer.

The door cracks open, so I stuff the empty cereal box under my covers.

I turn to face Mom. There are smears of mascara under her red-rimmed eyes.

When she speaks, her voice sounds like a deflated balloon. "I assume you've heard."

I nod.

Mom opens her mouth. This is the point in the conversation where she generally lapses into TherapistSpeak, offering a Dr. Phyllis Shreves professional explanation. But nothing comes out.

We stare at each other for several seconds.

Mom wipes under her eyes with the side of her finger. "Byron is moving home tomorrow."

I continue staring at her.

"He'll be living here until we can get this straightened out."

I turn to the window.

"There must be some mistake," Mom says. "I've known Byron for his entire life. I know who he is and how his brain operates and what he's capable of. And my son is certainly not capable of something like this. *That* I can guarantee."

There's a red light flashing in New Jersey.

"What's wrong, Virginia? Why aren't you saying anything?"

I concentrate on numbing my ankles and wrists.

"How do you feel about this?"

Now my hands and feet. Now my fingers and toes.

Mom switches off my light as she leaves my room.

VIRGINIA: It's 1:12 a.m. in NYC and I can't sleep. Are you there? If not, I'm going to keep texting you all night.

SHANNON: I'm right here! I was about to text you because Liam and Nina gave back my phone tonight and I wanted to tell you that you'll ALWAYS be my spiritual twin no matter what . . . hold on! What's up? Is everything okay?

VIRGINIA: No. But I'm still in shock. I can't talk about it.

SHANNON: Talk.

VIRGINIA: It's too horrendous.

SHANNON: Talk.

VIRGINIA: Consider yourself warned.

SHANNON: Warned.

VIRGINIA: Byron was found guilty of date-raping a girl at Columbia.

SHANNON: Holy shit.

VIRGINIA: He's suspended for the rest of the semester. He's moving home tomorrow.

SHANNON: Do you know who she is? Do you know when it happened?

VIRGINIA: All I know is that it has something to do with this Bros and Hos party he went to a few weeks ago.

SHANNON: Now I'M in shock. Bros and Hos? Gross.

VIRGINIA: I can hardly breathe. I have a huge lump in my throat. I just ate half a box of Ritz crackers. Do you know how many calories that is?

SHANNON: Screw your diet. Are you going to be okay?

VIRGINIA: I'll either be okay or I'll drink a bottle of Clorox.

SHANNON: Please tell me you're not serious.

VIRGINIA: I'm not serious.

VIRGINIA: For the most part, anyway.

13

I barely sleep all night. Every time I roll over, I grind against cracker crumbs and Frosted Flakes. But I don't feel them. I don't feel anything. I'm working extremely hard at being numb.

I'm going to stay home sick today. I hardly have the energy to sleep, much less take a shower, get dressed, and deal with school.

The home phone rings around 6:45 a.m. I can hear Mom answer it and put it on speaker, which is what she always does when she's doing her makeup. I'm surprised to hear Shannon's voice on the other end, stuttering up a storm. For some reason, Mom always makes her nervous. I glance at my phone. Three missed calls from Shannon. Damn. I accidentally turned it to silent last night.

"I'm c-c-c-calling for V-V-V-Virginia."

"I'm not sure she's awake yet," Mom says.

I shout from my room. "I'm up, Mom. Tell Shannon I'll call her from my phone."

"I'm so sorry for c-c-c-calling this early, Ms. Shreves. I mean, Doc-Doc-Doc-Doc—"

"That's all right."

"Virginia!" Shannon shouts as soon as I call her. "I set my alarm for the middle of the night, Walla Walla time, so I could catch you before you left for school."

"I'm not going to school today, but I'm glad you called." It's great to hear Shannon's voice. It's been a while since we've had a real conversation. Shannon prefers texting because phones make her stutter more.

"I wanted to make sure you didn't swallow any Clorox. I was worried."

"I'm still alive," I say. "Unfortunately."

Shannon ignores my comment. "Why aren't you going to school?"

"I just don't want to deal."

"Not to sound preachy, but you should go. Do you really want to be there when Byron moves in?"

I hadn't thought of that. I'm definitely not ready to see him yet, to acknowledge that this whole thing is happening. "I guess not."

"Well, hurry along then."

"Okay, Mommy." I wedge the phone between my ear and shoulder as I cross the room to my dresser.

"Before you go, can I read you something?"

"What?" I ask. As I root around in my top drawer for a

pair of undies, my hand brushes against my cedar chest, the one where I keep my treasured possessions.

"I came across this quote on a box of Sleepytime tea last night," says Shannon. "Someone named John Muir. I think he saved forests."

I sit on the edge of my bed.

"Here goes: 'When we try to pick out anything by itself, we find it hitched to everything else in the universe.'" Shannon pauses before adding, "I think it means that everything's connected. Or maybe that no single incident stands by itself."

"Are you saying you think Byron has done this to other girls?" I ask. I can tell my voice sounds sharp, but this is my big brother we're talking about, my hero. I'm not ready to start thinking of him as a serial rapist.

"No," Shannon says. "But *Bros and Hos*? Who goes to a party like that?"

"It was a joke," I say, remembering what Byron told me that day.

"Well." Shannon pauses. "I just thought of you when I read it . . . but maybe I was a little dopey from the tea."

"I don't know," I say.

"Neither do I."

ᧁ ᧁ ᧁ ᧁ

I can't believe I make it to school. I'm in a total daze. All I want to do is crawl into my locker and fall asleep.

My first class is Global Studies II. It should be called Murder Studies II. Last year in Global Studies I, we learned about every mass slaughter in history—from the Native Americans to the Holocaust. This year we're focusing on contemporary world issues. We have to read the *New York Times* at least twice a week. I thought it would be more upbeat than last year, but Mr. Vandenhausler has once again focused on death and destruction. We've just finished learning about the genocide of millions in the Congo. Next, we're starting a unit on the war against terrorism.

I'm settling into my seat when Mr. Vandenhausler skips to the front of the classroom.

"I have something exciting to announce!" he sings. "I'm squeezing in a special mini-unit on Nepal."

My ears perk up. Nepal is a small country in the Himalayas, right on the border of China.

Mr. Vandenhausler's mustache starts twitching. *Oh no.* That's what happens whenever he's talking blood-and-guts. I brace myself as he adds that we'll learn specifically about how the crown prince shot and killed the king, queen, and seven other members of the royal family during a Friday-night dinner.

"It was such a shock," chirps Mr. Vandenhausler. His mustache is vibrating so much it looks like it's going to pop off his upper lip. "Prince Dipendra was their beloved firstborn son. No one ever expected he'd do anything as brutal as this."

I think of Byron, of last night, of the phone call from Dean Briggs.

By the time the bell rings, my palms are slick with sweat. Mr. Vandenhausler has described the automatic submachine gun the prince used, the order in which the family members were shot, which parts of each body were penetrated. He even projected onto a screen video clips of wailing Nepalese people mourning the loss of their royal family.

The last thing I can imagine doing right now is "Shoots and Ladders," but I skipped gym on Monday so I can't ditch twice in a week. I've just entered the locker room when Teri the Tiny Gym Teacher walks in. She's wearing a slate-colored warm-up suit, cross-trainers, and a whistle dangling from a chain around her neck.

"PEEEEE-PULL," Teri bellows, blowing her whistle.

She proceeds to tell us that a fuse blew in the gym, so we're going to be sprinting up and down the hallway instead of doing "Shoots and Ladders."

Everyone groans.

"Make sure to wear sneakers," Teri adds. "Because we're going to work you."

I want to strangle myself with a shoelace. I hate doing sprints. I hate being worked. I hate being worked doing sprints a thousand times more than I hate climbing ropes and hanging from rings.

Teri turns to leave, but then she blows her whistle again. "I need one volunteer," she shouts. "Someone to record times."

I shoot up my arm faster than a bullet from an automatic submachine gun.

"Good reflexes, Shreves!" says Teri as she hands me a stopwatch and a clipboard.

One point for Shreves.

I get to be Teri the Tiny Gym Teacher's trusty assistant, timing sprints and clutching the clipboard as my classmates heave and pant and sweat their way down the hall. At one point Brie Newhart stumbles into a locker, moaning that she feels faint. Her pale cheeks are splotchy, and she looks like she's on the verge of tears.

But even that doesn't make me feel much better.

⑥ ⑥ ⑥ ⑥

Third period is French. I don't feel like seeing Froggy, having to smile and act like everything's okay. He's talking to another guy when I walk in, so I give him a quick wave and take my seat.

Ten minutes into class, Mademoiselle Kiefer distributes our weekly quiz. I scan the page. *Passé composé* as far as the eye can see. We have to list the seventeen verbs that use *être* in the past tense. I glance at Froggy and Brie and the other kids chewing their pen caps and scribbling answers. I know I'm going to bomb this quiz, so instead of attempting it, I write:

Why Past Tense Makes Me Tense.

I stare at my potential list, but nothing comes to mind. My brain feels as empty as the cereal and cracker boxes hidden under my bed.

I spend the rest of the period drawing spirals and three-dimensional boxes on my paper so Mademoiselle Kiefer won't notice I'm not writing and subject me to some form of torturous public humiliation. One time this girl named Alyssa Wu forgot her pen and had to sing "Frère Jacques" in front of the entire class.

When the bell rings, everyone drops the quiz on the corner of Mademoiselle Kiefer's desk. I slip mine into my notebook and dash out the door.

I can't handle another minute of school.

I consider visiting Paul the School Nurse and feigning yet more menstrual cramps, but I already burned a favor with him this week. Ms. Crowley wouldn't condone my skipping chemistry lab. Anyway, I think she's got senior composition fourth period.

I dump my notebooks in my locker and grab my backpack. Then I do something I've never done before. I walk out the front door of Brewster at a little before 11 a.m.

I've left school early for a doctor's appointment or to go home sick, but I've never ditched. There are kids who cut classes on a regular basis—the stoners, the slackers, the trench-coat wearers, but it always sounded vaguely dangerous, definitely not something I would ever do.

That's why I'm surprised it's so easy to walk out. One moment I'm an inmate at Brewster Penitentiary, and the next I'm strolling up Eighty-Fourth Street, the sun on my back, Bunsen burners and bubbling beakers a billion miles away.

I head toward Central Park. It feels like a typical day, except that no one on the street is over five or under twenty. The sidewalks are bustling with stressed-out executive types jabbering into phones and sliding on lipstick.

I walk in the direction of the Great Lawn and find a sunny bench to sit on. As I stare up at Belvedere Castle, this little castle in the middle of Central Park, I think of the movies I've seen where kids ditch school. *Ferris Bueller's Day Off*, of course. That's the classic. One summer Byron and I watched *Ferris Bueller* so many times we could recite the dialogue along with the characters.

I pull my phone out of my bag. I'm about to look up other skipping-school movies when I catch sight of my hands. A queasy feeling surges through my body. Last night, when we received the call from Dean Briggs, I was in the middle of painting my fingernails. I'd only polished my left hand when the phone rang.

I stand up and start walking again, but all my ditching-school excitement seems to have disappeared. I feel aimless and lonely and cold. I'd like to go back to our apartment, but Byron is probably moving in at this very moment and I don't want to be there for that.

Where do you go in New York City when you can't go home? I once read this book about a brother and sister who hide out in the Metropolitan Museum of Art. I always thought it would be more fun to stow away at Bed, Bath & Beyond. You could sleep in their elaborately made-up beds and raid the canisters of flavored popcorn or boxes of Good & Plenty if you're having the munchies.

Munchies. I can go to the movies.

I pull out my wallet. I only have three dollars and forty-seven cents, but my ATM card is tucked behind my school ID.

I walk over to Citibank and withdraw money from my savings account. As the receipt is printing, I feel slightly guilty. Mom and Dad are always emphasizing that the one thousand dollars in my bank account is mine, to do with what I want. It's mostly from birthdays and relatives and cat-sitting gigs. But I know they want me to put the money toward taking an Outward Bound course next summer, like Anaïs and Byron did after their sophomore year of high school. Some sort of trailblazing, pooping-in-the-woods occasion. Definitely not my idea of a good time. Not to sound like a city slicker, but I don't like to go too long without my phone or computer.

I head to the multiplex cinema near Mom's hair salon. When I approach the counter, I ask the woman for a ticket to the first movie I see on the sign.

"That started ten minutes ago," she says.

I push my money across the counter. She gives me a strange look as she hands me a ticket. Once I'm upstairs, I buy a tub of popcorn with extra butter.

As soon as I'm settled into my seat, I space out. I barely follow the story, but it does the trick of numbing my mind. As the credits roll, I wipe my greasy hands on the chair. Then I dart out of the theater, march into the neighboring one, and slip into an aisle seat.

Midway through my third movie, I run to the bathroom to pee. I quickly text Mom that I have a club meeting after school and won't be home until later. She writes back that that's fine. I try not to feel bad about the fact that she doesn't even know I'm not in any clubs. I pay another visit to the concession island.

This time I buy nachos with melted cheese, a jumbo pack of Sour Patch Kids, and a Diet Coke.

Diet Tip #6: Do not discover that your beloved brother has been found guilty of date rape.

I end up sneaking into seven different movies—some for the whole show, some for random snippets. It's 7:40 p.m. by the time I finally leave the theater. As I'm walking home, I realize that my stomach aches. My eyes ache. My ears ache. My tongue is raw, and my braces are crammed with kernels.

When I arrive home, it's after eight. The apartment is quiet and dark. Mom and Dad must be out for the evening. I'm heading down the hallway when I notice a strip of light coming from under Byron's door. My stomach flips nervously as I dash into my bedroom and burrow under my covers without undressing or brushing my teeth.

14

Early in the morning I hear dishes clanking and coffee grinding, but by the time I get out of bed, nobody's home. My parents must be in Connecticut already. They have that big golf tournament next weekend, so they're probably hitting the green early. The door to Byron's room is open. I peek inside. His bed is neatly made and there aren't any suitcases scattered around, nothing out of place.

I still feel popcorn in my braces, so I head into the bathroom and pull out the special dental floss that my orthodontist gave me. As I maneuver a string through my wires, I start thinking that maybe yesterday was just a nightmare, a blunder of my imagination.

I spit some kernel shards into the sink. The next time I see Byron, I'll have to tell him about it. He'll be shocked by the scenario that my brain conjured up, but he'll quickly find humor in the situation. He'll say something like, *You've been smoking too much weed, Gin.* Then we'll have a good laugh at my expense.

As I swish out my mouth with water, I think of ways to convince Mademoiselle Kiefer to let me make up the French quiz from yesterday. And I bet I can stay after school next week and do the lab on chemical reactions that I missed.

A few minutes later, I'm watching television and peeling an orange. I'm stacking the peels on the coffee table. My eating went a little haywire yesterday, but I've already decided to rein it in again. I'm going to drink two gallons of water today, so much that my pee will be clearer than a mountain creek. And I'll just have some lettuce later, maybe a few honey-nut rice cakes.

The front door unlocks. My tower of orange peels tips over.

"Hey, Gin."

I turn reluctantly, but my throat is too tight to speak.

Byron nods in my direction, but he doesn't smile. He's got a strange look on his face, something I've never seen before. It's a blend of embarrassment and exhaustion. I turn away. I really don't want to see him like this. I wish I could just close my eyes and open them again and have my perfect big brother back.

Dad comes through next. He grunts as he sets a milk crate onto the floor.

"Use your knees, Mike." Mom appears behind him with blazers and shirts draped over her arm.

Dad hunches down, his hands cupped on his knees. "Ginny,

what do you say about lending a hand? We've got a U-Haul van that needs unloading."

I stand up, but I don't say anything. I'm still processing the fact that they're not in the country. They go to Connecticut almost every weekend, rain or shine, sleet or hailstorm. They even went last spring when I won the creative writing award at Brewster's National Honor Society banquet. I ended up sitting at a table with Shannon and her parents instead.

"You might want to grab a sweatshirt," Mom says. "There's a nip in the air."

As I head into my room to get a sweatshirt, I can't stop thinking about how normal my parents just acted. It doesn't seem right. I mean, Byron has been suspended from school for *date rape*. In movies there would be a lot of crying and finger-pointing, maybe a few emotional hugs. So why is my family acting like it's a normal everyday morning?

No one says much during the next half hour, as we lug boxes and bags upstairs. At one point, as I'm helping Byron maneuver his futon mattress through the lobby, I try to catch his eye. I'm hoping he'll tell me this has been a huge mistake, but whenever I look at him, he turns away.

Dad and Byron drive off to return the U-Haul.

Mom and I take the elevator upstairs.

As soon as we get to the apartment, I head into my room and lock the door.

ⓖ ⓖ ⓖ ⓖ

I remain in my bedroom for the rest of the weekend. Mom and Dad knock a few times, but I pretend I'm sleeping. I don't feel like dealing with anything or anyone right now.

The only times I leave are when I'm sure no one's home or when they're all sleeping. Then I dash into the kitchen to scavenge cashews or gingersnaps or Diet Coke.

A few times I caught sight of myself in my new mirror, cramming food into my mouth, surrounded by all those diet tips that I stuck into the frame. Finally, on Sunday morning, I removed the tips and crumpled them into the trash.

Now it's Sunday afternoon. I've spent the day dozing and watching shows and doing homework. For "Ostracism and Oppression," we're reading this amazing book called *Caucasia*. It's about a light-skinned black girl whose mom is running from the law so she has to pretend she's white. Sometimes I wish I could pretend I were somebody else. I don't know who I'd be. Maybe Helen Keller, since she never had to see her reflection in the mirror or hear nasty things that people said about her.

I've kept up with baseball news on my phone. At this point, New York and Seattle have each won once, so there's a decent chance next weekend's game will be happening. Dad hasn't said anything more about giving the tickets away, so I'm still hoping I'll be able to go.

The only human contact I've had are my texts with Shannon. I've been writing her nearly every hour. She always writes back, not quite as frequently.

It's hard. Shannon is currently having a love affair with her

Walla Walla friends. Well, not romantic love. I double-checked that in my last text. I got a bunch of responses back:

SHANNON: Regarding your question about love, no such luck. Hunter and Evan are interested in each other. THEY don't know this yet, but Sabrina and I think that once they leave conservative Walla Walla, they'll move to Seattle and profess their undying love for each other.

SHANNON: Speaking of Sabrina, I finally asked about the "Mom" tattoo on her arm. She said it actually spells "Wow" and it's only meant for when she's doing handstands.

SHANNON: How are you? Have you left your bedroom yet?

I'm relieved that Shannon isn't getting a boyfriend on top of everything. Even so, it's hard to hear about these great additions to her life. Especially since all I've got is a failed diet and a kink in my lower back from remaining sedentary for the past twenty-nine hours.

15

On school days I set the alarm on my phone for 6:15 a.m. I always hit snooze, which starts waking me up. Snooze lasts for nine minutes, so I do it twice. If I'm up by 6:33 a.m., in the shower by 6:35 a.m., and out the door by 7:00 a.m., I can make it to school on time.

When my alarm rings this morning, I turn it off altogether. Then I collapse onto my pillow again and conk out.

I don't know how much time has passed when I hear a knock on my door.

I roll onto my stomach.

"Can you open up, Virginia?" Mom says from the hallway.

I tug a pillow over my head.

"I gave you your space for the entire weekend. I just want to talk for a minute."

I roll onto my side.

"Are you awake?" Mom asks. "It's after seven. You're going to have to take a cab to school."

"I'm not going to school," I grumble.

"Please unlock your door, and we'll discuss it."

I unlock my door and scramble back to bed before Mom can see me in my shirt and undies. As I dive under the sheets, a cashew jabs into my shoulder blade.

Mom walks in. She's dressed for work, but her hair is damp and she's not wearing any makeup yet.

"You don't feel well?" Mom presses her palm to my forehead. Her hand feels so soft it makes me want to cry.

"No," I whimper.

Mom sits on the edge of my bed. "Does it hurt somewhere specifically?"

I gesture to my stomach. "Maybe here. Sort of all over."

"Do you have any tests today? Anything you can't miss?"

I shake my head. We're starting a unit on atomic theory in chemistry, but I doubt I'll be able to pay attention.

"I've got to get running. I'm meeting Nan for an early yoga class. But I'll give the principal's office a call. It sounds like you need a personal day."

What I really need is a hug. I lift my hands, like a toddler asking to be picked up. Mom leans over, wraps her arms around me, and rocks me back and forth. I can't remember the last time she gave me a hug like this. Tears start running down my cheeks.

"You're having a hard time with this, aren't you?"

I nod and wipe away some tears.

Mom sits back. She inhales through her nose and exhales through her mouth. I call this her TherapistBreath. It's how I assume she always looks around her patients—calm, cool, composed.

"This isn't an easy ordeal we're facing," she says. "But we all love Byron, so we have to stick by him."

A fresh crop of tears pours out of my eyes. "How could he have done something like that?"

Mom presses her lips tightly together. I have no idea what she's thinking. If some people's faces are open books, Mom's is one of those leather-bound diaries with a lock on the front and a long-lost key.

"I don't know what to say, Virginia." Mom is quiet for a long time, then she takes another TherapistBreath and says, "Let's just keep going about our lives, and pretty soon everything will be back to normal."

I wipe my nose with the back of my hand.

"Do you think you can do that?" Mom asks.

"I'll try," I say quietly.

Mom gives me a quick hug. "I'm glad we had this talk. It's all going to be fine."

As soon as Mom is gone, I lapse into a fitful sleep. I have bizarre nightmares, one right after the next. I'm having a particularly creepy one about being chased by wild boars when I jolt awake. My phone says 10:21 a.m. I stare out my window at the cloudy sky.

That's when I hear grunting noises. I get out of bed and press my ear against my door. The grunts become longer, throatier. I grab some sweatpants from my laundry heap and pull them on. Then I tiptoe across the hall and stand in front of Byron's door.

"Grrrrrrr. Grrrrrrrrrr. *AAAARGGGHH!*"

My legs feel weak. Is Byron jacking off in there? Or worse, is he having sex? Oh God, I really don't want to think about that.

I hear a barbell knock against his floor. I dash into my room and slam the door.

So Byron was lifting weights. While I'm relieved that he wasn't exercising a *lower* portion of his body, I'm still a little shaken.

I slip into my sneakers, grab a sweatshirt, and scurry to the elevator.

It's overcast outside with a tinge of winter in the air. I zip my sweatshirt, pull up my hood, and shove my hands into the pockets. As I walk over to Broadway, I realize I forgot my bank card. I scrounge around in the change purse attached to my key chain and extract a crinkled five-dollar bill.

I head down to Dunkin' Donuts. It's about a ten-minute walk. Whenever I pass a college-aged woman on the sidewalk, I find myself wondering if she's the one. No one has given me details, other than what Dad told me after the phone call from Dean Briggs, about it being the girl Byron brought to that Bros and Hos party.

The door to Dunkin' Donuts is propped open. I head inside and am comforted by the sweet aroma of doughnuts. As I stand in the line, I try to remember her name. I think it was fairly generic. Maybe Amy? Or Abby? Or Ashley?

I order a glazed, a blueberry, and one with chocolate frosting. I've already polished off the glazed doughnut by the time I reach the door.

It's drizzling outside. I lick some sugar off my fingers. I remember Byron's friend, the one who looked like a hamster, mentioning something about the girl. That she was a math major. A cute math major.

As I take a right on Broadway, I try to imagine what happened that night.

Let's say Byron took a shower. He shaved and worked gel through his hair. He only wore a pair of boxers, so he could flaunt his new pecs. But they were nice boxers, like navy-blue silk.

I eat the blueberry doughnut. The drizzle is turning to rain—cold, driving droplets. My sweatshirt is getting wet, so it's clinging heavily to my body.

By the time Byron met up with her, she was flying high. It's not every day a math major goes out with a rugby god like Byron Shreves. She almost chickened out of wearing the leather bustier and fishnets, but her roommate convinced her to go for it.

They stopped by Hamster Boy's party, had a few beers, and headed over to Bros and Hos. They drank. They danced. Maybe it was the spiked punch, but she didn't feel as nervous as before. They started grinding their hips to the music.

I finish off my last doughnut, crumple the bag, and toss it in a trash bin. It's pouring by this point. My hair is sticking to my ears. My sweatpants are heavy with water. My feet are sloshing in my sneakers. I know it's time to yank the plug on my imagination, but I force myself to watch the next scene.

When the party wound down, Byron invited her back to his room. She'd had a lot of punch, so she knew she shouldn't go. But her brain was too murky and Byron's aftershave smelled too good.

Maybe Byron lit candles. Maybe he played jazz. Either way, they started making out. At first, she thought it felt good, but soon she noticed that Byron was moving really quickly. They'd barely started kissing when one of his hands undid her bustier, the other pushed down her fishnets. She asked him to slow down, but she was so drunk that her words were garbled.

The next thing she knew, Byron was rolling on a condom. She said no, but he was already inside of her. She told him to stop, but his eyes were closed as he pumped into a body that didn't feel like hers anymore.

"Are you okay, sweetheart?"

I blink several times. My vision is blurred, but I can make out a middle-aged woman with a concerned look on her face. Until she stopped me, I hadn't realized I'd been bawling my head off.

"Can I help you?" she asks.

"No," I say. "I'll be fine."

She nods reluctantly, so I dodge into a nearby Starbucks and head for the bathroom.

I glance at my reflection. My hair is drenched. My saliva and tears and snot are streaming together.

I dry my face with a scratchy napkin.

This is so confusing. For as long as I can remember, I've looked up to Byron more than anyone in the world. If he's the sun, I'm a planet revolving around him. Everything I've done in my life—from where I chose to go to school to how I feel about myself—has been because of my big brother.

But now that Byron has done something this horrible to a girl, I don't know what to make of anything. I mean, if you take away the sun's light, the planets won't know where to go or what to do.

I start sobbing again. As I lean against the filthy bathroom wall, I remind myself to be numb.

It's the only way I'll be able to carry on.

16

Where were you yesterday?" Froggy asks as I hang my jacket in my locker.

It's Tuesday morning. I wanted to take another personal day, but Mom reminded me of our "keep going about our lives" talk. So here I am, keeping going.

"I didn't see you in French, but I waited on the front stoop anyway." Froggy leans against the locker next to mine. "I waited for more than twenty minutes."

I fish a few textbooks out of my backpack. "I was sick."

"Again?" Froggy asks as he snaps and unsnaps his three-ring binder.

I don't respond.

"So you'll be there next Monday?"

When Froggy says that, my stomach does a flippy thing. I

think about how his neck smells up close and what it feels like to nuzzle my face against his lips. But then I get a sharp pain in my gut. I don't want to think about fooling around right now. I don't want to think about anything that will remind me of Byron's ordeal. I don't want to think about it so much that if a certain sexy shortstop came up to me and said I was the love of his life and he wanted to elope to the Bahamas with me, I'd tell him I was a nun.

"No," I say.

"What do you mean?"

I stare into the dark void of my locker. Last year Shannon and I stayed after school to line our lockers with wallpaper and hang up pictures and postcards, but this year I didn't do anything at all. "I won't be there next Monday."

"Are you saying it's over?" Froggy's voice cracks on the word "over."

Just then Mr. Moony hobbles by. He's got a Band-Aid across the bridge of his nose. He hasn't been in top form these days, colliding with lockers, tripping down stairs, sleeping in class. But his song archives are still as sharp as shattered glass.

The next thing I know, Mr. Moony starts rasping, *"Froggy went a-courtin' and he did ride, a-huh, a-huh."*

People stare at us. Froggy drops his notebook and scoops it up again. Normally, I would have croaked from mortification, but I'm instructing every muscle in my body, every cell, every emotion to be numb.

As soon as Mr. Moony is out of earshot, I turn to a

red-cheeked Froggy and say, "It can't be over because it never began."

Froggy takes a step backward. "So what was the last month, Virginia? Wasn't that anything to you?"

I want Froggy to go away. I need Froggy to go away. If he hangs around for another second, my self-inflicted anesthesia is going to wear off.

"Did you think that was something?" I ask curtly. "Because you sure didn't act like it when we were in school."

Froggy tweaks his nose a few times. "I thought that's how you wanted it. I mean, you always seemed to—"

I cut him off. "Well, *stop* thinking, okay?"

Then I grab my notebooks, slam my locker, and march away, leaving Froggy rubbing his nose and staring in my wake.

ⓖ ⓖ ⓖ ⓖ

I can barely pay attention in Global Studies. That's probably a good thing because Mr. Vandenhausler is knee-deep in the carnage in Katmandu. As soon as the bell rings, he announces that we're going to learn the process by which they inhumed the bodies of the Nepalese royal family. I'm not sure what "inhumed" means, but judging by the amount that his mustache is twitching, I don't *want* to know.

I keep replaying the interaction with Froggy in my head. I was just a total rotten bitch to him, which he didn't deserve in the slightest. But I couldn't help it. The words spewed out of my mouth. The idea of any guy, even Froggy, coming near me makes my skin crawl. It reminds me too much of my brother and that girl.

At lunchtime I grab a pack of Chips Ahoy! and snarf them on the way up to Ms. Crowley's office. I stop briefly in the second-floor bathroom to throw out the cookie wrapper. I'd never hang out in a stall again—too many bad memories from the Bri-girls episode—but I still come in for a quick pee or to remove food from my braces.

As soon as I walk in, I hear movement in a stall. I freeze when I notice that the person in the stall is wearing high-heeled magenta boots. Those are Brie Newhart's boots. She's the only girl in school who has them because they came all the way from Paris.

My first thought is: What is Brie doing up here? She always spends lunch period at the sophomore royalty table—flanked by cute boys, far from the trash bins, close to the exits. Besides, there's a bathroom right near the cafeteria.

My second thought is: Stop thinking thought #1 and get out of here! Brie Newhart is the last person on earth I feel like seeing.

I toss the wrapper in the trash and hurry out of the bathroom.

ⓖ ⓖ ⓖ ⓖ

"I've missed you these past few days," Ms. Crowley says. She's sitting at her desk, marking up an essay test with a red pen. "Were you braving the cafeteria?"

"Nope." I sink into the spare chair. "I was out sick."

"Are you feeling better?"

"I guess."

"Did being sick have anything to do with your diet?"

I think about the masses of sugar and chocolate and carbs I've consumed these past five days. I think about how I crept into the kitchen last night and tore the Food Police off the fridge.

"No." I sigh. "My diet is over."

"What happened?"

I gnaw at a hangnail on my thumb.

"Other stuff going on in your life?"

I nod.

"And eating helps you deal?"

I nod again.

"I've been there," Ms. Crowley says. "All I can say is, you'll figure it out eventually. It has to be the right time in your life. You don't want to diet to make someone else happy." Ms. Crowley is quiet for a moment. "Do you want to talk about it?"

"Talk about what?"

"What else is going on in your life."

I yank at the hangnail with my teeth, so hard it tears off a strip of skin. I wish I could tell Ms. Crowley about Byron being kicked out of college and how I'm so confused about everything. But I can't. Byron was a star student at Brewster, four-time MBS winner and overall legend. So who am I to drag his reputation through the mud? Besides, it's a Shreves family policy to not talk about our dirty laundry—in public and usually not even in private. It's sort of like if you don't discuss it, it didn't happen.

"No thanks." I grab a tissue from Ms. Crowley's desk and dab it on my thumbnail, which is dotted with blood. Then I repeat what Mom said the other morning. "It's all going to be fine."

Ms. Crowley looks unconvinced.

"Really," I say, flashing her my best imitation of a smile.

⊚ ⊚ ⊚ ⊚

SHANNON: I hate to think of you crying outside in the rain. How are you coping?

VIRGINIA: Meh.

SHANNON: Guess what?

VIRGINIA: ?

SHANNON: Liam just got royalties from the shoelace book, so he and Nina have decided to live it up. We're going to Seattle for Thanksgiving. Three nights. Two rooms at the Hotel Andra. One room for them and one for us.

VIRGINIA: ?????

SHANNON: Us = YOU AND ME!!!!!!!!!!!!!!!!!!!! My parents said your parents would only have to get the plane tix and they'd cover the rest. PLEASE SAY YES!

VIRGINIA: Don't you want to bring your new friends?

SHANNON: Don't be an idiot, Virginia. So . . . can you come?

VIRGINIA: Yes! Yes! Yes! Yes! Yes!

No."

"Mom, come on. Please. *Pleeeeeeeease.*"

"Absolutely not."

"Why not?" I sink to my knees and clasp my hands into the praying position. I'm not religious, but there are times in life when God comes in handy—taking off in airplanes, final exams, weekend jaunts to Seattle. "Is it because you don't like Shannon's parents? Because they're really nice if only you'd give them a—"

"Get up, Virginia. I don't know where you got that crazy notion about Liam Newman and Nina Malloy. They're perfectly decent people. I don't want you to go to Seattle because there's too much going on right now. Besides, I've already invited the Lowensteins and Nan Grossman, so I want to have as normal a Thanksgiving as possible."

I lean against the kitchen counter where Mom is mincing basil leaves. "What's the"—I make quotation marks with my fingers—" 'too much going on'? Are you talking about Byron?"

Mom sweeps the basil into a measuring cup and doesn't say a word.

I pluck up a leaf and pop it into my mouth. "What about what you said, about how we have to"—I curl my fingers into quotes again—" 'keep going about our lives, and pretty soon everything will be back to normal'? If that's the case, then why should Byron's ordeal affect what *I* do for Thanksgiving?"

Mom slams the knife onto the cutting board. "What's gotten into you? You're starting to sound like Anaïs."

"I'm sorry. I just don't think it's fair."

Mom slips on her reading glasses and squints at the cookbook. "Life isn't always fair."

"So why do I have to get the brunt of it?"

"You should meet some of my patients," Mom says. "Then you'd see teenagers who've had it hard. Not being able to go to Seattle for the weekend isn't getting the brunt of *anything*."

I grab another piece of basil, head into my bedroom, and slam the door. This leaf must not have been washed yet because I wind up with a mouthful of sand.

This only contributes to my week from hell. It's Saturday afternoon. Ever since Shannon's texts, I've been begging my parents to let me go to Seattle. I want to go so badly it hurts. Mom nixed it from the start—too much going on, need a normal Thanksgiving, blah, blah, blah. At first, Dad suggested using his frequent flier miles and arranging for a free flight, but

Mom vetoed that idea. Later that evening I heard them arguing, though I'm not sure whether it was about Seattle or all the other things going on. There's been a lot of tension around the apartment recently.

Over the past few days, details of Byron's date rape have been trickling out. No one has talked with me about it, but my parents and Byron have been having late-night conversations in the living room. I've developed supersonic listening skills, which work especially well when I'm sitting on the floor of my bedroom with the door cracked open ever so slightly.

On Tuesday night I was reminded that the girl's name is Annie Mills. She's a junior at Columbia. And she's from Saskatchewan. I knew that was somewhere in Canada, but when I was in Global Studies the next morning, I flipped to the page in my textbook with the world map. I was surprised to discover how far west it was, all the way above Montana.

On Wednesday night I overheard Byron admit to my parents that he slept with Annie on the night of the Bros and Hos party. Byron was explaining how Annie had reported the incident to the Office of Sexual Misconduct rather than going to the police. From there, it all happened quickly. They convened a panel of university people who heard the case and voted to suspend Byron for the rest of the semester. Dean Briggs seconded the decision. It sounds like Byron has thirty days to appeal. I was falling through my door by this point, straining to catch every word.

I heard Mom ask Byron about the likelihood of winning an

appeal. I couldn't make out a response, so I inched forward on my butt until I was in the hallway.

"I'm not sure," Byron said. "I drank way too much that night. We started fooling around and it went too far. How can I say whether it was consensual? I couldn't remember anything the next morning."

Neither Mom nor Dad said anything. I wished they would yell at him, tell him that, wasted or sober, he had no right to force himself onto Annie Mills.

But then Byron said, "Let's say I made a mistake. Let's say I messed up. Have I completely fucked up my entire life?"

I could hear little sobs. I slid to the end of the hallway and peeked into the living room. Byron was sitting on the couch with his head bowed. Mom and Dad were on either side of him.

"We'll figure it out." Mom rested her hand on his shoulder and then added, "We're in this together."

Dad tousled Byron's hair. "That's right, Son."

I rubbed my knuckles against my braces until I shredded the skin.

On Thursday my parents took Byron to their lawyer so they could get a professional opinion on whether he should appeal. I didn't find this out until my nightly snooping session. I was crouched at the end of the hallway when I heard Dad say that he agreed with the lawyer, that an appeal was probably not the best idea.

"It could just open you up to a stronger penalty," Dad said.

"Or provoke the girl to take it up with the police department," Mom added.

I picked at a small scab on my knuckle where my braces had torn the skin the night before. I wanted to chime in that "the girl" has a name, and it's Annie Mills.

By Friday Byron descended into a depression. He was just getting out of bed when I got home from school. I half waved into the kitchen, where he was slurping down a bowl of Cheerios, but I didn't say anything and neither did he. That's how it's been since he moved back. To be honest, I don't know what to say to him. *It'll be all right?* Not for Annie Mills. *I'm sorry?* For Annie Mills, but not for you. *How's the weather?* It sucks—cold, gray, and drizzly.

The skies finally cleared last night, but even so, Mom and Dad bailed on their golf tournament. The Yankees and Seattle are three and two in the playoffs. This afternoon's game could determine who's going to the World Series. Dad decided to take Byron as an attempt to get him out of his funk. When I learned that, I was stunned. That's the game *I* had originally been invited to. Besides, my parents have been anticipating their golf tournament for months.

But what really blew me away was what happened with Mom. As soon as Dad and Byron left for Yankee Stadium, she dashed outside and returned an hour later with bags of groceries and a baguette wrapped in white paper.

I watched as Mom washed her hands and rolled back her sleeves. Then she unpacked fresh mozzarella, a bunch of basil, tomatoes, garlic, and a slab of meat. I was completely speechless. Mom denounced cooking when Anaïs left for college five years ago.

"I've paid my motherly dues," she'd said as soon as they returned from dropping my sister off at Dartmouth. "We'll let the delivery guy pick up the slack."

Over the past five years, Mom has only cooked on special occasions, like Thanksgiving or Christmas or if we're having company over.

But I can't for the life of me figure out how this constitutes a special occasion.

ⓖ ⓖ ⓖ ⓖ

"Phyl, you've outdone yourself!" Dad exclaims. He drains his first glass of red wine and pours himself a second.

I eye Dad taking a long swig. Ever since Byron's been home, Dad's been drinking more than usual.

"I thought a home-cooked meal would cheer everyone up," Mom says. "But it doesn't look like you need it."

Dad and Byron were in high spirits when they arrived home an hour ago. I boycotted watching the game for obvious reasons, but when they came through the door singing "New York, New York," I knew we were headed to the World Series.

"To the Yankees." Dad raises his wineglass.

Mom and Byron clink with him.

I survey the candlelit table. Mom made veal Parmesan, linguine, and a mixed green salad. I only took a sliver of meat and a heap of salad, no bread or pasta. I still act like I'm on a diet when I'm around my parents, which is such a joke because I've been gaining weight again. I can only fit into my Fat Pants, the ones I save in the back of my closet for when I'm really bloated.

We're just finishing dinner when Dad says, "Guess what Byron and I were discussing this afternoon?"

"What's that?" Mom picks at the lettuce on her plate. In the past week, Mom has been munching a lot—pretzels and rice cakes and even some of Dad's olive oil potato chips. Last night Dad joked about Mom plumping up for winter. When he said that, Mom spit her mouthful of chips into a paper towel. Now I guess she's back to her usual regimen of lettuce and water.

Byron wipes his mouth with his napkin. "I'd have to double-check with the lawyer about the legal implications, but I'm thinking about going to Paris until the beginning of next semester."

"When would you leave?" Mom asks.

"As soon as possible. In the next two or three weeks."

I do some quick calculations. That would have Byron out of town by mid-November. I set down my fork. "But what about—"

"I think it's a fine idea," Mom says, cutting me off. "You've always wanted to spend time in Paris, and you could use the change of scenery."

I clench my fists. "But what about Thanksgiv—"

"Virginia," Mom says. "We're talking about completely different circumstances."

"But—"

Dad jumps in. "Hey, Ginny, maybe I could take you on that

shopping spree we were talking about, get you something nice to wear for Thanksgiving dinner."

I shrug. "I don't know."

Dad has this lopsided grin on his face. I think he's had too much to drink tonight. "Have you gotten any closer to the body goal that Mom was talking about?"

I stare at my empty plate.

"I'm going to take off," Byron says, pushing back his chair.

As Byron heads toward his bedroom, Mom raises her eyebrows at me. "I hope you're still taking this diet seriously."

Dad rises from his chair, using the edge of the table to steady himself.

"Make us proud," he says.

Mom gathers together some dishes. "Make *yourself* proud."

They head into the kitchen. I hear water running. I stare at the flames flickering atop the candlesticks.

How is it that Byron is allowed to go to Paris for Thanksgiving and I can't visit my best friend who I haven't seen in over three months? He gets kicked out of college for date rape and still gets a Yankees playoff game *and* a change of scenery? All I've done is gain a few pounds, and suddenly I'm the one being penalized.

I feel bile stinging my throat, anger seeping through my body. Before I know it, I'm holding my hand over a candle. It's warm on my fingertip. I lower it until my pointer is touching the flame. I can smell the stench of burning flesh.

I hear Mom approaching the dining room so I pull my hand away.

"What's that smell?" she asks. "Does something smell funny in here?"

I don't answer. She leans over and blows out the candles.

As Mom heads into the kitchen again, I rock back and forth, cradling my hand in my lap. My finger is searing in pain. But at least the pain is concentrated in one spot rather than dominating my entire body.

18

I'm having a hard time writing to Anaïs. Her twenty-third birthday is on November seventeenth. Mom is putting together a care package to send to Africa, so I want to include a letter. It'll take a few weeks to arrive in Ouagadougou, the capital of Burkina Faso, and several more days to make it to her rural hut.

There are two reasons why writing this letter is impossible. For one, my finger is burned pretty badly. It's been more than a week, and it's still raw and oozing. It hurts all the time, especially when I'm on the computer. That's why I'm handwriting Anaïs's letter. For the past hour, I've been sitting on my bed with a stack of stationery on my lap. I've churned out four attempts, but I keep crumpling them up and tossing them onto my rug.

Which ties into the second reason why this is so difficult. When I told Mom I wanted to include a letter in my sister's package, she asked that I not mention Byron being home from Columbia.

"Keep it upbeat," Mom said. "Anaïs is witnessing hardship on a daily basis. The last thing she needs is something else to worry about."

I was tempted to say, *So you want me to lie?*, but I kept my mouth shut.

I'm already on Mom's bad side because I've been begging on a daily basis to go to Seattle. It's more than three weeks away, so I'm still clinging to a shred of hope that she'll change her mind.

But that doesn't make it any easier to write to Anaïs. In my first four attempts, I embellished on my life so lavishly I could have won a Pulitzer Prize for fiction. They all made me queasy. Recently, I've been finding it harder to pretend that everything is A-okay.

I begin attempt #5.

Dear Anaïs,

Here's a juicy piece of news! I had a fling this fall. His name is Froggy Welsh the Fourth. He's also a sophomore at Brewster, and he's in my French class. At first, I didn't think he was that cute, but the more I got to know him, the more he grew on me. Has that ever happened to you? Well, it doesn't matter because those days are over. Byron date-raped a girl at Columbia, and now I'm repulsed by sex or anything leading up to it. I told Froggy to get lost, and now he won't even look in my direction or talk to me . . .

I fling the paper onto my rug and embark on my sixth attempt.

Dear Anaïs,

Tomorrow is Halloween! I've decided to go as the woman who sings the arias at the Metropolitan Opera. Yes, the FAT LADY. I was on a diet, but those days are over. I'm the heaviest I've ever been. Even when I'm wearing my Fat Pants, I have to keep the top button undone. I've been pigging out so much, ever since Byron got kicked out of Columbia for date rape and . . .

Another crumpled letter on the floor. I take a deep breath and flex my hand a few times.

Dear Anaïs,

The Yankees won the World Series!! Normally, I'd be freaking out, but those days are over. My heart wasn't in it this year. I watched a few of the games with Dad and Byron, but every so often I'd glance at our brother and I'd be filled with intense anger. How can a date rapist casually munch a handful of pretzels and sip a beer when a girl's life has been destroyed?

I crumple attempt #7.

Then I grab my jacket and walk over to Cardeology. I check out a dozen cards before finding the right one. It's got two smiling girls on the front, one with blond hair and one with brown hair. They're embracing each other amid a field of wildflowers. On the inside it says *Hugs and kisses on your birthday.*

When I get home, I write:

Dear Anaïs,
    I hope all is well in Burkina Faso.
    I miss you.
    Love,
    Gin

6 6 6 6

I'm sitting in the auditorium waiting for the annual awards ceremony to begin. They hold it on Halloween every year. It was originally intended to be a costume contest, but it's evolved into an occasion to spotlight Brewster's best and brightest. This is the day they give out plaques to all the Model Brewster Students.

Woo-hoo. I'm sure I'm totally in the running.

We had to report to our last-period class before heading downstairs. Most likely Brewster's ploy to get us to climb more stairs. I'm sitting next to Alyssa Wu, the girl who had to sing "Frère Jacques" in French that time. She's in all my classes. She's nice but definitely a strange bird. She's got long hair, almost down to her butt, and tiny bangs snipped across the top of her forehead. And she's always knitting, even at her desk.

I was relieved to get out of math today. Math is my second favorite subject, after language arts, but my mind has been wandering a lot recently. It's actually to the point where my grades are starting to slip.

I scan the crowd. The right quadrant of the auditorium is the popular section. Brie Newhart is dressed as a queen, complete with a tiara and a velvet cloak lined with faux fur. Brinna and Briar are wearing skintight cat suits and headbands with pointy ears. They must see Halloween as a prime opportunity to flaunt their own personal skeletons.

The front row is all faculty and staff. Mademoiselle Kiefer is attempting to flirt with the sexy male physics teacher. The only problem is, he's ogling Teri the Tiny Gym Teacher, who's dressed as a high school cheerleader. I'm trying to determine whether Teri is shaking her pompoms at the physics teacher when I spot Froggy.

He's seated to my left, surrounded by a group of his friends. That's when I notice that Froggy is sitting next to a ninth grader named Sarah. She has a ski-jump nose and a slight overbite, giving her an overall rabbity look. I tighten my fists, even though it causes extreme pain to my burned finger. I know I have no claim to Froggy. We're not even talking anymore. But it's not like I want to see him with another girl.

"Byron Shreves is your older brother, isn't he?"

I turn to face Alyssa. She's knitting an orange-and-brown square.

"Yeah," I say tentatively.

"Didn't he win an MBS award every year he was here?"

I nod.

"That's impressive," Alyssa says. "I've heard he's a great guy."

"Who said that?"

"Lots of people."

"Don't believe everything you hear."

Alyssa misses a stitch.

The principal strides onto the stage. She's wearing a wizard's cape, half-moon glasses, and a silver beard. She's dressed as Dumbledore, the headmaster in the Harry Potter books. I'm relieved when she taps her wand on the microphone to signal the beginning of the awards ceremony.

6 6 6 6

The crosstown bus doesn't come for fifteen minutes, so I decide to walk home across Central Park. The sky is bright blue, and there's a chilly wind slicing down the avenues. I hug my arms across my chest and keep a fast pace.

Of course, Brie Newhart won an MBS award. She got it for being an overall positive addition to our school. She delivered such a tear-filled acceptance speech—half of which was in French—you'd think she'd won an Oscar. Mademoiselle Kiefer actually gave her a standing ovation.

They also presented MBS awards for athletics and community service. Every other school does awards in the spring, but Brewster has this theory that if you highlight exemplary talent at the beginning of the year, it will raise the bar for the rest of us slackers. But as I slouched in my chair and listened to how Hannah Hajost built houses for Habitat for Humanity and Kyle

Bartz was the Most Valuable Runner on the varsity cross-country team, it only made me want to curl up and take a nap.

Just when I thought the torture was over, the principal announced that she had some exciting news.

"One of our sophomores has just won an extremely competitive graphic design award," the principal said. "Over seven hundred high-schoolers submitted designs and the prize went to . . ."

I held my breath, distinctly remembering that day back in September when Froggy told me about a design competition he had entered.

"Froggy Welsh the Fourth!" she exclaimed, flapping the sides of her cape like wings. "Please join me onstage for a special MBS award, young man."

Everyone applauded, but Froggy was stuck to his chair. After a few moments, Sarah tugged him to his feet and shoved him down the aisle. The principal shook Froggy's hand and told him to continue making Brewster proud.

I enter Central Park near the Met. The air is freezing, but I'm pretty wound up, so it feels good to be walking home.

Making people proud. Is that what life is about? That's what Mom and Dad told me a few weeks ago. Make them proud. Make myself proud. But I've spent my whole life trying to win their praise, and where has it gotten me?

As I walk along the Great Lawn, I pass the bench where I sat the day I ditched school, the day after I found out about Byron.

Take my brother. He gets kicked out of college for date rape and, as Alyssa Wu pointed out, he still has a great reputation. Or Brie. She's a total ice queen, and she still wins an MBS award.

I'm walking faster by this point, my heels clomping against the path. What if for one second I didn't care what people thought of me? What if I weren't so eager to please Mom and Dad? What if I didn't always try to blend in, go with the flow, be the good, obedient girl?

What on earth would I do?

As I reach Central Park West, the answer hits me as certain as the gusts slapping my cheeks.

I'd visit Shannon Iris Malloy-Newman.

I'd go to Seattle for Thanksgiving.

ⓖ ⓖ ⓖ ⓖ

There's a Liberty Travel a few blocks from our building. I've walked by it a million times, but I've never gone inside. As I step through the door, I'm greeted by a bored-looking guy digging through a bowl of Halloween goodies.

"Hey," he says as he nibbles off the top of a candy corn.

I glance at the cardboard witches, the plastic jack-o'-lanterns, the cotton spiderwebs obscuring posters of Jamaican beaches.

"How much would a plane ticket to Seattle cost?" I ask.

He decapitates another candy corn. "That all depends on when you want to go."

I rub my hands together. "Over Thanksgiving."

He wheels his chair around so he's facing the computer. I

can't believe I'm here. As he begins typing, I'm tempted to bolt back onto Broadway.

"It'll be a minute." The man pushes the bowl of candies in my direction. "Why don't you take a seat?"

I pop a sugary pumpkin in my mouth and settle down across from him. I have to clutch the sides of my chair to keep from running away.

"Were you thinking Wednesday to Sunday?" he asks.

That would mean missing a day of school. I'd better not give my parents any extra reasons to say no. "Is there anything that leaves on Thanksgiving Day?"

"I've got a flight leaving LaGuardia at eight forty-two on Thursday morning. It transfers in Denver, which will get you to the Sea-Tac Airport at two thirty-five that afternoon."

I scoop up a few candy corns and mash them between my molars. "How much is it?"

"With all applicable taxes, it comes to four hundred and fifty-eight dollars."

I'm quiet for a second. That's nearly half my savings account.

"Do you want me to ticket it?" he asks.

"Do I need a credit card?"

He yawns and rattles off all the ways I can buy plane tickets: credit card, debit card, cash, money order.

"Can you give me a few minutes?" I ask.

"Sure," he says. "But I'd recommend moving quickly because there are only four seats left on that flight. It's a holiday weekend."

I spell out my name for him and then jog to a nearby Citibank. If I'm going to do this, I'd better do it now. And cash feels like the best way to go, the most certain. I enter my PIN number and take out five hundred dollars. My hands are trembling as I count out the crisp twenty-dollar bills.

This is my money, I keep telling myself. *Mom and Dad have always said I can do whatever I want with it.*

Twenty minutes later I exit Liberty Travel with the plane ticket in my hand. As I walk home, I want to tell every person I pass, *I'm going to Seattle in a few weeks! I'm spending Thanksgiving with my best friend! Can you believe it? Can you* fucking *believe it?*

I know nothing major has changed. Brie Newhart is still an MBS. Byron will still be moping around the apartment, resisting my parents' attempts to cheer him up. I'm still wearing Fat Pants with the button open and two inches unzipped.

No, nothing major has changed.

But everything feels different.

19

I still haven't told my parents about Seattle. Today is November seventeenth. Six days before Thanksgiving. Six days before I'm scheduled to board a westbound flight. I have to tell them soon. I've *almost* done it about fifty times these past few weeks, but just as I'm readying the muscles in my mouth, I wimp out. I'm afraid they'll simply say, *No, absolutely not, and—by the way—you're grounded for life.* Until I devise a more foolproof plan, I've kept it a secret.

The plane ticket is stashed in my cedar box in my top dresser drawer. Every morning I take it out and hold it in my hands. I do the same thing as soon as I get home from school and right before I go to bed. I doubt I'll be allowed to actually use the ticket, but it makes me feel better to know that for one brief instant, I was bold and courageous.

It was a mistake to waste my money on it. An *impulse buy.* That's what Mom called it the time she purchased an eight-hundred-dollar dress from Saks. But she went back the next day and returned it. I bought a nonrefundable ticket, so I'll just have to suck up the loss.

It's not like I've completely given up yet. I'm planning to tell my parents tonight. Everyone will be in a good mood because it's Anaïs's twenty-third birthday. Dad is bringing home dessert, and we're going to celebrate in her honor.

Around 9 p.m. Dad lifts a carrot cake out of its box and sets it in the middle of the table. I poke twenty-three candles into the thick white frosting.

"Byron?" Mom shouts from the kitchen, where she's scavenging the freezer for the nonfat sorbet that she's going to have instead of cake.

No answer from my brother.

I add a twenty-fourth candle for good luck.

"Byron?" Mom sets some mango sorbet on the table. "Don't you want to come to Anaïs's birthday party?"

Byron peeks his head out of his bedroom. "I'm not up for it tonight. Go ahead without me."

No one says a word, but it dampens the mood. We light the candles and sing "Happy Birthday," but the song trails off somewhere in the middle.

That exemplifies the gloom that's pervaded our apartment these past few weeks, ever since Byron got depressed again. He mopes around the apartment all day. I don't even think he's lifting weights anymore. It all started when my parents' lawyer recommended that Byron not go to Paris. Something about how he should give Columbia the impression that he's remorseful about this incident rather than viewing it as vacation time.

"I don't see why that's Columbia's business," Byron said to Mom as soon as he got off the phone with the lawyer. "I do feel remorseful. Of course I wish none of this was happening. I just don't see why it matters what continent I'm on."

I was sitting at my computer, searching for information on how to get your parents to agree to something they've already nixed. I was tempted to call into the other room, *I doubt ANNIE MILLS gets to decide on which continent she nurses her wounded soul.*

Mom murmured something to Byron that I couldn't hear followed by a heavy sigh. She's been sighing a lot recently and chain-chewing Tic Tacs, which is what she does when she's stressed.

I think Byron is also depressed because the reality of his situation is finally hitting him. One day he was Big Man on Campus, and now his life has come to a screeching halt. Usually when my brother is home, his phone is ringing and chiming and vibrating—friends inviting him to parties, girls asking what he's up to, guys organizing football in the park. But now, hardly anyone calls or texts him. Mom says it's because they're all at school, wrapped up in their own respective lives. But I think they've gotten wind of what Byron did to Annie Mills, and they're as repulsed as I am about it.

As I lick the cream cheese frosting off my fork, I review my strategy for telling my parents about Seattle. I've decided to take the casual route, so I don't raise their defenses. As in, *Hey, guys, I'm going to Seattle next Thursday morning*, the way Dad announces last-minute business trips.

Mom must have read my mind. She spoons some sorbet into her mouth and says, "Well, the upside of Byron not going to Paris is that the four of us will be in town for Thanksgiving. Too bad Anaïs can't be here, too."

I choke on my frosting.

"Are you okay?" Dad asks.

I nod as I chug a glass of milk.

Mom starts rambling on about how she's determined to make homemade cranberry jelly and smooth mashed potatoes.

I help myself to another slice of carrot cake.

SHANNON: Why don't you tell your parents that you bought a one-way ticket to Seattle and you're not coming home? That way, when they discover that you're flying round trip, they'll be so relieved they'll allow you to come.

VIRGINIA: If I tell my parents I'm going to Seattle, I may as well have bought a one-way ticket because there won't be a home waiting for me after the weekend.

SHANNON: Liam and Nina have offered to call your parents and reassure them that the plan is legit.

VIRGINIA: Please thank Liam and Nina for their offer, but I'm afraid there's nothing anyone can do to convince them.

VIRGINIA: Maybe you should invite Sabrina to Seattle.

20

On Monday morning, as I reach into my cedar box for the plane ticket, I pull out the pictures that Byron and I took in a photo booth at Grand Central Station a few years ago. It's hard to look at us, our arms slung around each other as we crossed our eyes and flashed our teeth. We'd just come back from spending the night with my parents out in Connecticut. Byron had to return to the city for an early rugby practice the following morning, so I offered to take the train with him and keep him company.

I tuck the photos back in the box and pull out the plane ticket.

Ms. Crowley is the only person in New York City who knows about Seattle. I broke down and told her after she grilled me for five lunch periods in a row. She kept commenting that I had a secret smile on my face.

"Is there a new guy in your life?" she asked last Tuesday.

"Not a new one or an old one," I said.

Ms. Crowley nodded sympathetically. I'd recently told her about Froggy. Not the graphic details, but just that there used to be something going on and now he'll barely look in my direction.

"Have you taken up Wicca?" Ms. Crowley asked on Wednesday. "Do you know where rainbows come from? Are you getting a ladybug tattooed onto your ankle?"

I laughed. "No, no, and *definitely* no."

On Thursday, when I finally told her that I secretly bought a plane ticket to Seattle, she said, "You are a brave woman."

"Brave enough to throw away five hundred bucks."

"Don't be so quick to doubt yourself, Virginia."

"Whatever," I said.

When I go to Ms. Crowley's office today, there's a Post-it stuck to her computer monitor:

V—
Did you tell them over the weekend?
I'm in a meeting. See you tomorrow!
E.C.

I reach into my backpack and pull out my math notebook and a poppy-seed bagel with cream cheese. I've just conquered the congruent triangle when the bell rings. I head into the second-floor bathroom to pick the poppy seeds out of my braces.

As I open the door, I hear puking noises. The toilet flushes, and then there's silence. I'm about to ask if the person is okay when I peek under the stall.

I suck in my breath.

High-heeled magenta boots all the way from Paris.

This is the fourth time I've seen Brie Newhart's boots in this bathroom in the past few weeks. Until now, I'd never really thought about it.

I stand there for a second, adding two and two together. *Second-floor bathroom. Far from the cafeteria. Puking. Skeletally skinny. Feeling faint in gym class.*

Could Brie have an eating disorder?

I mean, she and the other Bri-girls are always bragging about dieting and exercise, but that's one thing. Throwing up your tater tots on a daily basis is another.

I hurry back into the hallway. Maybe I'm blowing the whole thing out of proportion.

Then again, she *did* say that if she looked like me, she'd kill herself.

And I know from Mom that if an eating disorder gets out of control, that's exactly what can happen.

ⓖ ⓖ ⓖ ⓖ

I'm still thinking about Brie on the bus ride home from school. I can't get those vomiting sounds out of my head. I know I have every reason to hate her—she's gorgeous, she's popular, she treats me like a pigeon dropping. But I actually feel sorry for her. I mean, we're on opposite ends of the weight spectrum, but

I know what it's like to hate your body so much that you want to hurt it.

When I come through the front door, I hear the TV blaring. I glance into the living room. Byron is conked out on the couch, his hair oily, his face coated in stubble. He has a half-eaten bag of Oreos nestled into the crook of his arm. I get a knot in my stomach when I remember how we used to split open Oreos, fill them with ice cream, and make cookie sandwiches.

These are the kinds of things I can only think about when Byron is sleeping. When he's awake, all I want to do is shake him by the shoulders and ask how he could have treated a girl so badly.

⟟ ⟟ ⟟ ⟟

An hour later I'm sitting on my bed, attempting to concentrate on manganese and titanium and unununium. My chemistry textbook is propped open in my lap. We have a huge test tomorrow on transition elements on the periodic table, but I keep spacing out, wondering if Brie is bulimic, how I'll tell my parents about Seattle, whether Annie Mills celebrates Thanksgiving even though she's Canadian, who in their right mind would name a metal "unununium."

There's a knock on my door.

"Come in," I shout.

Mom walks in. She's wearing a tailored black pantsuit. And she must have gotten her hair touched up today because it's blonder than usual.

"How was school?" she asks.

"Fine."

"Anything interesting happen?"

"Not really."

"Do you have a lot of homework?"

"Some," I say. "Why?"

"I'm getting interviewed at the Ninety-Second Street Y tonight. Would you like to come along?"

"What's it about?" I ask.

"They're doing a special series about raising healthy teenagers, so it's mainly geared for parents, how to handle various problems that arise," Mom says. "I thought it would be nice to bring one of mine along."

I'm tempted to ask whether she means one of her teenagers or one of her problems. "What about Byron?"

"What about him?" Mom asks. "Can you be ready in ten minutes? We'll grab sushi on the way."

"Okay," I say, pushing aside *The Study of Matter*.

Just before Mom leaves my room, she glances at me. "Why don't you change into a dressier outfit? Some press will be there and maybe even a literary agent."

"Okay."

"How about that beige sweater from Saks?"

"Okay," I say again.

As soon as Mom is gone, I head over to my closet and pull out the beige sweater. Mom is always buying me clothes from the plus-size department at Saks. The styles aren't trendy or cool.

In fact, sometimes it seems like I have the wardrobe of a fifty-two-year-old woman.

As I yank off my sweatshirt, I think about how I don't care that Mom probably would have brought Byron to the lecture if he weren't so depressed. And I don't care that tomorrow's test on the periodic table will count for 20 percent of my chemistry grade.

I'm just happy to finally get invited to one of Mom's events.

6 6 6 6

Mom is going to be interviewed by a woman named Joy Lassiter. She introduces herself to me as a television journalist. She has the whitest teeth I've seen in my entire life, like a row of peppermint Chiclets.

As forty or fifty people file into the small auditorium, a cluster of us mill around near the stage. Mom is talking to a woman who introduced herself as a literary agent and is wearing black leather pants and a black leather jacket. Mom's face lit up when she heard that. She's always saying how she wants to write a book about being an adolescent psychologist.

A guy with a bushy ponytail sets up a video camera.

Joy Lassiter squeezes my shoulder and exclaims, "Aren't you a lucky girl!"

"Lucky?" I ask.

"To have Dr. Shreves as your mother. She really understands what it's like to be a teenager."

Mom? Mom refuses to even *talk* about her own adolescence.

And as far as *my* teen years, I wouldn't exactly say Mom understands what I go through every day. But rather than telling Joy Lassiter that, I mumble, "Thanks."

As the interview begins, I settle into a chair near the front. It's impressive to see Mom in the spotlight. Joy Lassiter asks about how she became a therapist and then highlights her career accomplishments. The audience is enraptured; some people are even taking notes.

When Joy starts addressing the nitty-gritty of relating to teenagers, I shift uncomfortably in my chair and attempt to follow the conversation.

> **JOY LASSITER:** What are the most important things for parents of teenagers to keep in mind?
>
> **MOM:** Above all, it's important to have open and honest communication. You can't talk enough with your teenagers—even if it's hard for you, even if the subjects are controversial or taboo.
>
> **JOY LASSITER:** How would you recommend doing all this open and honest talking?
>
> **MOM:** What I always tell parents of my patients is that they must remember that their children aren't children anymore. They're complex, independent individuals with needs and desires that must be acknowledged and respected.

I can't believe this. First of all, there's very little open and honest communication going on in our family. No one even says the phrase "date rape." We just refer to it as "the ordeal." And if Mom viewed me as an independent individual whose desires must be acknowledged and respected, I'd totally be on a plane to Seattle in three days.

I feel like I can hardly breathe. I suck in some stale air, but all that makes me do is cough.

I need to get out of here.

I grab my jacket and tiptoe toward the exit. I trip over the literary agent's black leather satchel on my way, but I don't stop moving until I've hit the lobby.

It's chilly outside, and the air smells like snow. I stand on the front steps, watching my breath emerge in cloudy puffs. My braces are icy against my gums, so I run my tongue over the brackets.

I walk down to East Eighty-Sixth Street, where there's a bustling strip of movie theaters and restaurants. As I weave through the throngs of people, I think about how hypocritical Mom sounded back there, acting like she's this cool parent who partakes in cozy gabfests with her children.

A few summers ago, Anaïs and Mom got in a big argument. Anaïs called Mom Cleopatra, Queen of the Nile. I didn't understand why that made Mom so furious until I realized that Anaïs actually said Queen of *Denial*. As Mom stormed into her bedroom, Anaïs shouted after her that she always sweeps everything under the carpet and never deals with what's really going on.

When I think about it now, it makes sense. Like how Mom's been acting like life is normal even though Byron got kicked out of college for date rape. Or how she never talks about her childhood. Or how she always finds ways to skirt around the fact that I'm heavy. It's like Mom wants our family to be perfect even when we're not.

I've always had so much respect for Mom—how she looks so together, how she has a successful career. But maybe I haven't been seeing her for who she actually is. That is, the Cleopatra part.

I don't think I've been seeing Byron for who he is either. I've spent fifteen years considering him the ideal human being. But when I stop to think about it, I remember a lot of less-than-ideal things, too. Not the date rape, but smaller incidents, things he did to me. Like when I surprised him with Rice Krispie treats up at Columbia and he acted so cold. Or how he's always making little remarks about my body. Or that day we took those photos at Grand Central Station. I'd ridden back from Connecticut with him so we could hang out that evening. But as soon as we arrived at the apartment, he got a text from a rugby buddy inviting him to a party. Before I could say *dissed and dismissed,* Byron was in the shower and out the door.

There's a guy on the corner selling hot drinks from a cart. As I reach into my pocket for some bills, I remember something Ms. Crowley told me last week.

Don't be so quick to doubt yourself, Virginia.

As I sip my hot chocolate and walk uptown again, I finally understand what she meant when she said that.

🌀 🌀 🌀 🌀

Mom is standing on the front steps of the Ninety-Second Street Y. She glances around to make sure no one is watching and then hisses, "Where the *fuck* were you?"

I take a few steps backward. Mom only swears when she's really upset.

"I needed some fresh air," I say.

"My interview ended twenty minutes ago. I've been standing here in the freezing cold, calling and texting you." Mom's face is pinched, and she's jabbing her finger in my direction. "Also, Joy announced that my teenage daughter was in the audience and asked you to stand up. She kept calling out your name. Everyone was looking around. A reporter joked about how teenagers are so unpredictable. It was mortifying."

"I'm sorry. My phone was on silent. I didn't know she was going to do that. I just—"

Mom flags down a passing cab. As it pulls up to the curb, she slides to the far end of the back seat. I get in after her and stay over on my side.

As the cab takes off, Mom starts rambling on about how she's worked so hard to get to this place in her career and how it's important to present the image of a solid family and why did I think I was entitled to chase after whatever whim came over me, especially when I should be honored that she invited me to such an important event?

I watch the traffic lights changing, the cars darting in front of each other. It's not like I'm about to tell Mom that I've realized she's a Queen of Denial who doesn't practice what she preaches.

"Don't you have anything to say?" Mom asks.

I count the different license plates within view. Three New Yorks. One New Jersey. Another New Jersey and a Connecticut.

"Say something, *dammit.*"

"Okay," I finally say. "I'm going to Seattle for Thanksgiving."

"Excuse me?"

I turn to face Mom. "I'm going to Seattle for Thanksgiving."

"That's three days away! There's no way you could get a ticket at this point, even if Dad and I gave you permission."

"I already have one," I say.

"Excuse me?"

"I bought a ticket. I'm leaving on Thursday morning. I'll get back on Sunday evening. I won't miss any school. And I'll pay for the cab fare to and from the airport, so you don't have to worry about that."

"I don't give a damn about the cab fare *or* the plane ticket! You are *not* going to Seattle."

"Yes, I am."

Mom lowers her voice. "Virginia, I forbid you to go."

I take a deep breath, count to five, and say, "I'm going."

21

I'm on the plane to Seattle.

I can't believe this.

The pilot just announced that we might encounter turbulence. I double-check my seat belt. The flight attendant collects our trays. Today is Thanksgiving, so they served dry wedges of turkey and powdery mashed potatoes. It seemed like a strange menu, since everyone will be eating the same meal tonight, but they could have given me raw Brussels sprouts and I'd still be elated.

I slept for the first leg of the trip, from New York to Denver, but I'm wide awake during this stretch. At first, I tried memorizing words from my SAT Hot 100 list. We have a vocabulary test the day after break. But after reading the definition of "pedantic" twelve times, I decided that I'm too wired to think about SAT words, so I put away my homework and stared out my bubble window. I watched as the plane glided over jagged expanses of the Rocky Mountains. Now we're flying over a patchwork quilt of green-and-brown earth, roads that stretch for hundreds of miles. I think it's Idaho or maybe Oregon.

The Rocky Mountains. Idaho. Oregon.

I really can't believe this.

I was convinced that I wouldn't be allowed to come. On Monday night, after I dropped the news, Mom got on the phone with the airlines, only to confirm that my ticket was nonrefundable. Then she left a frantic message on Dad's phone. And then she called Shannon's parents in Walla Walla. Liam and Nina must have been reassuring because Mom seemed calmer by the time she hung up.

"Well?" I asked. I was lingering in the hallway, ready to dash into my bedroom in the event of a major eruption.

"Well, *nothing.*" Mom headed into her room without saying good night.

I slept fitfully all night. The anticipation was gnawing at me. But when I woke up on Tuesday morning, Mom had already left for yoga. As I was pouring myself a bowl of cereal, Dad entered the kitchen.

"Mom and I talked last night," he said. "We've decided to let you go to Seattle."

"Daddy!" I flung my arms around his waist.

"Mom wanted me to tell you that she's still not happy with the way you handled this."

Dad was trying to look stern, but I could tell he was suppressing a grin.

Dad has been coming through a lot recently. He insisted on getting the car out of the garage to drive me to the airport this morning. He invited Mom, but she said she was too busy preparing Thanksgiving dinner. I think the real reason is that she's angry I'm going to Seattle. Mom likes to call the shots in the Shreves household, after all.

Dad and I didn't say much on the drive out of Manhattan. He listened to the weather forecast on 1010 WINS. I watched the shadowy city streets come to life. But as we hit the RFK Bridge, Dad reached into his wallet and pulled out some twenties.

"Have fun in Seattle," he said, handing the bills to me.

I stuffed them in my backpack. "Thanks."

Dad turned down the volume on the radio. "I know it's been a difficult last few months, with everything going on with your brother. I just hope you've been okay."

I fiddled with the zipper on my bag.

Dad continued. "Our family doesn't talk about things very much. It's hard for Mom." He paused. "It's hard for all of us."

I thought about Dad's recent drinking. He's curbed it a lot in the past few weeks, but this whole ordeal must be taking a toll on him, too.

"Dad?"

"Yeah?"

"Do you think maybe we could . . ." I paused for a second, trying to figure out how to put it. "Do you think maybe you and I could try to communicate a little more about everything going on?"

Dad was quiet for a long time. I was about to say *forget it* when he turned to me. There were tears in the corners of his eyes.

"I would love to, Ginny," Dad said quietly. "Let's make a deal, you and me, to try to talk about things more."

I squeezed Dad's shoulder. He reached up and rested his hand on top of mine.

⑥ ⑥ ⑥ ⑥

The pilot announces that we're beginning our descent into Seattle. We'll be landing at the Sea-Tac Airport in approximately thirty minutes. My ears are clogging up, so I yawn a few times to clear them. I tap my fingers up and down the tray table. My finger doesn't hurt anymore, but there's still a splotch on the tip that'll probably become a scar. I unwrap a piece of gum and grind it between my teeth. I cross and uncross my legs. I continue tapping my fingers along the armrest.

I guess I'm anxious about seeing Shannon. I'm nervous that Walla Walla has changed her, that her new friends have made her snobby or sophisticated. I mean, Shannon is the most grounded person in the world, but you never know what three thousand miles will do to someone.

The first thing I notice when I enter the airport is a small figure with long hair as bright as a new penny. She's waving a big round object over her head. It looks like a softball, but as I get closer I realize it's an onion. Shannon sprints toward me, places it in my hands, and squeals, "Welcome to Washington State!"

We wrap our arms around each other and start crying.

"Did-did-did you know that some people eat a Walla Walla onion like an apple?" Shannon asks.

As I hug Shannon, my anxiety evaporates. She must have been nervous too because she hardly ever stutters around me. Her hair has gotten longer and she may have gained a few freckles, but this is definitely the Shannon Iris Malloy-Newman that I know and love.

"When do we get a go at Virginia?" Nina asks.

I daub my eyes. Liam is wearing a T-shirt that says Feminist Chicks Dig Me. Nina is wearing a baseball cap that says Visualize Whirled Peas. I have to laugh. Liam Newman and Nina Malloy are the complete opposite of my parents.

We hug and kiss and cry some more. Liam grabs my suitcase and the four of us walk, arm in arm, to the short-term parking lot. As Nina pulls onto the highway, Shannon explains that if it weren't so drizzly, we'd be able to see Mount Rainier, the nearly fifteen-thousand-foot mountain southeast of Seattle.

I clutch my onion and look out the back window. *Holy shit.* I'm in the Pacific Northwest—land of mountains rather than skyscrapers. I'm three thousand miles away from New York City, Mom, Dad, Byron, everything.

I really can't believe this.

ⓖ ⓖ ⓖ ⓖ

As we approach Hotel Andra, Shannon bounces around in her seat.

"What?" I ask.

"My lips are sealed," she says, sliding her finger and thumb across her mouth.

"We stayed at the Andra in August," Nina says as she switches on her left blinker. "It's in downtown Seattle. And you wouldn't believe this, Virginia, it's on—"

"Neen!" Shannon catapults through to the front seat. "Don't you remember *anything*? That's a surprise."

"*What?*" I ask again, but Shannon shoots me a mysterious look.

We pull up in front of the brick building. As Nina gives the keys to the valet and Liam checks in, Shannon steers me toward the street.

"Look where we're staying." Shannon gestures up to the sign.

"We're on the corner of Fourth Avenue and—" I suck in my breath. "We're staying on Virginia Street!"

"I know!" Shannon shrieks.

Shannon and I start singing, "We're staying on Virginia Street! We're staying on Virginia Street!" I pull out my phone, and we take a bunch of selfies under the street sign.

Liam summons us into the lobby. "Rules for Seattle," he says, handing Shannon our room cards. "Stick together all the time. I know you girls run around Manhattan, but we're talking about an entirely new city. Rule number two. Make sure you have a cup of coffee every day. Even if you don't like coffee, you'll love it here. And lastly, paint the town red by daylight, but meet us in the lobby every night at six."

"Are we excused?" Shannon asks, rolling her eyes.

Liam swats her with a Seattle guidebook. "You're excused."

Our room is small but elegant, with antique cherry furniture, two double beds, plush white bathrobes, and a collection of miniature Neutrogena products. Shannon and I flop onto one of the beds and talk for over an hour. Around five thirty, Shannon pulls out a tube of silver glitter and we roll streaks onto our temples and cheeks. As I brush my hair, Shannon braids hers into pigtails. We decide not to change our clothes because Nina said the dress code in Seattle is casual with a capital "C."

When we arrive in the lobby, Liam and Nina are sitting on a couch in front of the fireplace. Liam is reading the *New Yorker*. Nina is reading a manuscript. She's a freelance copy editor, so she's always buried in a laptop. Shannon is the physical clone of Nina, down to the red hair and the Milky Way of freckles, but when it comes to energy level, she's totally her dad.

"The glitter girls!" Liam gives us both a hug. "Do either of you feel like turkey? Because although Nina and I are having major Thanksgiving guilt, we're craving Asian food."

"How unpatriotic," Shannon says wryly.

Liam turns to me. "Virginia, do you have any thoughts on the matter?"

I shrug. "Anything's fine with me."

"Not good enough," Liam says. "We need an opinion. We need to be swayed."

"I had turkey on the airplane," I say.

"Then it's settled!" Liam claps his hands together. "Neen! Put away that computer. We're having Thai food tonight."

We drive up to a neighborhood called Capitol Hill. It reminds me of the East Village, with tons of restaurants and tattooed twenty-somethings milling about. Liam leads us to a Thai place, where we devour a vegetarian meal and declare it our best Thanksgiving dinner ever. I can't help but think about the traditional Thanksgiving that took place on Riverside Drive tonight—turkey and stuffing and Mom rambling on about how she's thankful for a *wooonderful* family and *wooonderful* friends and a *wooonderful* life.

After dinner we wander down Broadway, which is the main street running through Capitol Hill. Liam and Nina are holding hands and reading dessert menus at various cafés. As Shannon and I trail behind, we tally up the various bodily locations where we've seen piercings this evening. So far, it's cheeks, eyebrows, lips, ears, chins, tongues, and one shirtless guy with a ring through his nipple. We're just musing about below-the-waist possibilities when we stumble upon an arrangement of small bronze footprints embedded into the sidewalk. Upon closer inspection, we realize they're marking the steps for the rumba. Shannon and I start following the numbered footprints, doing the rumba. As soon as Liam and Nina spot us, they join in and the four of us dance until we're laughing so hard that our stomachs cramp up.

When we get back to the hotel, Shannon and I scrub our faces with the tiny bar of Neutrogena. She strips down right in front of me, pulling a T-shirt over her head. I head into the bathroom to change into my flannel pajamas, but Shannon doesn't make me feel self-conscious about the fact that I prefer to undress in private.

We decide to share one of the double beds. Shannon pulls back the covers. I crawl in after her and slide over, so we're lying shoulder to shoulder.

As soon as Shannon switches off the light, she says, "Do you want to play Fairy Godmother?"

"Sure."

We always used to play Fairy Godmother during sleepovers in junior high. The game goes like this: If you had a fairy godmother who could wave a magic wand over your head and grant you three wishes, what would you ask for? The only rule of Fairy Godmother is that you have to be completely honest.

"You start," Shannon says.

"My first wish is easy. I wish I were thin. I wish I had the perfect body."

"Kazam," Shannon says, tapping my forehead with her finger. "And your second wish?"

"I want a boyfriend who loves me and accepts me and we're great friends and he has a sense of humor and he's totally hot. And please, Fairy Godmother," I add, "if you decide to make him play shortstop for the Yankees, I wouldn't have a problem with it."

Shannon giggles as she pats my forehead. "One ball-playing boyfriend, coming right up."

"For my third wish . . ." I let that thought trail off. Shannon and I haven't talked about my brother at all since I arrived.

I've been enjoying the vacation from all the drama in New York. It's a relief not to have it occupying my brain every single second. Even so, the rules of Fairy Godmother are strict. You must be honest about your wishes.

"I wish this whole ordeal with Byron never happened," I say quickly. "I wish it would disappear and we could go back to the way things used to be."

When Shannon reaches over, I assume she's going to touch my forehead, but she slides her arm under the covers and squeezes my hand.

"Before I grant that wish, I want you to say it out loud. I've never heard you say it out loud."

"Say what?"

"What your brother did."

I turn to face Shannon. The room is dark, so I can only see the silhouette of her profile. Could she possibly be right? I've been obsessing about the date rape so much these past six weeks, but I don't think I've ever actually said those two words out loud. I guess we've all just followed Mom's lead and called it "the ordeal" or "why Byron got suspended from Columbia."

"Okay." I take a shallow breath. "Rape. Date rape."

"Who? What?"

"Byron. Byron date-raped a girl. No, not a girl. Annie Mills. Byron date-raped Annie Mills."

"And you wish it never happened?"

"Yeah. I mean, shouldn't I?"

"Of course you should wish he never did it." Shannon pauses before adding, "But he did."

I'm quiet for a long time. I think about that quote Shannon read me from the tea box, about how everything in life is tied together, that nothing stands by itself. She shared it with me the morning after I found out about the date rape, so I was like, *What on earth are you talking about?* But I've learned so much about Byron since then. I mean, it's not like he's done to me what he did to Annie Mills, but he hasn't exactly been the perfect big brother these past few years. And I probably wouldn't have even realized that if it hadn't been for this big-time wake-up call.

"Did you ever think Byron could do something like this?" I ask.

"I never considered rape," Shannon says. "But I can't say I thought he walked on water, like you did. Maybe it's different because he's not my brother, but I'd hear the things he'd say to you or watch the way he'd blow you off all the time."

"I know, Shan. I've been thinking about that so much recently." I choke up, making it hard to talk. "It's just . . . I don't know . . . it's just confusing to see this all so clearly for the first time."

I'm really crying by this point. My nose is running and my stomach is heaving. Shannon wraps her arms around me.

"I've missed you, Virginia," Shannon whispers.

"I've missed you, too," I say, wiping my wet cheeks on the sheet. "More than you can imagine."

22

It's Saturday afternoon. Shannon and I are sitting on a pier sipping hazelnut lattes and watching ferries shuttle to Bainbridge Island. Over the past two days, we've done everything under the sun. Or I guess I should say rain. It rains constantly in Seattle. The hotel loaned us a huge black umbrella and, fueled on various coffee concoctions, we explored Pike Place Market— an open-air market on the waterfront where fish vendors fling salmon through the air. We trekked back up to Capitol Hill. We even had Liam and Nina drive us past the headquarters for Amazon.

I took a picture of it for Froggy in case he ever talks to me again. That's the kind of thing he would think is cool. It's been over a month since the incident at my locker, and he still hasn't said a word to me. Shannon thinks he's probably licking his wounds, that guys have sensitive egos that way. I'm convinced that Froggy was legally blind in September but sold his trombone so he could get laser surgery on his eyes. Now that he can see what I actually look like, he can't believe he ever came near me.

Yesterday Shannon and I rode an elevator to the top of this futuristic tower called the Space Needle. The skies were clear, so we got a stunning view of Puget Sound, the Cascade Mountains, and the Olympic Mountains. Looking south, I was blown away by Mount Rainier. It's the tallest, widest mountain I could ever imagine, just like those snowcapped peaks I drew when I was a kid. As I gaped at Mount Rainier, I was both speechless and elated.

That's how I've been since I arrived in Seattle. Not speechless as much as elated. For the first time in months, I've been laughing at even the silliest things. I'm not distracted all the time. And being around Shannon, who rarely talks to strangers for fear of stuttering, makes me more outgoing. I've been babbling to every person on the street, asking for directions or striking up random conversations. The strangest thing is that I'm not thinking about food all the time. Rather than constantly munching, like I do at home, I'm just eating when I'm hungry. I'm not back on my diet, but I may have lost a few pounds because my Fat Pants are feeling a little loose.

Shannon and I have decided we want to do something special to commemorate this weekend. That's what we're discussing now, down at the pier.

"Friendship rings?" Shannon suggests.

"Too overdone."

"Toe rings?"

"My toes are really sensitive," I say. "It would drive me crazy."

I hear a foghorn blaring in the distance. A guy wearing combat boots passes our bench. He's got a shaved head, dozens of studs in his ears, and a ring through his nostril.

"Hey, you!" I shout to him.

I don't know who looks more surprised, the guy or Shannon. He freezes in his tracks and stares at me.

"Where do you get body piercing done around here?" I ask.

Shannon grabs hold of my hand and squeals.

"Lots of places." He scratches his bare head. "How old are you?"

"Seventeen," I lie.

Shannon digs her fingernails into my palm.

"Unless your parents come along, most places won't pierce you until you're eighteen."

Shannon and I must look devastated because the guy sits down on the bench with us. Shannon adjusts the umbrella so it's covering him as well.

"I know a guy named Sage at a place on Capitol Hill," he says. "It's called Holy Moly. He's the one with the lime-green Mohawk. If you tell him I sent you, he'll hook you up."

"What's your name?" I ask.

"X," he says.

"X?" Shannon and I ask in unison.

The guy smiles sheepishly. "My real name is Matthew, but don't tell Sage that."

Shannon and I walk to the corner, where we hop on an electric bus that's attached to overhead cables. On the ride to Capitol Hill, we discuss the factors of a potential piercing.

There's the legal issue, but we both agree that we won't be deterred by age limits. It's not like they can send someone to jail for getting a nose ring.

Then there's the parental factor.

"Liam and Nina will love it. They're always saying they want matching belly button rings." Shannon gives me a sympathetic look. "What about yours?"

"They'll hate it," I say. "But they can't exactly make me live in a refrigerator box, so what's the worst that can happen?"

Then we discuss the most pressing element—bodily location. I've decided to get an eyebrow ring. I want something on my face, but nose rings are too gross, what with the booger factor. Chin studs look like zits. And I'm worried a lip ring would get torn out by my braces.

"What about you?" I ask.

Shannon stares out the bus window. "My tongue," she says quietly.

"You're getting your *tongue* pierced?"

Shannon nods. "I've spent my entire life hating my tongue because it makes me stutter. It's time to start bonding with it."

We find Holy Moly right away. Sage, the only person in the shop with a lime-green Mohawk, is discussing aftercare with a woman who has just gotten a stud through her cheek. We linger around the counter for a few minutes, admiring tattoo templates. When Sage finally comes over, we explain our situation and tell him that X thought he could help us.

"For X," Sage says, "I'll do anything."

Sage starts by examining what he calls "the webbing" on Shannon's tongue, which he proceeds to deem pierceable. Then, as he reviews prices and procedures, I count my money. With the cash from Dad, I've got enough for the eyebrow ring. Sage writes down our names and tells us to return in a half hour.

We walk over to Broadway and grab some pepperoni pizza. Sage recommended that Shannon eat a fortifying meal, since she might not be able to deal with solid foods for a few days after the piercing. Once we're done, we wander into a funky vintage shop. Shannon buys a plastic ring. I buy a polyester orange shirt with horizontal green stripes. Mom's always telling me I should stick to neutral colors. And definitely no horizontal stripes, since they reveal extra poundage. But something about the shirt beckons me. Besides, it's only five dollars so I can always toss it if I change my mind.

On our way back to Holy Moly, Shannon asks, "You sure you want to do this?"

"Surer than ever."

Twenty minutes later, I have a silver ring in my left eyebrow and Shannon has a stainless steel barbell through her tongue. The pain wasn't bad, at least for me. Sage fastened on clamps to hold the skin in place and told me to take a deep breath. It felt like a sharp pinch when the needle went through. I definitely flinched, but it was over pretty quickly.

Shannon went next. As Sage marked a dot on her tongue,

she was trembling like a dog during a thunderstorm. I didn't blame her for being anxious because although Sage reassured her that he was quite experienced, he *did* explain that there are risks involved when piercing a tongue, like hitting a vein. It hurt so badly that Shannon teared up. I held her hand as she winced in pain. Sage said it'll be healed in no time, like six weeks, so she took some comfort in that.

Then he launched into a lecture about cleaning and maintenance. I promised him I would be scrupulously sterile, but even so he warned me that it'll take three months to heal.

I don't care if it takes three years because I love my eyebrow ring. I loved it the second Sage held up the mirror so I could see the new addition to my face.

"I can't believe it," I kept repeating as I stared at my reflection.

It was like I was seeing myself for the very first time.

⟨ ⟨ ⟨ ⟨

"Here's to facial ornamentation!" Liam raises a glass of water in the air.

"Here, here." I clink with him.

"Heee, heee," Shannon says. It's hard for her to talk with a swollen tongue.

Nina sips her beer. "Will you please tell your parents we had nothing to do with this?"

I dip a piece of bread into olive oil. "I'll take all the blame."

"Tell them we're furious with Shannon," Liam says as he studies the menu.

We're eating at a restaurant called the Pink Door. It's on Post Alley, which is walking distance from the Andra. There's no sign outside, so you just have to look for the pink door.

While we're waiting for the waitress to come over, I tell them the story of Sage and X. Shannon nods and makes guttural noises.

"After I've finished my book on onions," Liam says, "I'm thinking of proposing a book about people with unusual names."

I consider mentioning Froggy Welsh the Fourth, but then the waitress arrives to take our order.

After dinner we head right back to the hotel. My flight leaves at eight thirty tomorrow morning, so Nina is giving us a wake-up call at five thirty. They're going to drive me to the airport and then continue on to Walla Walla. Nina makes both of us take Advil before we go to our room, in case the pain increases overnight.

Shannon switches on the television and starts sucking an ice cube. I go into the bathroom and turn on the shower. I glance into the mirror. I can't believe how much I love my eyebrow ring. It makes me look unique and interesting. I stare at my reflection for about five minutes, checking out my face from every possible angle.

I step into the shower. It's one of those contoured tubs with a detachable nozzle. As I run the nozzle over my chest, I think about Froggy. I've been thinking about him a lot since I've been in Seattle. Whenever I do, I get a pang in my stomach. I wish I could make things better. I miss kissing him, but I also just miss the way I felt in his presence—sort of giggly and girlish.

I probably shouldn't have denounced everything having to do with the opposite sex. What Byron did was horrible, but I have to remember that that was date rape. And forcing yourself onto someone is *completely* different from consensual fooling around, which is what Froggy and I were doing. I think I got them jumbled together in my head.

I lower the nozzle so it sprays a stream of warm water between my legs. This is the first time I've touched myself like this in months. I don't hold the nozzle there for long, just enough to send a tingling sensation through my body.

That's when it dawns on me.

At some point over the past few days, I've stopped feeling numb.

Mom and Dad are waiting for me at the airport. I think they're even smiling. Liam and Nina overnighted them fresh salmon packed on ice, so maybe that cushioned the blow of my running away to Seattle.

As I get closer, Mom's smile fades. "What's on your face?"

My hand wanders to my eyebrow. I'm about to touch the ring when I remember that Sage told me not to fiddle with it. "An eyebrow ring."

"I know what it is. But what is it doing on *your* eyebrow?"

"I like it," Dad says.

"Don't encourage her, Mike."

Dad reaches for my suitcase.

"Let's go," Mom says. "We'll discuss it later."

None of us talk much on the ride home. Mom says they appreciated the salmon from Liam and Nina. Dad asks if I went up in the Space Needle. I tell them that we stayed on Virginia Street. Dad says he bought capers to eat with the salmon. Mom asks when the Space Needle was built. I repeat that we stayed on Virginia Street.

As soon as we get back to the apartment, Mom grabs a book and disappears into their bedroom. Dad joins Byron on the couch, where he's watching a Knicks game. I go into the kitchen and devour two slices of leftover pumpkin pie drenched in homemade whipped cream.

As I'm heading into my bedroom, Byron calls out, "Welcome home, Gin."

"Thanks."

In the old days, I would have paraded over and shown him my eyebrow ring. If he liked it, I would have been the happiest person on the planet. If he said it looked dumb, I would have taken it out instantly. But now I couldn't care less what Byron thinks.

ⓖ ⓖ ⓖ ⓖ

I'm on my way into school the next morning when I run into Ms. Crowley.

"A true Seattle babe!" she exclaims, admiring my eyebrow ring.

I give her the quick scoop on my trip, promising to fill her in at lunch.

As soon as the bell rings, I scurry up to Global Studies. We're midway through the terrorism unit. Mr. Vandenhausler spends the first several minutes explaining how the best way to trap terrorists is to get inside their heads, to understand the nuts and bolts of their operations. His mustache twitches like a rattlesnake's tail as he instructs us to break into small groups and pretend that we are masterminding a terrorist attack.

I wind up in a group with Alyssa Wu and three guys. The guys are debating whether to hijack an airplane or go the biological-warfare route. Alyssa is knitting. She must have noticed me watching her because she leans toward me and whispers, "I love your eyebrow ring."

"Thanks."

"Did you get it done downtown?"

"No, it was at a place in Seattle. That's where I went over Thanksgiving."

"Lucky," she says. "All I did was go to Delaware, where my family fought for four days and my dad was only thankful that he wasn't the turkey."

I crack up.

"Alyssa Wu! Virginia Shreves!" Mr. Vandenhausler marches over to our desks. "Terrorism is not a laughing matter. Do you think the FBI and the CIA are giggling right now? As a matter of fact—" Mr. Vandenhausler stops when he notices my eyebrow ring. "Virginia, when did you get your eyebrow pierced?"

"Over Thanksgiving break."

Mr. Vandenhausler's mustache twitches ever so slightly. "Did it hurt?"

I nod.

"Serious pain?" he asks.

"Not that bad."

Mr. Vandenhausler looks disappointed. "Well, get back to terrorism, girls. You've got a world to save."

That's how it's been all day. People who I never thought noticed me before have been telling me how great my eyebrow ring looks. It's funny. I always assumed an Iron Rule of the High School Way of Life is that only the cool crowd is allowed to take fashion risks and if a regular/dorky person does something wacky, then everyone will call them a poseur or a wannabe. But the strangest thing is that that hasn't been happening at all.

Even Brie Newhart notices my eyebrow ring. We're sitting in French, waiting for class to begin. I can tell she's staring at my eyebrow, so I turn and smile at her.

"I want to get my nose pierced," she says, "but I'm scared of needles."

"It wasn't that bad. It took under thirty seconds."

"Really? That's all?"

I nod.

If someone told me a few months ago that Brie and I would have a normal human exchange, I would have been like, *Yeah, right.* But I'm not so floored now. I guess I'm feeling a little different about things, like how outside appearances can be deceiving and sometimes people aren't all they're cracked up to be. Speaking of appearances, Brie looks pale and worn out, like a T-shirt that's been in the dryer too many times. She's not quite as intimidating as she was back in September.

Mademoiselle Kiefer claps her hands together. I glance at Froggy. He got a haircut over break, reducing his cowlick to a little ridge on his forehead.

If only Froggy would notice my eyebrow ring. Now *that* would make my day.

⑥ ⑥ ⑥ ⑥

It's the second-to-last day in November. I just got home from school. I'm in my bathroom cleaning my eyebrow. I've been following the aftercare instructions to the letter. I start by removing crusty matter around the pierce hole. There's not a lot, just a few flakes of skin. I dip a Q-Tip into warm water, wet down the area, and apply a smidgen of Dial.

The door to the bathroom is cracked open. No one's home, so I have the music pumped in my room. I'm singing along as I lather the antibacterial soap.

Mom peeks into the bathroom.

I stop singing. "What are you doing home?"

"I have to pick up some files," she says. "Can you talk for a minute?"

I nod quickly and continue soaping my eyebrow.

Mom sits down on the toilet lid and takes a TherapistBreath— in through the nose and out through the mouth. "I've been thinking a lot about your recent rebellions," she says. "Buying that ticket to Seattle and now this." Mom gestures in the direction of my face.

Ashanti starts singing "Foolish." My music is on loudly, so Mom has to raise her voice to be audible.

"I realize that the teen years are a time to assert your autonomy, to establish an identity separate from your family. Anaïs went through this stage, just a few years later." Mom takes another TherapistBreath. "I just want you to think carefully about your actions. I don't like to see you being so impetuous."

"Impetuous" is on my SAT Hot 100 list. It means "sudden and spontaneous," which is *exactly* what I'd like to be. I decide not to inform Mom of that. Instead, I lean over the faucet and rinse my eyebrow.

"Having a ring through your eyebrow seems so barbaric," Mom says. "I can hardly look at it without wincing."

Ashanti is singing about how she keeps running back to someone even though he treats her badly. I carefully slide the ring back and forth to make sure the pierce is clean.

"When women first started getting their ears pierced, everyone thought *that* was barbaric," I say. "But now it's as normal as necklaces. I think it's the same with facial piercings. It'll just take time to get used to them."

"The two aren't comparable, Virginia. Piercing your ears is easy and relatively painless. Getting a hole through your eyebrow . . . that's just, well, unattractive. You looked much better without it."

"In your opinion," I say. "Besides, my eyebrow was easy and relatively painless, too."

Mom clenches her jaw. "I just wanted to say that I'd like you to—"

I cut her off. "If you're trying to convince me to take out my eyebrow ring, I'm sorry. It's here to stay."

Mom stands up so quickly that a towel hanging on the shower rack slips to the floor. "I don't know what's gotten into you, but I don't like it."

As she marches out of the bathroom, I pat my eyebrow with a cotton ball.

"I'll tell you what's gotten into me," I call after her. "I'm finally having a little fun in my life."

But Ashanti has launched into a chorus of *"never gonna change,"* so I don't think Mom hears me.

One of the side effects of not being numb anymore is that I'm starting to realize what I want, and I'm sticking to it. Which pisses the hell out of Mom.

ⓖ ⓖ ⓖ ⓖ

I'm dreading our shopping trip today.

It's been over a week since the bathroom showdown, and Mom and I are still on pins and needles. We haven't had a blowout, though we've been making a lot of snippy comments back and forth. But the Lowensteins' annual holiday party is less than two weeks away, and Mom is insisting that I get something new to wear and that it come from Saks. I know what that means. The plus-size department.

It's Sunday afternoon. Dad and Byron are at a Knicks game. Mom and I are riding the elevator downstairs.

"Why can't we go to Torrid?" I ask. I've browsed in there before, but I've never had the guts to buy anything. I like that they have cool clothes in every size, so the fat girls aren't banished to the fat floor where the dresses look like gunnysacks and the mannequins resemble embalmed grandmothers.

"Torrid?" Mom scrunches her nose. "It's so cheap-looking. We're going to a holiday party, not the Jersey Shore."

"What about Old Navy?"

"Too casual," Mom says.

We step onto Riverside Drive. There's a bitter wind whipping in from the river. The doorman flags a cab. Mom tells the driver to take us to Saks.

Saks is swamped with holiday shoppers. We weave our way to the elevator bank. Mom presses the button for the tenth floor. The plus-size floor. The fat floor.

"Mom?"

"Yes?"

"Maybe we can check out the teen section instead?"

"But . . ." Mom glances uncomfortably at the other shoppers in the elevator.

I press the button for the fifth floor. I'm not sure what's come over me. I guess I just want to wear something more fun for my holiday outfit this year. More colors. More curves. Maybe even a little flesh exposure.

When the elevator arrives on the fifth floor, I head into the teen section. Mom hesitantly follows.

The only way to compare the teen styles to the plus-size styles is likening it to the East Village and Queens. Completely different universes only an arm's length apart.

"Do you really think we'll find something flattering for you?" Mom asks as I eye a stretchy black dress with sequins around the chest. "I mean, these aren't exactly . . ."

"You never know," I say, plunking the black dress off the rack.

I gaze at a row of sparkly red velvet gowns. They're really

glamorous, like something a movie star might wear to the Academy Awards.

"I don't know, Virginia," Mom says. "Red isn't really your color. Why don't we find something a little less attention-grabbing?"

"I like red," I say, taking the gown in two different sizes.

Mom digs her Tic Tacs out of her purse and pops two into her mouth.

I'm just checking out some silky kimono-style dresses when Mom holds up a pale-green-satin number. It's very roomy. And very pale green.

"What do you think?" she asks.

"It looks like a bridesmaid dress," I say.

Mom grinds the Tic Tacs between her teeth. "You don't have to try it on."

"No, I will."

Once we've selected five dresses, we follow signs to the dressing room. It has an abundance of mirrors, which are thankfully *outside* the stalls. They're piping an orchestral version of "Silent Night" over the sound system. I settle into a stall and strip down to my undies and socks.

I can hear Mom pacing nervously outside my door. I try on the black sequined dress. Even though it's stretchy, I can barely tug it over my hips. I wriggle out of it, toss it on the little bench, and move on to the largest of the red velvet gowns.

"So?" Mom asks.

"Still trying."

The red gown is too snug. So is the kimono. The only one

that actually fits is Mom's pale-green selection. And even with that one, I can only zip it halfway up my back.

I glance down at myself. I look like an overgrown avocado.

"Any luck?" Mom asks. I hear another Tic Tac crunch in her mouth.

"None are quite right."

"What's wrong?"

"They don't exactly fit."

I hear the saleswoman suggesting we check out the plus-size department.

"Honey," Mom says, "let's go up to the tenth floor. That's where we should have started in the first place. We can look for something a little more layered."

"I don't want to," I say, sitting on the bench and folding my arms across my chest. I sound like a brat, but I don't care. I mean, do I have to write it in blood? I. Do. Not. Want. To. Wear. Any. More. Ugly. Fat. Girl. Clothes.

"Why not?" Mom asks. There's an edge in her voice, like she's losing her patience.

"Because the clothes make me look like a dumpy old great-aunt."

Mom takes a few steps closer to my stall, so she's right against the door. "With your body type, Virginia," she whispers, "it's better to go for layers. I should know."

"The tenth floor has a lot of attractive plus-size clothing," the saleswoman chimes in. "You'd be surprised at the . . ."

"What body type are you talking about?" I ask, standing up. I'm on the verge of tears.

"We'll talk about this later," Mom says in a hiss-whisper.

I fling open the door, even though I'm half squeezed into the avocado dress. "Why can't you say it out loud, Mom?" I shout. "I'm fat, okay? F-A-T. But that doesn't mean I have to hide beneath layers of fabric. That doesn't mean I'm exactly like you used to be, ashamed of showing my body. That doesn't mean I have to get my dress from the stupid old tenth—"

Mom cuts me off. "I've had quite enough of you this afternoon," she says curtly.

I slam the door and start crying. My face is hot, and my nose is streaming.

"Meet me at the elevators as soon as you've changed," Mom says through the door. "We're going home."

Mom's footsteps recede from the dressing room.

I kick the wall of my stall. It leaves a small indentation. I kick it again, harder this time. I'm only wearing socks, so I bash my toes pretty badly, sending a jarring shock through my whole body.

As the orchestral "Silent Night" hits the sleep-in-heavenly-peace part, I collapse to the floor and sob for five minutes straight.

I think the second toe on my right foot is broken. It hurts so badly that I can't put any weight on that foot without shrieking. When I texted Shannon about it, she instructed me to go to the emergency room immediately. But Dad left for a business trip yesterday evening, and Mom is so angry that if I asked her for anything, she'd probably go after my nine intact toes.

On Monday morning I hobble to school and wince my way through first period. When I arrive in gym, Teri takes one look at me and sends me to the nurse's office. Paul hands me an ice pack and tries my parents' phones. He can't reach Dad and Mom is with patients all morning, so her assistant gives him the number for my doctor.

Dr. Love's office says they can fit me in right away. I give Paul my locker combination. He retrieves my jacket and backpack, helps me outside, and loans me cab money.

Now that I know this can get me out of school so easily, I'll have to make a career out of breaking my toes.

That's a joke.

Sort of.

6 6 6 6

As soon as Dr. Love enters the examination room, he compliments my eyebrow ring.

"How's it healing?"

"Pretty well," I say. "It doesn't hurt that much."

"Mind if I take a look?"

"Go ahead."

Dr. Love washes his hands. As he approaches the table, I pull aside my eyebrow ring so he can get a better look at the pierce.

"What happened to your finger?" Dr. Love asks.

I lower my hand to my side. "I burned myself."

"How?"

"Truth?"

Dr. Love nods.

"On a candle."

As he examines my finger, his face looks concerned. "You should rub vitamin E oil on it every night. That'll reduce scarring." Dr. Love checks out my eyebrow ring and then sits on his rotating stool. "So what's up with your toe?"

"I think it's broken."

"How did it happen?"

"I was pissed at my mom so I kicked a wall in Saks."

"If you've got to kick somewhere," Dr. Love says, laughing.

I crack up, too.

He gingerly unlaces my sneaker and rolls off my sock. After examining my toe, he says that while he's almost certain it's broken, he's not going to send me for x-rays because either way he'll just have to tape it up.

"Speaking of your mom," Dr. Love says as he tapes my wounded toe to my third toe, "I owe you an apology."

"Me? Why?"

"When you were here for your last visit, I regretted involving her in that discussion. Weight is such a dicey issue, especially for mothers and daughters. I firmly believe that it's about feeling good, regardless of your body type. I'm not sure your mom understands that."

I choke up. I can't believe what a relief it is to hear this out loud, like I'm not a factory defect or something.

Dr. Love hands me a tissue. "Going through a hard time with your family right now?"

I nod.

"I bet you're pretty angry."

I blow my nose.

"Anger is a healthy emotion," Dr. Love says, "as long as you can find ways to channel it where you don't hurt yourself in the process."

I glance at my burned finger, my broken toe.

"Have you ever tried kickboxing?" Dr. Love asks.

I wipe my eyes. "Is it like CrossFit? Because that's really not my thing."

"No, it's nothing like CrossFit. Kickboxing combines traditional martial arts with boxing, stretching, and breathing techniques. A friend of mine teaches a class geared for teenage girls." Dr. Love reaches for a Post-it and jots down the name and address of the gym. "It's a great way to release anger, not to mention build strength and flexibility."

"It sounds interesting," I say.

"Give your toe a few weeks to heal and then check it out."

By the time I leave Dr. Love's office, the temperature has plummeted. My toe feels a little better now that it's taped up. I zip my jacket and limp toward the subway station.

As the train pulls into 125th Street, I realize that the next stop is Columbia. I haven't been to Columbia since late September, when I surprised Byron in his dorm room.

My heart is pounding as I get off the subway at 116th, carefully walk up the steps, and limp to the main entranceway of campus. I stare up at the imposing gate, topped with golden crowns and flanked by toga-wearing statues.

Somewhere inside there, Annie Mills is living, breathing, suffering.

I shuffle through the gate and nimbly navigate the brick pathways, which are slick with ice. It's hard to imagine that Annie Mills is a real person. No one in my family ever talks about her, so she exists only in my imagination, a tragic figure whose life was destroyed by my brother.

My heart is punching against my chest as I stop a woman

on the path and ask where I can find a student directory. She points me toward a glass building and tells me to look for the information desk.

By the time I make it into the building, my ears are frostbitten and my neck is stinging. I thaw out for a second before asking the person at the information desk how I can find what dorm someone is in. He surprises me by saying it's all online and open to the public. I must be gaping cluelessly at him because he takes my phone from my hand and loads up the Columbia student directory. Thanking him, I step aside, touch the box for name, and enter A-n-n-i-e M-i-l-l-s.

It pops up on the screen, just like that.

Her dorm and room number and everything. My knees are buckling. Annie Mills lives in Wallach, the same dorm as Byron. I glance nervously over my shoulder before scribbling the information onto the back of the Post-it from Dr. Love. It feels surreal, like Annie Mills's information is going to disappear at any second.

As soon as I get home, I put the paper in my cedar box, strip down to my T-shirt, and crawl into bed, where I remain for the rest of the day.

My toe has healed steadily over the past ten days. Even so, I've been excused from gym. Brie Newhart has been complaining of dizzy spells, so Teri won't let her participate either. Some mornings we set up cones or inflate volleyballs, but usually we just do our homework together.

Brie has been helping me understand the difference between a relative pronoun and an object pronoun in French. And I have a better grasp on the books we've been reading for "Ostracism and Oppression," so I give her pointers for her language arts papers. It's not like we chat much, but I think we've established a silent peace treaty. At least I have. I'm not so obsessed with what she said about me in the bathroom anymore. I mean, I've heard her puking in that same stall three times now, so I hardly think she's in a position to judge *me*. Mostly, I just appreciate her help with my French homework.

I'm really suffering in French. I may get my first C ever. My mind wanders so much during class. I can't stop looking over at Froggy. I've spotted him walking out of school with Sarah, the freshman girl with the ski-jump nose. Seeing that she's most likely Froggy's girlfriend, I shouldn't spend French class pining after him. But I can't help it.

I wish I could memorize French pronouns the way I've memorized Annie Mills's information. I take the Post-it out of my cedar box all the time just to look at it, to think about how Byron once visited that dorm room.

Speaking of Byron, he's in a good mood today. It's Wednesday afternoon, less than a week before Christmas. I'm on the couch with my computer watching these live YouTube concerts that people at school have been talking about and munching chocolate-covered pretzels when the buzzer rings.

Byron jogs into the foyer, humming one of the songs I was just watching.

"Who's here?" I ask.

"A friend texted earlier to see if he could swing by."

It turns out to be that guy I met in Byron's dorm, the one who looks like a hamster. He's holding hands with an Indian woman wearing a knee-length skirt and tall black boots. Byron offers to get them something to drink, but Hamster Boy coolly explains that he just stopped by to return some money my brother loaned him last fall.

They're in and out in less than five minutes, not enough time for the slush from their boots to melt into puddles.

As soon as they're gone, Byron knocks around the kitchen, clanking dishes and slamming cupboards.

"Could you keep it down?" I pump the volume on my laptop to its highest setting.

"Get off my back," Byron barks from the kitchen.

"What's gotten into you?"

"Why do you care?"

"I care because I can't hear the concert," I shout.

"Fine." Byron stomps into the living room. "I was interested in that girl, and Shawn, the little asshole, chased after her as soon as I was out of sight."

Before I can stop myself, I say, "Well it's not like anyone will want to go out with you anymore."

"What are you talking about?"

"You know what I'm talking about." I give him a knowing look. "Annie Mills."

Byron pales. "Don't go there, Gin."

"Why not?"

"Because it's none of your fucking business."

"Maybe it's none of my fucking business," I say, "but I'm just saying that I'm probably not the only person who thinks you're the asshole for date-raping someone."

Byron lurches toward me. I tumble over the back of the couch, truck into my bedroom, and turn the lock.

Byron pounds on my door. "Come out, you fat piece of shit!"

"Fuck you!" I shout. I'm trembling all over.

"No, fuck *you!*"

Byron goes into his bedroom and blasts his music. I dig that photo strip of us out of my cedar box, tear it to shreds, and chuck it into my trash. I'm looking around my room for other remnants of my brother when I spot a paper clip on my desk. I'm tempted to unbend the wire and run it across my wrist until I break the skin. I can picture the blood oozing to the surface, releasing the anger inside my chest.

That's when I remember what Dr. Love said about not hurting myself anymore. Instead, I grab my jacket and hurry out of the apartment before Byron hears me and pummels me to a pulp.

⑤ ⑤ ⑤ ⑤

I take the subway up Broadway and walk across Columbia's main campus. The sky is hazy, and snowflakes litter the air. They're forecasting a blizzard this evening, four to six inches of snowfall.

I find Wallach right away, but I have to wait on the front stoop for nearly twenty minutes, shivering and rubbing my hands together, until enough students are crowded into the entranceway for me to slip past the security guard.

Annie Mills's room is 209, so I take the narrow stairs to the second floor. I make my way down several hallways, past the 230s and the 220s. As I get closer, my heart is beating so hard it feels like it's going to crack my ribs.

Room 212 . . . 211 . . . 210 . . .

There it is. Room 209.

I raise my hand and knock on the door.

"Who is it?" a voice calls from inside.

Is that Annie Mills? Or maybe her roommate?

I knock again.

I can hear footsteps crossing the room. The woman who opens the door has blue-green eyes and tangly brown hair that reaches her waist. She's wearing an off-white undershirt, overalls, and no makeup.

"May I help you?" she asks.

"Are you Annie Mills?"

"Yeah."

"I'm Virginia Shreves. My older brother is By—"

"Byron Shreves." Annie frowns. "What are you doing here?"

I chew on a fingernail, even though it's already ground down to the skin. I prepared what I was going to say on the subway, but now my mind is blank.

Annie twists a long strand of hair around her finger. "I'm not exactly sure you should be . . ."

"You're right." I choke up. "I'm sorry . . . it was a stupid idea."

I turn and take off. Once I reach the stairwell, I plunk down on the top step. I'm shaking all over—from nerves, but also from being cold. My hair is damp and my sneakers are soggy and freezing. I can't believe I'm sniffling and shivering in a dingy stairwell of a dorm.

Hang on. No. I came to Columbia for a reason. Partially, I

needed to see Annie, to confirm that she's a real person. But I also wanted to apologize to her. I know I'm not responsible for Byron's actions, but she deserves to have sympathy from one of the Shreves.

I stand up, take a few deep breaths, and head back toward room 209. When I reach her door, I wipe my eyes and nose, take a calming breath, and knock.

The door opens right away.

"Hey," I say.

Annie looks confused.

"I'm sorry to bother you." I stare down at my wet sneakers, willing myself not to cry. "I just wanted to say I'm sorry for what my brother did to you. If it makes any difference, I think he's an asshole for wrecking your life like that."

Annie doesn't respond, so I quickly add, "Well, that's all. I guess I'll head . . ."

"Wait. You look freezing. Do you want a cup of tea?"

I shiver and hug my arms to my chest. "Are you sure?"

"Mint or apple spice?"

"Apple spice," I say, "if it's not a problem."

Annie opens her door a little. "Come on in."

I unlace my sneakers and leave them in the hallway before stepping into Annie's room. The first thing I see is one single bed. *How strange.* I always pictured Annie having a roommate.

As she fills an electric kettle with bottled water and plugs it into the wall, I settle onto her rug. It's a cozy room, with a fuzzy beanbag chair, a lava lamp, and photos of friends and people I'm guessing are her family plastering the walls. I notice a half-packed suitcase by the closet. She must be leaving for break soon.

"Do you want honey in your tea?"

"Sure."

"That's how I like it, too."

Annie hands me a mug.

"Thanks."

"Virginia, right?" Annie says, settling onto the beanbag chair.

"Yeah."

"Virginia, it was brave of you to come up here, though I have to admit it weirded me out at first."

I attempt to sip my tea, but it's still too hot.

"How did you find my room?" Annie asks.

"The student directory."

Annie is quiet as she blows the steam off her tea. "Can I say one thing about your . . . about Byron?"

Annie pronounces "about" the Canadian way: *a-boot*.

I shrug. "Sure."

"What you said at the door, about him wrecking my life . . ."

"Yeah?"

"He hasn't."

"Really?"

Annie shakes her head, and her hair spills over her chest like a shawl. "What Byron did was awful. That's why I reported him to the campus authorities. I don't want him to think he can ever do that to another woman." Annie pauses and looks around her room. I can tell this is hard for her to talk about. "But as much as this has been a horrendous experience, my life isn't wrecked. I won't let him have that kind of power over me."

"What do you mean?"

"I had no control over what Byron did that night," Annie says. "But what happened the next morning, what will happen every morning for the rest of my life, that's up to me. I think people can choose to be victims or they can choose to be empowered and to carry on. That's what I want. To be empowered."

I stare at Annie. I'm completely speechless. I can't believe how much I identify with what she said—just with how things are in my family, how I've always let myself get treated.

"May I play a song for you?" Annie asks. "It's an early one by Ani DiFranco."

I nod.

Annie reaches for her phone and taps a few times before setting it on the floor between us.

"It's called 'Gratitude,'" she says. "It's really helped me get through this semester."

It turns out to be a song about a guy who invites a girl to sleep in his bed, promising it'll be platonic, and then starts pressuring her to fool around. You can tell that Ani is angry, but at the same time she's also funny and strong and sassy.

By the time the song is over, I've got goose bumps on my arms.

"You remind me of my older sister," I say. "You'd like her a lot."

Annie smiles. "I bet I would. Because I already like her sister."

It takes me a few seconds to realize that she's talking about me.

🌀 🌀 🌀 🌀

As soon as I get home, I write a letter to Anaïs. I tell her about Byron, my crash diet, my burned finger, Seattle, my broken toe, Annie Mills. I write and write until I've filled nine sheets of pale pink stationery. Then I fold the pages into an envelope and head into Mom's office to search for my sister's address.

Mom's desk is covered with papers and Post-its and books on adolescent psychology. After poking around for a few minutes, I locate her address book. I flip to the S's and there it is: Anaïs Shreves, care of the Peace Corps.

I always thought Mom was the gatekeeper to my sister, that I couldn't write her without Mom's permission. But Anaïs's address has been here all along. I just had to look.

26

The day before winter break has dragged more slowly than a snail on sleeping pills. I'm so exhausted that I've spent the entire day in a state of perpetual yawn. I stayed up until two in the morning studying for today's Global Studies exam. We had to regurgitate everything we learned all fall, complete with names, dates, and puncture wounds.

I set my alarm for five thirty this morning so I could memorize the various nationalities in French for our test today, but I didn't rouse until ten to seven, so I skipped my shower, rushed to the bus, and bombed the quiz. The only nationality I could remember was *chinois*, which is Chinese.

In language arts we had to write an in-class essay about "Ostracism and Oppression," comparing and contrasting the various books we read this fall. In chemistry we were tested on stoichiometry, which I can barely pronounce, much less define.

I've decided that Brewster teachers definitely missed the lesson on holiday spirit.

Even Mr. Moony scheduled a test for today. I spent all of lunch memorizing circle theorems, but as I arrive in last period, Mr. Moony is sleeping at his desk. Behind him on the chalkboard, he's written:

Class —
I'm not feeling well this afternoon. The examination is rescheduled for after break.
Happy Holidays,
Clive Moony

A few kids fling their notebooks into the air. One guy erases "after break" and writes "never." Alyssa Wu suggests we send for Paul the School Nurse, but she's outvoted by the rest of the class, who point out that he might report it to the principal, who might replace Mr. Moony with a new geometry teacher who might actually make us work. As everyone rearranges their desks into clusters of three or four, I forge Mr. Moony's signature on a pass and take the back staircase down to Ms. Crowley's office.

I didn't see her during lunch period because she had a holiday party with the other language arts teachers, so I want to make sure to give her the card I bought for her. It has a picture of eight Great Danes pulling Santa's sleigh across a rooftop. Ms. Crowley and her husband are total Great Dane freaks.

I wrote a long note inside, thanking her for being there for me this fall.

Ms. Crowley explodes into laughter as she slides my card out of the envelope.

I smile. "I thought you'd like it."

As she reads my note, I fiddle with my eyebrow ring. I was in a gushy mood when I wrote it, so I hope I didn't go too far.

"Oh, Virginia," she says, patting my arm, "it's been such a pleasure having you up here so much."

"Thanks."

Ms. Crowley traces her finger along the spine of the card. "I hope I'm not out of line saying this . . ."

"Saying what?" I ask, my shoulders tensing up.

"I've enjoyed spending all these lunch periods together, but I want to make sure you're not isolating yourself from your peers. There are lots of nice kids at Brewster, if only you reached out, gave them a—"

Adrenaline surges through my body, propelling me to my feet. "I thought I was welcome here."

"You were." Ms. Crowley makes an uncomfortable face. "You still are. I'm just saying this because I care about you."

"If you cared about me, you wouldn't say something like that!" I shout.

I storm out of Ms. Crowley's office and race down the stairs, two at a time. I'm almost at my locker when I smack into Paul the School Nurse.

"Are you okay?" he asks.

"Perfect!" I shout.

I'm about to add *lovely, fine, and great* when I notice that Paul is wringing his hands together and staring anxiously out the front doors of Brewster, which are propped open.

That's when I see the ambulance parked on the street.

"What's going on?"

"It's Clive Moony," Paul says. "A student called 911 because he was complaining of chest pain."

I suck in my breath. I was up there only ten or fifteen minutes ago. It must have happened right after I left. I can't believe it. I wonder who called 911. I wonder who ran down and got Paul. I wonder what the other kids did.

"Do they think it's a heart attack?" I ask.

"No one knows for sure," Paul says.

Paul and I walk to the front stoop. The air is so bitterly cold that it's hard to breathe. We watch as two paramedics slide a stretcher into the back of the ambulance. There's an oxygen mask on Mr. Moony's face. One person crawls in after him. Then the other jumps in and slams the door shut. Seconds later the ambulance is speeding down the street, lights flashing and siren wailing.

The final bell rings.

Winter break has begun.

My parents' friends, Marcia and Brad Lowenstein, always have their holiday party on the Saturday before Christmas. She's Baptist and he's Jewish, so it usually lands on one of the days of Hanukkah. They're raising their twin boys in both faiths, so they adorn their Connecticut house with dreidels and menorahs, Santas and mangers, five-pointed stars and six-pointed stars. Everyone gets dressed up. The parents drink too much eggnog. The teenagers pretend they've drunk too much eggnog. I wind up in the kiddie room with the preschool crew, watching *Frozen* and wishing I could get run over by a reindeer.

And it's all happening tonight.

I still don't have a dress. Ever since the Saks incident, Mom hasn't mentioned my holiday outfit. But I've decided I want something new to wear, so I wait until Mom has left for her spin class to ask Dad if I can borrow his credit card.

I take the subway down to Torrid, where I try on about thirty dresses before finding the perfect one. It's purple stretch velvet, low cut, snug around my chest and loose in the tummy-hip-thigh region. The saleswoman tells me that if I pass it up, I'll regret it forever. I study my reflection in the mirror. I've never worn anything this risqué, but it strikes me that my breasts actually look vaguely sexy when they're not lost beneath layers of baggy clothing. I decide to go for it.

As soon as I get home, I slip on the new dress and peek into my parents' room. Mom is unpacking her gym bag.

"What do you think?" I ask, twirling around her room. The skirt billows out like an upside-down tulip.

"Very nice," Mom says.

"Thanks."

"It's not your usual style, is it?"

Actually, Mom, I want to say, *it's not YOUR usual style.*

"That's what I like about it," I say.

"Where did you get it?"

"Torrid."

Mom places her sneakers in the rack hanging over her closet door. "Do you really think you should have gotten purple?"

I stop twirling. "Why not?"

"Purple doesn't go with your hair. Blonds should wear yellow or beige, something that isn't so domineering."

Fifteen minutes later, Mom leaves for a hair appointment. That's when I decide to have a little hair appointment of my own. I zip up my jacket and walk down to Ricky's, this wacky store that specializes in leopard-print undies and glittery makeup. The sales guy recommends a brand of hair dye called Special Effects. He explains that it lasts for three to six weeks, possibly longer with light hair. I select the shade "Pimpin' Purple."

As soon as I get home, I dig some rubber gloves out of the supply closet and lock myself in the bathroom. I turn on the shower, strip down, shampoo my hair, and follow the instructions on the Special Effects bottle. Forty minutes later, I emerge from the bathroom. My hair resembles a wad of grape-flavored Bubble Yum.

"Oh my God!" Mom gasps upon entering the apartment a few hours later.

I'm in the kitchen making a cup of hot chocolate. I'm wearing one of Anaïs's old Dartmouth sweatshirts and my flannel pajama bottoms.

"What have you done?" Mom clutches her collarbone. She appears to be asphyxiating.

"You said my hair didn't go with my dress," I say matter-of-factly.

"Please tell me it's not permanent. That's all I want to hear."

"It's not permanent." I pour boiling water into my mug and watch the mini-marshmallows bob to the surface.

"Really?"

"No. You just asked me to say that."

Tendons are straining out of Mom's neck like taut violin strings. "How long will it last?"

"Three to six weeks, possibly longer."

"Well," Mom says after a long silence, "at least you didn't dye it green."

Special Effects had a particularly offensive shade called "Iguana Green." I kick myself for not going that route.

❦ ❦ ❦ ❦

Everyone at the Lowensteins' party gushes over my hair. With that and my cleavagey dress and my eyebrow ring, I make an impressive entrance. Dad escorts me around the room, commenting that the purple hair comes from *his* side of the family.

While we're in the buffet line, Byron makes a sniping remark about how I look like one of those Teletubby characters from the show we used to watch when we were really little. He emphasizes the word "tubby." Before I can stop myself, I kick him in the shin really hard. I can tell it hurts because he looks like he wants to smack me. He slams down his plate of latkes and stomps away. I help myself to one of his potato pancakes.

Near the end of the evening, I'm trapped in a corner with Nan the Neurotic Nutritionist. She's spent the past ten minutes warbling on about organic produce and the chemicals they put into prepackaged foods.

"Speaking of chemicals," Nan says, gesturing to my purple head, "how did you decide to take the plunge?"

I glance at Mom. She's standing a few feet from me, sipping spiked punch and talking to a small, bespectacled woman. I can hear her explaining how Byron took time off from Columbia to reevaluate his life, how it's hard always being an overachiever.

"I'm taking time off to reevaluate my hair color," I say. "It's hard always being a blond."

⑥ ⑥ ⑥ ⑥

We're in the car on the way home from the Lowensteins'. Dad is driving. Byron is up front keeping him company. Mom drank too much punch, so she's resting in the back with me. I'm staring out my foggy window, checking out Christmas decorations in people's yards.

"Ginny?" Mom says.

I turn toward her. Mom hasn't called me Ginny since I was five or six. "Yeah?"

"Remember what you said when we were shopping, about how you're not like me when I was younger?"

I nod as I think about that scene in Saks. My toe is nearly healed, so I'd rather not dwell on it anymore.

"I wish I'd had the nerve to dye my hair purple when I was your age."

I can't believe I'm hearing this. "You like my hair?"

"I'm not saying *that* much." Mom smiles sheepishly. The punch definitely has loosened her up. "But I do admire your chutzpah."

I stare at Mom. She stares back at me. We sit there for a second, staring and smiling at each other.

"Did Mom just use the word 'chutzpah'?" Byron laughs hoarsely. "Ms. Ozark, Arkansas, goes to a Hanukkah party and suddenly she's speaking Yiddish."

Mom looks out her window.

I look out mine.

"I like the word 'chutzpah,'" Dad says. "It means courage and strength, but it sums it up in a way that only Yiddish can do."

"But *Mom* speaking Yiddish? She's so white bread."

I wipe the condensation from my window just in time to spot a huge plastic Santa propped on a rooftop, his tomato-red cheeks blinking in the night.

Yes, Mom.

Speaking Yiddish.

About me.

28

Christmas has never been very deck-the-hallsy around the Shreves household, and this year is no exception. I give Mom a gift certificate to Banana Republic. I give Dad a gift certificate to Patagonia. I give Byron a gift certificate to Amazon. He gives me the same gift certificate for the same amount, so we both keep our own. I use my gift certificate to buy a book of poetry and art by Ani DiFranco, the woman who wrote the song that Annie Mills played for me.

My parents give me a high-quality digital camera. That's what I asked for. I've been mulling over the idea of starting a blog with writing and pictures, so I thought a real camera would come in handy instead of just using my phone. At the very least, I can send Shannon shots of my purple hair. She's already texted me a bunch of goofy pictures of her sticking out her completely healed tongue.

The day after Christmas, Mom and Dad fly to the Caribbean, where they're spending a week at a tropical golf resort. As soon as they leave, Byron takes over the apartment, strewing towels on the bathroom floor, leaving the TV on all the time, clogging the kitchen sink with crusty dishes.

I relocate to Mrs. Myers's apartment on the ninth floor. She's visiting her grandnephew in Florida, so I'm feeding her Siamese cats. I don't sleep in her bed, but I spend all my waking hours down there reading, baking brownies, and watching shows. The only times I go up to our apartment are to sleep or shower.

I haven't spoken with anyone from school, so I don't know what happened with Mr. Moony. I don't know if he had a heart attack or if he's in the hospital or what. I still can't believe I saw him a few minutes before he was rushed off in an ambulance.

I considered calling Ms. Crowley to see what she knows, but then I remembered that she's spending the break with her in-laws in Vermont. I feel awful that I stormed out of her office last week. I know she only wanted to help me, but I guess it struck a raw nerve. As they say, the truth is always the hardest thing to hear.

ⓖ ⓖ ⓖ ⓖ

It's New Year's Eve afternoon.

I've just arrived at the kickboxing class that Dr. Love recommended. For my New Year's resolution, I'm vowing to do something good for my body and soul. A daily hot fudge sundae almost won out, if it weren't for the body aspect. Then I

222

considered another crash diet, but that seems to trash my soul.

It's a small class, only nine other girls. They're all around my age. The teacher's name is Tisha. She's got cornrowed hair, a full figure, and an orange spandex outfit. She looks like she could kick some serious ass.

Tisha has us jump rope and do jumping jacks to warm up. After we stretch, she hands out gloves and this long, black cloth material. She shows newcomers how to wrap the material around our hands to protect them. It's supposed to go around each finger, our knuckles, and our wrists, but it's so confusing that one girl jokes by binding her hand to her foot, which makes us all crack up.

We spend the rest of the hour learning how to punch and kick various bags. At one point, as we're punching what she calls the "heavy bags," Tisha tells us to visualize someone who pisses us off and let them have it. I think about Byron and end up punching so hard that Tisha has the other girls pause to admire my efforts.

After class I'm drenched in sweat, but I feel energized. It's strange how taking all that anger out on the punching bag actually makes me feel better than I have in a long time.

"I'm thrilled to have you join us," Tisha says to me as I pull my sweatpants on over my shorts. "I can tell you have a lot of potential."

"Thanks," I say.

Tisha and I discuss the schedule and fees and then I head to the subway with two other girls from the class. They introduce themselves as Sammie and Phoebe. Phoebe is really small and chatty. She says she started this class a few months ago, after her parents insisted she take up an athletic activity. Sammie is much quieter, but she smiles at me a few times and I can tell she's nice, just more on the shy side.

We all chat for a few stops on the subway. They both rave about my purple hair. Phoebe gets off at Ninety-Sixth Street. Sammie and I ride down to Seventy-Ninth Street together. She tells me how her dad is in town for the holidays, so she's showing him around the city.

When we get to my stop, I wave good-bye.

"See you at the next class," she says.

"Yeah," I say. "Happy New Year!"

🌀 🌀 🌀 🌀

Shannon and I have promised to call each other tonight, have a bicoastal celebration, ring in the New Year.

I call Shannon around ten. Liam and Nina have just left for the evening, so our first order of business is intoxication. I put my phone on speaker and carry it into the kitchen because Dad keeps the vodka in the freezer. I narrate my bartending prowess to Shannon as I pour some vodka into a glass and fill the rest with orange juice.

"Well, I'm taking white wine," Shannon says, giggling, "and mixing it with cherry Kool-Aid."

"Shannon Iris," I say, "you are such a boozer."

Neither of us has ever raided our parents' alcohol supply before, so we're buzzed just from the excitement of it. I carry my drink into my bedroom. Shannon and I chat for about an hour, and then we decide to take a quick bathroom break.

"I'll call you back in five minutes," Shannon says.

"Make sure to fill up your wineglass!"

"Who's the boozer now?"

I teeter a little when I stand up. After peeing, I head into the kitchen and pour another shot of vodka. This time I mix it with cranberry juice.

"Go easy on Dad's vodka," Byron calls from the living room. "It's not cheap stuff."

Byron is slumped on the couch, watching the ball drop on TV. He's been grumpy all day because no one invited him out tonight.

"Whatever," I say, pouring some additional vodka into my glass.

My phone rings, so I spring for it.

"Shan?"

"Drunk yet?"

"Getting there," I say.

"Me too!"

Shannon and I giggle and tell stupid jokes until the clocks hit midnight in New York. Then we shriek and scream and jump on our beds. We're both a little sloshed. And it doesn't help that we've been pretending to slur our words for the past twenty minutes.

"Happy New Year, shhhwweeetheart," Shannon garbles.

"Shhhame to you, Shannon Ireeeeesh."

After we hang up, I make my way into the kitchen to get

some water. I'm so wobbly that I have to clutch the walls. My cheeks feel flushed, and I'm smiling for no reason in particular.

"Feeling okay?" Byron asks. He's clutching a fork and staring into the open fridge.

I scowl. "Why should you care?"

I attempt to pour a glass of water, but half of it splashes onto the counter. Ever since our argument a few weeks ago, there's been some serious tension between Byron and me. In the past I would have been the one to back down, but now I'm more than happy to keep my pistols drawn.

"It's just that your first time drinking can be the worst," Byron says.

"How do you know it's my first time?"

"I'm remembering back from when I was in high school."

"And what does *that* have to do with me?"

Byron shrugs as he takes a container of potato salad out of the fridge. "It's crazy thinking about high school, Gin. I thought I had my whole life set, but then one wrong turn and look at me now."

I hold on to the dishwasher to steady myself. "Do you regret what you did to Annie Mills?"

Byron stabs a potato chunk with his fork. "Sure. I mean, I regret that whole night."

"Well, you definitely let me down," I say. Normally, I wouldn't be this honest with Byron, but the vodka is doing strange things to my brain.

"What do you mean?"

I stare at my brother. In the past several months, I've been so upset because he hurt Annie Mills. But it hits me that I'm angry on my own behalf, too. Partially because of the date rape, but mostly for how Byron has acted toward me over the past several years.

"I used to worship you," I say, "even though you didn't treat me with the same respect that I treated you."

"You can't put people on pedestals." Byron snaps the lid back on the container. "They'll just disappoint you."

"You let me put you up there, so you've got to take some responsibility."

Byron leans against the counter. He doesn't respond, but I know that he heard me.

I head into my room and collapse on my bed. The walls start spinning around me. I feel like I'm in that twister scene from *The Wizard of Oz,* but instead of farmhouses and witches on bicycles whizzing through the air, it's ideas.

I'm thinking about Ms. Crowley's comment about how I isolate myself from my peers. I'm thinking about my new camera. I'm thinking about how much I've enjoyed trying new things, like my eyebrow ring and my purple hair. I'm thinking about those girls from kickboxing and how easy it was to meet new people, much easier than I always thought it would be.

All of a sudden, I feel nauseous. I stumble into the bathroom, open the toilet lid, and puke.

Happy New Year, I think to myself as I swish a mouthful of water and spit it into the sink.

29

I'm actually excited about starting school again. Today is our first day back, so I'm wearing the polyester orange shirt that I bought at that vintage shop in Seattle. I wore it once over break, and I like the way it looks.

I factor in some extra time to do my hair. It's faded a little, so I want to jazz it up for school. I experiment with a few styles before settling on two antenna-like pigtails sprouting from either side. I rub purple glitter around my eyes to add to the cosmic effect.

I'm on my way to my locker when I pass Alyssa Wu. She's wearing a cream-colored sweater and a matching cap. I bet she knitted them herself. They look great with her shiny black hair.

"Cool hair!" she says.

"Thanks."

Alyssa walks to my locker with me. As I turn my combination, I ask, "How was your break?"

"Fine. Boring. Same as usual," she says. "What about you?"

The principal's voice comes over the intercom. She summons us to the auditorium for an assembly before first period.

I slam my locker shut. "Do you know what that's about?"

Alyssa shrugs. "Not a cluc."

As Alyssa and I settle into some aisle seats, I notice that Brinna Livingston is sitting in Brie's usual Queen Bee spot. To her right is Briar Schwartz, Lady in Waiting #1. To her left is a skinny sophomore named Brittany Felsen.

I glance around for Brie, only to see her sitting a few rows back. She looks awful—pale and small, like a flutter of wind could blow her away. I wonder if she's been bumped from her position of power, if Brinna now holds the throne, if Brittany Felsen is the replacement Bri-girl.

The principal walks onto the stage and taps the microphone a few times.

"Welcome back, students and faculty," she says. "I'm sorry to start the new year with tragic news, but as most of you know, Clive Moony had some heart trouble the day before break." The principal daubs her eyes with a tissue. "It turned out to be a major heart attack that took a toll on his body. Mr. Moony passed away on New Year's Day."

The auditorium is completely silent. I glance at Alyssa, but her face is sinking into her hands. My eyes and nose sting like I want to cry, but the tears won't come. The principal launches into a speech about how Mr. Moony taught math for forty-one years, directed the school choir for thirty years, won Model Brewster Teacher seven times. When she tells us that condolence cards can be sent to his widow, I'm shocked by the realization that Mr. Moony had a life outside of the Pythagorean theorem.

"In honor of Clive Moony," the principal says, "I'd like to have a moment of silence."

As we sit in silence, I can't help but feel like something is wrong. I mean, Mr. Moony was *never* quiet, what with his never-ending parade of songs with our names in them.

Suddenly, a guy near the back belts out, *"Mr. Moon, Moon, bright and shiny moon, oh won't you please shine down on me?"*

A few kids crane their necks to stare at him, but most people join in the song.

"Mr. Moon, Moon, bright and shiny moon, oh won't you please shine down on me?"

Those who don't know the lyrics hum or sway from side to side. I sing, even though tears are trickling down my face. Most people in the auditorium are at least sniffling, if not all-out crying. I have a feeling we're all thinking the same thing. We hated the way Mr. Moony serenaded us, but we're going to miss it now that he's gone.

As I'm filing out of the auditorium, I pass a teary-eyed Ms. Crowley.

"Virginia." She wraps her arms around me.

"I'm so sorry for how I acted before break," I say. "I don't know what—"

Ms. Crowley cuts me off. "No, *I'm* sorry. I completely overstepped my boundaries. I've been feeling horrible ever since I said it."

"I'm glad you did. I needed to hear that, especially from someone I respect."

Ms. Crowley squeezes my shoulder. "What have you got first period?"

"Global Studies. Why?"

"I've got something for you. I was going to give it to you before break. Can you come up to my office? I'll write you a late pass."

On our way upstairs, I tell Ms. Crowley about my new idea. I've decided that rather than having my own blog, I want to start a student blog where kids can rant about anything on their minds. I want to make it an official Brewster club, so I'll need a teacher to sponsor the idea.

"I'd be happy to," Ms. Crowley says as she hands me a wrapped present. "Just bring me the forms and I'll sign away."

I rip open the paper. Ms. Crowley has given me a book called *Body Outlaws*. There are several pictures of women on the cover—all shapes and sizes and races—flexing their biceps, chowing down, flaunting tattoos.

"It's a fantastic book," Ms. Crowley says. "All essays by young women who are rebelling against body norms."

I thumb through the index. There's a chapter called "The Butt" and another called "Fishnets, Feather Boas, and Fat."

"Make sure to read the inscription," Ms. Crowley adds.

I flip to the inside flap, where she's written:

"I thought at last that it was time to roll up the crumpled skin of the day, with its arguments and its impressions and its anger and its laughter, and cast it into the hedge."
—Virginia Woolf, *A Room of One's Own*

I've never really *gotten* Virginia Woolf before, but this passage seems to make sense. It's about throwing out old notions and reevaluating what you've always thought. At least I think so. I guess it makes more sense on an emotional level than on an intellectual one.

Maybe that's the way it's supposed to be.

As soon as I've read *Body Outlaws*, I think I'll give my namesake another chance.

30

I can't believe how much has changed in the first week back at school. I don't know whether it's Mr. Moony's death or just my perception of things, but the climate at Brewster feels much warmer. Popular kids are waving at regular kids in the halls. Regular kids are helping dorky kids gather papers if they drop a notebook down the stairs. Dorky kids aren't smirking behind their hands when a popular kid screws up in class.

When I pointed this out to Alyssa Wu, she summed it up as "the Postdeath Touchy-Feely Period."

"It's like how my whole family got along for a few weeks after my uncle died," she said one morning as we were waiting for Global Studies to begin. "Don't be fooled by it, though."

"But isn't it a good thing?"

"Rule number one of the Postdeath Touchy-Feely Period:

Enjoy it while it lasts," Alyssa said. "Rule number two of the Postdeath Touchy-Feely Period: It doesn't last."

I had to laugh. It was surprising to hear that someone else in this world thinks the way I do, in terms of lists and rules. I haven't written a list in forever, not since everything happened with Byron. But I'm starting to feel ideas come into my head again.

"I still can't believe I was in his class a few minutes before the heart attack," I said.

"I know," Alyssa said. "It was so scary. I kept thinking that I shouldn't have listened to everyone. I should have gotten the school nurse at the beginning of the period."

"There's no way you could have known."

"But still."

I've been eating lunch with Alyssa and a few other girls every day, even though Ms. Crowley keeps reminding me that I'm welcome in her office. I'm really starting to like Alyssa. She comes across as a little weird at first, but she's actually pretty cool. She fidgets constantly—her fingers, wrists, ankles—every joint is always in motion. That's why she knits. She says she needs to be doing something with her hands, otherwise she'd drive herself and everyone in her vicinity crazy.

Alyssa is a music junkie. She's the one who told me about the concerts I've been watching on YouTube. She goes to live pop-up concerts around the city almost every day after school to join the crowds cheering anywhere from Union Square to the Oculus subway station. She invited me to join her at one in Prospect Park yesterday afternoon. As we jumped and hooted and froze our butts off, I learned another thing about Alyssa. She can scream louder than anyone I know.

That's why I've asked her to get everyone's attention today.

It's lunchtime. I'm about to make an announcement about my new blog. Over the past week, I've filled out all the necessary paperwork to make it an official school club. I've even received a modest budget, enough to buy a domain name and get it hosted. The only things I need now are writers, editors, and people who can do graphic design.

Alyssa stands on a chair and cups her hands around her mouth to create the megaphone effect.

"Romans, cafeteria-men!" she bellows.

People pause midbite and glance curiously up at her.

She continues. "Virginia Shreves has an important announcement, so lend her an ear."

I take a sip of Diet Coke, swish the taco shell out of my braces, and climb on a chair next to Alyssa. I tell everyone that I'm creating a blog where people can bitch, rant, and rave about whatever is on their minds.

"The first meeting is in the computer cluster after school today," I say.

Alyssa chimes in that it'll look good on college applications, something that would inspire most Brewsterites to dance on scorching embers.

A few people visit our table to say they'll swing by the meeting. One girl tells me she can't make it but gives me her number so I can let her know about future gatherings.

I'm tossing my napkin into the trash when I spot Froggy.

He's heading out of the cafeteria with some friends. We've spoken a little since school started again. He complimented my purple hair in the hallway. I borrowed his eraser in French. That's about the extent of it. I *did* see him lugging his trombone up the front steps of school, so that ruled out my sold-horn-for-laser-surgery theory.

"Hey, Froggy," I call out. "Wait up!"

Froggy glances over his shoulder. I can hear him telling his friends to go on ahead.

"What's up?" Froggy asks. He looks pretty surprised.

I feel my cheeks turning pink. "I was just wondering if you were coming to my meeting today."

Froggy tweaks his nose a few times. "I hadn't thought about it."

"I could really use your design skills."

Froggy doesn't respond.

"More than that," I add, "it would be nice to hang out again."

Before I can say anything I'll later regret, I turn and start toward my table.

"Virginia?" Froggy calls after me.

I spin around. "Yeah?"

"I'll be there."

ⓖ ⓖ ⓖ ⓖ

I race to the computer cluster after last period. Krishna said we can hold our meetings there. He's even offered to assist with the techie aspects of getting the blog up and running.

I'm so excited about the turnout—eight kids, including me and Alyssa—that I won't let myself feel bad that Froggy is a no-show. I glance at Alyssa, who gives me a sympathetic smile. I filled her in on the brief history of Froggy, so she had her fingers and toes crossed that he'd be at the meeting.

"One more minute," Alyssa mouths, gesturing to her watch.

We wait for two and a half minutes. Finally, I sit on top of a desk, cross one knee over the other, and turn my notebook to a fresh page. I'm just introducing myself when Froggy walks in, his hands jammed in his pockets. I wave at Froggy, take a deep breath, and suggest we go around the room and say our names.

After everyone's introduced themselves, I talk a little about my vision for the blog. I make sure to add that it will reflect what's going on in *all* our heads. Basically, I want us to voice the things that people don't ordinarily talk about.

Then I bring up the first order of business—deciding what to call it. Froggy rolls his chair over to a computer and volunteers to check which domain names are available.

"How about Rant?" suggests one ninth grader.

Froggy types it in. "Taken," he says after a moment.

A girl named Nikki asks, "What about DirtyLaundry, since that's what we're going to air?"

"Good idea," one kid says.

Froggy is quiet for a second. "Also taken."

This goofy junior named Hudson says, "We should call it MBS, like Model Brewster Student, except it would really stand for Major Bullshit."

"I wish," I say, laughing, "but they'd probably cut our school funding."

Alyssa is propped on the back of a chair, knitting something long and violet. "Do you have any ideas, Virginia?"

I'm quiet for a second. "What about something like Earthquake because we want to shake things up?"

A few kids nod, but after Froggy types "earthquake" into the computer, he says, "Taken by some science lab."

"What about Earthquack?" Alyssa asks. "We're shaking stuff up, but we're also going to expose things for what they are and what they aren't."

We all crack up. Hudson makes a duck sound.

Froggy types "earthquack" and then turns in his chair so he's facing everyone. "Surprisingly," he says, grinning, "Earthquack is up for grabs."

Everyone applauds.

"Let's have a show of hands," I call out. "How many people want Earthquack?"

The vote is unanimous.

Earthquack is born.

31

Life has become a blur of school, Earthquack, and wailing with Alyssa at various live concerts around the city. Even my parents commented that I'm rarely home anymore, and I didn't think they noticed those kinds of things.

What shocked me more than anything is that I didn't watch shows for three straight days last week. I didn't even realize it until I went to check out something on Netflix and spaced about my password. By the time I finally remembered it, I'd gotten a brainstorm for Earthquack, so I ran into my room to scribble some stuff in my notebook.

I've been putting so much energy into Earthquack. We agreed to convene once a week, but the core group of us have been sitting together at lunch every day, so it usually becomes an informal meeting.

We're shooting to launch Earthquack by the beginning of

February. People have already shown me drafts of their ideas. Nikki is writing the uncensored story of Theo Brewster, with an emphasis on his alcoholic, rum-running days. Hudson is writing a humorous call-to-arms, urging the regular and dorky kids to infiltrate the popular courtyard armed with candy cigarettes. Alyssa is gathering lyrics to Mr. Moony's favorite songs because we're going to post a special tribute to him. She's also writing a scathing essay about how because she's Asian, the Brewster administration always calls on her when they're taking pictures for their promotional fliers so they can flaunt their diversity.

When she told everyone that idea, Nikki laughed and said, "Me too!"

Nikki is black, so she's probably on the diversity roster as well. I was tempted to say something about how Brewster hasn't shown any interest in *weight* diversity, but I'm not quite ready to go there yet.

One day at lunch, Froggy brought along Sarah, that ninth grader with the ski-jump nose. I wanted to drown myself in an industrial-sized vat of chocolate pudding, but then I heard her tell Hudson that Froggy's parents and her parents are old friends, so she and Froggy are practically siblings. It also turns out that Sarah is a grammar whiz, so she's going to be our copy editor.

Froggy has put together some hilarious ideas for the design. My favorite is an image of a yellow duck taking a bite out of our planet. When it does, several ducklings jump out of the Earth's core and waddle across the screen, quacking wildly.

He printed out a screen shot for me, and I taped it up inside my locker.

I have to admit I still have feelings for Froggy. But since I can't imagine he'd ever want to go public with me, I'll have to settle for just being friends. My hormones are telling me to obey the Fat Girl Code of Conduct and invite Froggy to fool around in private again. Then I remember how hiding our relationship made me feel lousy. Even so, whenever I catch Froggy looking my way in French class, I feel a thrum-thrumming between my legs.

Speaking of French, I'm considering dropping it after this year. It's actually not that bad anymore because Mademoiselle Kiefer has undergone a hundred-and-eighty-degree transformation. It all started when our new geometry teacher—the one who replaced Mr. Moony—delivered a dozen white roses to the language office. They were addressed to *Joanne Kiefer, a natural woman*. Mademoiselle Kiefer must have had a whopping case of sexual frustration because she's now as sunny as Saint-Tropez. She's even talking about doing a special unit on Valentine's Day vocabulary. But I've finally come to terms with the fact that, regardless of my Shreves lineage, I'm simply not meant to *parler Français*.

I arranged a special meeting with the Chinese teacher. He said that if I take an intensive course over the summer, I can join the sophomores in September and thus complete my three-year language requirement by graduation. Alyssa's parents are from Beijing, so she's offered to tutor me. She's already taught me how to say *hello, thank you,* and *fuck off* in Mandarin.

I've gone to four more kickboxing classes. I love it, even though I'm so sore some days I can hardly sneeze. But it feels incredible to kick and sweat for a solid hour, to channel my aggression into a punching bag. I'm starting to feel stronger, to see my stomach and arms tightening up.

Dad must have noticed the difference. Last Sunday we went to a Knicks game together. I was surprised when he invited me because that's something he always does with Byron. But Dad and I have been communicating a little more recently, ever since he drove me to the airport on Thanksgiving morning. A few weeks ago, I worked up the nerve to tell him I felt bad he didn't bring me to that Yankees playoff game last fall, so maybe the Knicks tickets were his way of making it up to me.

We were at Madison Square Garden. I'd been cheering and springing up and down and lusting after a certain sexy forward. As I settled back into my seat, Dad turned to me.

"You know, Ginny," he said, "you really look like you're slimming down."

A few months ago, that kind of compliment would have made my day. But I don't want that kind of feedback from my parents anymore. I don't want them to think they can discuss my body like it's the weather forecast on 1010 WINS.

"Dad? We're trying to be more open with each other, right?"

Dad nodded, but his forehead was wrinkled in confusion.

"Then I have to tell you that I'd rather you don't talk about my body. It's just not yours to discuss."

Dad looked like he swallowed a basketball. "I'm sorry," he said. "I hadn't realized . . ."

"It's okay. Now you know."

ⓖ ⓖ ⓖ ⓖ

I've been thinking a lot lately about why I overeat. I've decided that food is my ultimate comfort. If I'm lonely or depressed, a bowl of pasta or a plate of cookies will cheer me up. I know I have to learn healthier ways to deal, but it can't happen overnight. And I can't do it for anyone but myself.

That's why I haven't told Mom I'm taking kickboxing. I'm paying for it out of my own money. I just don't want this to become something I'm doing to please her, to make her proud of me.

I *did* tell Teri the Tiny Gym Teacher. She gave me a form and said that if I have Tisha sign it after every kickboxing class, I can place out of gym.

Thanks to kickboxing, I've been able to go to the computer cluster during gym periods. My grades slipped a little last fall, so I'm determined to bring them up again. Especially since I've decided I probably don't want to go to college in the Arctic Circle. I think I'd like to apply to an artsy school with a good writing program, like Vassar or Wesleyan.

That's what my language arts teacher was talking about the other day. I'm really loving language arts now. We started a new unit a few weeks ago called "Women and Power," so we're reading this amazing book called *The Red Tent,* which is about biblical stories retold from the perspective of women.

Only when I'm completely done with my homework do I let myself work on Earthquack. I'm writing a list for the blog, my first one in months. It's also the first list ever that I'm going to show people. No, not just *people.* Many, many people. I still can't believe I'm going to take the plunge. It makes me jittery just thinking about it. But I'm tired of always hiding what's going on and acting like things are okay even when they aren't.

Here's what I've written so far:

THE EARTH, MY BUTT, AND OTHER BIG ROUND THINGS
by Virginia Shreves

1. My best friend moved to the other side of the earth for the entire school year. I thought I couldn't survive without her. While I still miss her like crazy, I think it's good that I've had to venture out on my own.
2. Besides, if she hadn't gone to Walla Walla (home of the big round onion!), I wouldn't have been able to run away to Seattle for Thanksgiving and get an eyebrow ring and escape my stress-filled home (see #4).
3. I've never been a fan of my butt. Too big, too round, blah, blah, blah. But when grooving to outdoor concerts in the middle of the winter, it's much more fun to shake your

booty when you actually HAVE a booty to shake, not just a bony excuse for a rear end.

4. Not all big round things are great. Definitely not the meteor-sized lump I got in my throat last October when I found out my brother was being suspended from college. But it gave me an important reality check about him, about my family, about myself.

5. Speaking of last fall, this isn't round, but it's definitely big. It's an apology. Last fall I was mean to someone special. I hope you know who you are (hint: Mondays after school). I wish I could say I was temporarily possessed by an evil alien, but the truth is just that I was going through a hard time.

6. Another big round, not-so-pleasant thing: a head of lettuce. I'm going to state it—here, now, and forever. I hate lettuce. I've always hated lettuce. So maybe my mom is a skinny, lettuce-eating fiend, but I don't have to be, too. There are ways to eat healthy that don't involve rabbit cuisine.

7. And finally, let's face it. If you had a small puny present and a big round present, which one would you open first? The big round one, right? Who ever said smaller is better? NO ONE, that's who!

32

It's an unseasonably warm Saturday afternoon. One of those days when the air is mild, icicles are dripping outside my window, and I want to throw all my winter clothes down the garbage chute. Of course, there will probably be a blizzard tomorrow, but on a day like this, it feels like the balmy weather will last forever.

I'm crouched in front of my mirror, trying on the tiny gold eyebrow ring that Mom brought me from the Caribbean. When I first opened the velvet box, I thought she was giving me a pair of earrings, but then I realized there was only one ring inside.

"Is this an . . ." I was so shocked I couldn't finish my sentence.

"If you're going to have facial jewelry, you shouldn't wear silver, not with your complexion."

"That's my Phyl," Dad said, tickling her waist. "If you can't beat 'em, at least make sure they have the right metal."

Mom swatted him playfully, and I cracked up. I'm realizing that sometimes it's easier to laugh off annoying Mom-isms than get angry at them. Besides, it's a cute eyebrow ring, much nicer than anything I could afford.

Byron is moving back to Columbia today. He's not going to the dorms, though. He'll be living in an off-campus basement apartment with a few grad students. It was Byron's choice, but he made it with strong pressure from Dean Briggs. It sounds like the rugby team will take him back, but he's been kicked off debate and has to undergo mandatory counseling for the entire semester.

Byron seems to be taking it all pretty hard—the off-campus stuff and the counseling and the debate team. The other day when he was grumbling about it, I overheard Mom tell him that he's lucky Columbia is giving him another chance. Dad added that the whole thing could have gone a lot worse. Byron didn't say anything back. He's still unaccustomed to Mom and Dad not applauding every little thing he does.

It doesn't help that Mom and Dad are skiing in Connecticut this weekend, so Byron has to move all by himself. And there's no big brunch today, like my parents have had at the beginning of every other semester. I could tell Byron felt bad when he woke up this morning. He kept making comments like, "They're gone?" and "They didn't even leave a note?" and "They just left without saying good-bye?"

I was tempted to say, *Join the club. That's how they've treated me for fifteen years*. But instead I toasted us both a bagel and made two mugs of hot chocolate.

Ever since New Year's Eve, Byron's been nicer to me than he's been in years. I still haven't forgiven him for what he did to Annie Mills, but he's the only brother I have, so I can't hate him forever. I don't think we'll ever be as close as when we were kids, but maybe that's okay.

I hear Byron heaving as he carries crates to the service elevator.

"Byron?" I call from my bedroom.

"Yeah?"

"Can you come here for a second?"

Byron approaches my doorway. He's wearing faded jeans and a sweat-soaked shirt. "What's up?"

"How would you like a full-length mirror for your new room?"

"You don't want your mirror?"

"I *never* wanted my mirror."

"I'll take it," Byron says. "But let me know if you ever want it back."

Byron and I lift the mirror together. Once we've loaded it into the elevator, I help him haul the rest of his stuff out of the apartment and into the rental van.

After Byron drives off, I walk into the lobby of our building and check the mail. I'm thumbing through a stack of bills for my parents when I come across a handwritten envelope from Anaïs, addressed to me. I step into the elevator.

Dear Ginny,

Thanks for your letter! I'm so sorry about everything that's been happening. It reminded me of why I had to escape to Africa. I was suffocated by Mom's denial, by our family's pressure to fit a perfect mold at all costs. I'm sure you know what I'm talking about.

I promise a longer letter very soon, but I just wanted to say that in spite of everything, you sound better than ever.

Love,

Anaïs

When I get upstairs, I put the letter back in its envelope. It's strange to see Anaïs writing about the whole perfect-family thing. I'm starting to wonder if that's changing, if Byron's date rape shook everything up.

My phone rings. I make a dive for it.

"Hello?"

It's Mom, calling from the car. "We're driving home from Connecticut."

"But it's only Saturday afternoon."

"The snow is too slushy for skiing," Mom says.

Dad says something in the background.

"Oh yes," Mom adds. "We've gotten last-minute tickets to a film screening this evening. Would you like to come along?"

"Thanks, but I can't."

"Why not?"

"I'm getting together with some friends for dinner."

"Can't you get out of it?" Mom asks. "This is a great opportunity."

"Nope," I say. "Sorry."

Mom laughs. "You really are a Shreves."

"What do you mean?"

"You do exactly what you want." Mom pauses before adding, "If I don't see you before you leave, have fun tonight."

"Thanks."

As I'm hanging up, I think about how I've always felt very *un*-Shreves, like I belonged in a clan of plump, blond underachievers. Now that I've been deemed an official family member, I'm not even sure I *want* that affiliation. Does "doing exactly what I want" mean not thinking about other people's feelings? Because that's just not the kind of person I am.

Maybe it can mean whatever I want it to mean, like taking care of myself and not letting people walk all over me.

Yes, that's much more like it.

⑤ ⑥ ⑥ ⑥

I wear jeans, a long undershirt, and my Walla Walla is for Lovers sweatshirt. I excavated it from under my bed last night and threw it in the wash. I'm also wearing the violet scarf that Alyssa knitted for me. It's so long I can wrap it around my neck three times.

I grab my new camera and head over to Central Park. I'm meeting up with the Earthquackers at Belvedere Castle. We're going to Pizzeria Uno for dinner, but first we're doing a photo shoot so we can post pictures of us on the premiere issue of

Earthquack. Froggy thought the castle would establish our regal status.

Most of the others are already there when I arrive. Some are climbing the stairs to an upper turret. Others are throwing ice chunks into Turtle Pond. Alyssa is chatting with Hudson. I know she has a crush on him, so I leave her alone.

"Nice sweatshirt." Froggy bumps his hip against mine.

"Thanks," I say, bumping him back.

"Virginia?"

"Yeah?"

"Do you know what they say about a frog in a castle?"

"No . . . what?"

Froggy gets a shy smile on his face and rubs his nose a few times. "If you kiss him, he'll turn into a prince."

I glance around at the other kids. According to the Fat Girl Code of Conduct, public displays of affection are a cardinal no-no.

"Right here?" I ask.

Froggy nods.

"Right now?"

He nods again.

So I lean forward, close my eyes, and kiss Froggy Welsh the Fourth.

Right on the lips.

Right in front of everybody.

ACKNOWLEDGMENTS

Thanks to my agent, Jodi Reamer, whose positive attitude drove this novel forward. Thanks to my US and UK editors, Deborah Wayshak and Mara Bergman, for loving Virginia as much as I do. Thanks to Liz Bicknell, Jane Winterbotham, and all the amazing people at Candlewick and Walker. Thanks to Cindy Loh and the entire Bloomsbury team for fulfilling my dream of an updated anniversary edition.

Thanks to everyone who gave me the scoop on private schools, plus sizes, piercings, and so much more. Thanks to Jenny Greenberg, Amber Kallen-Monroe, and Juliet Eastland for reading the manuscript and offering valuable suggestions. And a special thanks to my family and friends, for always making me feel welcome on this earth.

FOR FURTHER READING

If Virginia's story brought up strong feelings about body image or sexual violence, I've put together a few places where you can learn more—and get help if you need it. Please remember that you are not alone in your struggles. Reaching out always makes things better. —Carolyn

NATIONAL EATING DISORDER ASSOCIATION
NEDA handles all issues around food and body image, not
   just eating disorders.
www.nationaleatingdisorders.org
Helpline: 1-800-931-2237 or text the word "NEDA" to
   741741

ADIOS BARBIE

A website focused on healthy body image, body positivity, anti-fat-shaming, and much more.

www.adiosbarbie.com

RAPE, ABUSE, AND INCEST NATIONAL NETWORK

RAINN is the largest anti-sexual-violence organization in the country and has a hotline, live chats, and information for anyone in need.

www.rainn.org

National Sexual Assault Hotline: 1-800-656-4673

ABOUT THE AUTHOR

Carolyn Mackler is the acclaimed author of the YA novels *Infinite in Between, Tangled, Guyaholic, Vegan Virgin Valentine*, and *Love and Other Four-Letter Words*, as well as *The Future of Us*, cowritten with bestselling author Jay Asher, and the middle grade novel *Best Friend Next Door*. Her books have been translated into more than twenty languages. Carolyn lives in New York City with her husband and two sons.

THE VERY BEGINNING

Here are a few pages from a notebook I toted around when I was starting *The Earth, My Butt, and Other Big Round Things*, with descriptions of characters and flow charts for how Virginia would change through the course of the novel. I always think it's fascinating to see the process behind the process—and to try to figure out how random scribbles on paper somehow transform into a novel.

And now . . . turn the page for never-before-seen materials from my desk!

VIRGINIA'S FAMILY

On this page I was outlining the characters in Virginia's family and their essential traits. I originally called Virginia's brother Thornton, after Thornton Wilder, but I quickly changed him to Byron because he shares some less-than-savory qualities with Lord Byron.

<u>Mom</u>
- Teen shrink — know-it-all' about teens
- in denial about her own family
- won't say the word <u>fat</u> around V.

<u>Dad</u>
- distant, absent, thinks he can make everything better by snapping his fingers, saying a mean comment

<u>Thornton</u> — Too coddled, too cocky, too deserving

<u>Anais</u> — High expectations — had to flee to other side of world to become herself

<u>Virginia</u> — something always missing — eats to comfort herself

VIRGINIA

Here I was taking time to get to know my main character. This is a rough list of who I thought Virginia would be. I'd barely started writing the book yet. The BW4 was Barrington Welsh the Fourth. That was Froggy's original name before it hit me, early in the writing, that he was totally Froggy.

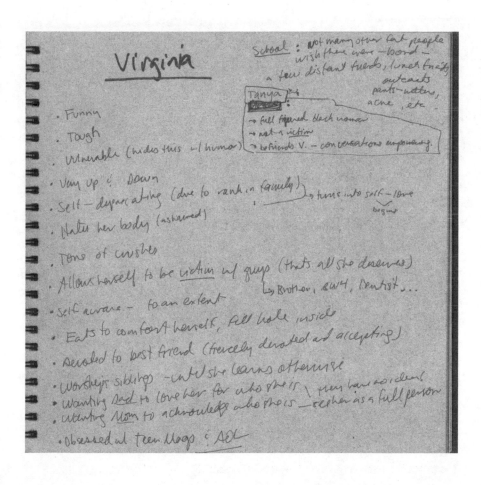

FAMILY TENSION

The "Family Tension" page was an important one for me to figure out because this was going to be Virginia's story—how she broke away from her family and defined herself on her own terms.

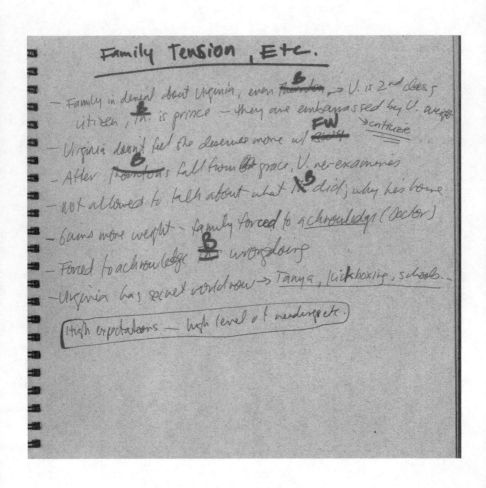

VIRGINIA'S JOURNEY

It was also necessary for me to map out Virginia's journey, to see how she would change from a "good girl" to a liberated person. Those three arrows represent all the things I needed to figure out between the first few chapters and the last!

OTHER RESEARCH

I love how this page has everything from questioning how Virginia's mom controls her weight to researching rumrunners and dorms at Columbia to writing down Virginia's fictional class schedule and teachers. This, to me, is the joy of novel writing.

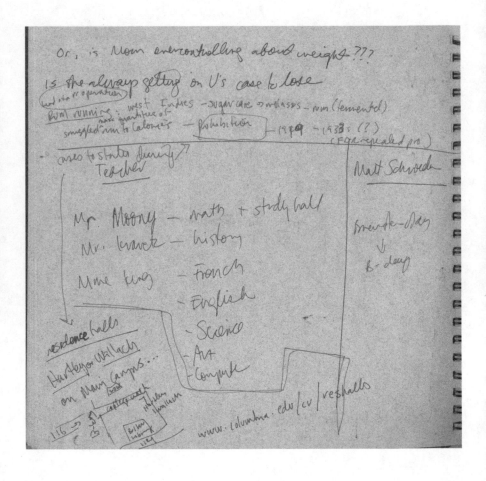

VIRGINIA'S APARTMENT

My very rough sketch of Virginia's apartment. I have no idea why I wrote that their television is in a walnut case, but I did know that I wanted Virginia's room facing the Hudson River. One of my favorite scenes is when she's bereft in bed and sees a red light flashing in New Jersey.

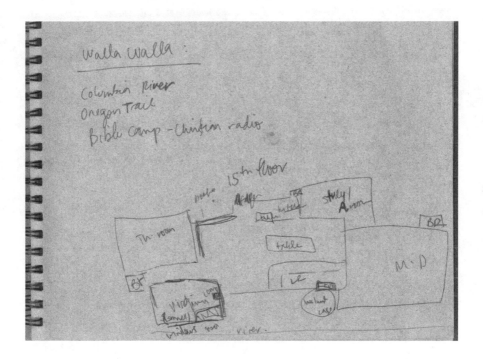

WHAT'S NEXT FOR VIRGINIA?

Find out in the long-awaited sequel to
The Earth, My Butt, and Other Big Round Things!

READ ON FOR A SNEAK PEEK!

Froggy Welsh the Fourth is trying to get inside my jeans.

That should be fine because he's my boyfriend and we've been publicly and officially together for five months and we were privately together for two months last fall and we've already made out and he's gone up my shirt and right now we're locked in my bedroom on a sunny Wednesday afternoon in early June while my parents are at work and my brother is at the gym and my sister is thousands of miles from New York City, finishing her two-year stint in Africa.

But there's a big problem.

The problem is that I've fallen out of like with Froggy. It was never love, but Froggy is my first boyfriend, and the fact that he wanted to be with me, publicly and officially, seemed like a miracle. So I was okay with like. I could deal with like.

To be clear, I'm not saying that *Froggy* is the miracle. He's a dorky-in-a-good-way sixteen-year-old guy. He's medium height and skinny with fluffy hair, pinkish skin, and a stubby nose. He's talented at trombone and graphic design, and not altogether unpopular in our tenth-grade class. That's where the miracle comes in. While I'm not altogether unpopular either and I have some attributes of my own, I'm definitely not skinny. On good days, I consider myself curvy. On regular days, more like chunky. On bad days, I'm plain old fat. In my prestigious private school on the Upper East Side of Manhattan, there aren't a lot of fat girls. And the few plus-size girls who amble apologetically around the hallways never score boyfriends.

So, yeah, I've been super grateful to have Froggy, and I've also liked the making-out and up-my-shirt aspects, especially kissing until our lips are numb and various quadrants of our bodies are wriggling with desire. But then yesterday, as we were making out on a bench in Central Park, a few blocks from school, I had this weird feeling that I was kissing a golden retriever. This was new. Not the kissing part, because we've done a lot of that. But the new sensation was that his tongue felt slobbery and long, like it was trying to retrieve a dog treat from behind my molars. After a few minutes, I wiped my face with my hand and made an excuse about how I forgot a final exam review sheet and had to run back to Brewster before our Global Studies teacher left for the day.

All last night I was stressed. I kept wondering why kissing Froggy had grossed me out. Was I not into him anymore? But how can that happen when nothing between us changed from Monday when we had a perfectly fine good-bye kiss in the empty stairwell near the computer cluster to Tuesday's slobber-fest on the bench? Also, if I truly wasn't into Froggy anymore, what was I supposed to do about that? Is canine-kissing grounds for a breakup?

As I was tossing in bed I decided that the slobbery kiss had to be a fluke. And the fluke had to be because Froggy was stressed about the end of school and therefore not exercising proper tongue control. Mom is an adolescent psychologist, and she frequently says that academic stress hits everyone in different ways. In our case, there are six days left of sophomore year and teachers are slamming us with homework. I decided I needed to forget yesterday and give Froggy and his tongue another shot.

That's why I invited him to my apartment today, and that's how we ended up making out in my room. But as soon as we closed my door, we sat on my bed and pressed our lips together and . . . nope. No chemistry. Not even a spark of physics or just plain human biology. And that's when I knew that—gasp, gulp, crap—I'm not into Froggy anymore.

This is a bad thing to realize as we're on my bed and he's sliding his hand across my stomach to the waistband of my jeans.

"Virginia." Froggy sighs, pushing up my shirt.

I used to cringe at the thought of him seeing my belly region. That was back when we were secretly hooking up. Once we publicly and officially got together, fooling around felt so good that I didn't stop him. But now that I've fallen out of like, I don't want to be doing this anymore. I glance longingly at my bedside table, at the cover of *Fates and Furies*. I wish I could be reading right now. Not only are the main characters, Lotto and Mathilde, the cutest couple ever, but they met at Vassar, which is where I want to go to college.

Froggy sweeps his hand south and starts fiddling with the button on my jeans.

"Uhhhh," I mumble. I clasp my hand over his and drag him back up north. Froggy and I have never been inside each other's jeans before, and I'm definitely not ready to start now.

"Hmmm?" he asks.

I cough and, for lack of a more imaginative word, repeat my brilliant earlier statement. "Uhhhh."

Despite the fact that Froggy and I have been together, on and off, since the beginning of sophomore year, we still suck at talking to each other about what our hands are doing.

"Is everything . . . ?" Froggy pushes his hair out of his eyes.

I know he's asking if I'm okay, if *we're* okay. I don't know what to say because even though I've fallen out of like with Froggy, I can't break up with him. That exact item is at the top of my current list. I often create lists in my head about important things in my life, and sometimes I even write them down. Here's rule number one of a list that I've been thinking about this spring:

HOW TO MAKE SURE SKINNY GIRLS AREN'T THE ONLY ONES WHO HAVE BOYFRIENDS, RULE #1:

It's no secret that the skinny girls score the bulk of the guys. It's not that I have anything against skinny girls as long as they're not bitchy and they don't make fat girls feel like slovenly slobs. But it's still not fair that skinny girls get first, second, third, fourth, and hundredth dibs on the pool of available guys. So if you're a chunky chick and you managed to get a nice boyfriend, don't ever let him go.

I know my lists tend toward the harsh, but whatever. There are very few places that girls, especially teen girls, especially fat teen girls, can be brutally honest. And my imagination is one of them.

Also, maybe it seems harsh when I call myself fat. The truth is that sometimes I *feel* harsh about it and I wish I were born into a skinny body with a kickass metabolism. The list I made up when Froggy and I first got together was called The Fat Girl Code of Conduct, and it smacked of low self-esteem. I've come a long way since then. In general I don't hate my body as much as I used to. I'll never be a twig, but I've learned to embrace my curves. Most days. Okay, some days.

"I have to pee," I say to Froggy.

That will buy me five minutes to figure out what to do. Maybe I can come back with a cold shower and push his horndog self into it.

But then, just as I'm standing up, I hear the front door unlock.

"Anyone home?" my brother shouts.

Froggy yanks down his shirt, rolls off my bed, and stands up so quickly he knocks into my lamp, which topples onto the floor. My door is locked, but I'm freaking out so much I can't hook my bra. And it's not like my boobs are cooperating. By the time I rein them in, my hands are sticky with sweat.

It's not that Byron doesn't know about Froggy. My family is aware I have a boyfriend. Froggy comes over to watch movies, though usually we go to his apartment.

"I didn't think . . . your brother . . ." Froggy picks up the lamp and adjusts the shade.

"Me neither," I say. "He's always at the gym until dinner."

My chest is tight, making it hard to take a good breath. The last thing I want is to be caught midhookup by my *brother*. It's bad enough that Byron smirks when I mention Froggy, like the fact that I have a boyfriend is a joke to him.

I consider suggesting we hide in my room until Froggy has to leave for jazz ensemble. Usually I walk him uptown and then I grab dumplings or scallion pancakes at Pearls on the way home. Not that Upper West Side dumplings compare to the ones in Chinatown. On the weekends that I'm not forced to go to our country house in Connecticut, my friend Alyssa Wu, whose grandparents live in Chinatown, takes me to insider dim sum places.

"What should we do?" Froggy asks. He peers out my window like he's contemplating alternate exit routes. Not an option. My family lives on the top floor of a fifteen-story building on the Upper West Side of New York City. We face west, which means we can see the sunset and the Hudson River and New Jersey stretching out to the horizon.

I shouldn't be blindsided that my brother is here. Now that Columbia has let out for the semester he's living at home, but he's mostly at the gym or hanging out in Brooklyn with old high school friends. In a few weeks he's flying to Paris for an international relations program at the Sorbonne where he'll make up credits that he lost when he got suspended from college last semester. Byron's suspension, in our family, is referred to as "the ordeal."

Translation: It happened, it's over, and now we're not supposed to talk about it.

My summer plans do not involve eating baguettes and strolling along the Seine. My parents wanted me to go on Outward Bound. That's a mountain-climbing, character-building, pooping-in-the-woods expedition. Both my older sister, Anaïs, and then Byron did Outward Bound after their sophomore year of high school. I flat out refused. Even if it didn't involve pooping into a hole and wiping with a leaf, it didn't sound like my idea of a good time. My parents finally agreed to let me stay Inward Bound as long as I agreed to two terms.

1. I get a college-application-enhancing internship.
2. I get my driver's license.

Term one is going to be awesome. Dad is lining up an internship at the company where he's the chief operating officer. Not just for me, but for my best friend, Shannon, who's been on the West Coast since last August but is coming home soon. Dad works in the music industry, creating streaming software. His company is called Ciel Media. *Ciel* means sky in French, my least favorite language, but I try not to hold that fact against the company. There's a pool table in the lounge area and a stocked fridge, and they sometimes receive free concert tickets and get to meet celebrities.

Fantasy: A hot celebrity guy, like a seventeen-year-old shaggy-haired drummer, notices me in the Ciel office and we fall madly in love and I drop out of Brewster and travel the country with him, the envy of drooling groupies.

Reality: I get a selfie with a hot celebrity guy's shaggy hair in the background.

The driver's license term is all sucky reality. I got my learner's permit when I turned sixteen in March, and every weekend since then my parents have forced me to take a driver's ed class at a driving school near our country house in Connecticut. Even with all that driver's ed, I still panic and forget what side of the road I'm supposed to drive on. Dad is determined to help me get my required forty hours behind the wheel, and he's already signed me up for my road test on July tenth.

So, yeah, that's the less-than-ideal part of my summer plan.

While Froggy is lacing his sneakers, I grab my phone and send a group text to Shannon and Alyssa. They don't know each other because Alyssa and I became friends while Shannon was in Washington State this year. But this is an emergency, and I need both of their advice as quickly as possible.

My brother just walked in on Froggy and me, I tell them both. Well, not IN-in. We're hiding in my bedroom, and he's in the living room. Help! What should we do?

Nothing from Shannon, but Alyssa writes almost immediately.

Too much info, she texts. *Spare me.*

"Let's get out of here," I say to Froggy as I slide my phone in my bag. "We'll wave and make a quick exit. No time for questions."

"What if your brother asks what I'm doing here?"

"We won't engage," I tell him, borrowing some of Mom's TherapistSpeak. Mom is always peppering her language with phrases from the world of psychology like "don't engage" and "comfort zone."

"Uh, okay. Okay." Froggy tweaks his nose and grabs his trombone case. He's nervous about seeing my brother. I wish I could tell him about "the ordeal," about how Byron isn't actually that cool after all. I told Shannon about it. She was already away in Washington State so I texted the drama to her as it unfolded. But with my New York City people, like Froggy and Alyssa, I didn't say a word about the trouble my brother was in. For one, I didn't want either one of them to dump me as a girlfriend/friend if they found out the horrible thing he did. But also my family is private about anything that doesn't make us look perfect. I'm already on the low end of the Shreves Family Totem Pole, and blabbering our business would plummet me to subterranean levels.